DIRECT EXAMINATION OF WITNESSES

DIRECT EXAMINATION OF WITNESSES

by

Howard Hilton Spellman, A.B., LL.B.
Member of the New York Bar

Prentice-Hall, Inc.
Englewood Cliffs, N.J.

Third Printing.....March, 1972

This publication is designed to provide accurate and
authoritative information in regard to the subject matter covered. It is sold with the understanding that
the publisher is not engaged in rendering legal, accounting or other professional service. If legal advice
or other expert assistance is required, the services of
a competent professional person should be sought.

*—From a Declaration of Principles jointly
adopted by a committee of the American
Bar Association and a Committee of Pub-
lishers and Associations.*

TO
Nick, Syl, Cole and Clay

Other Books by Howard Hilton Spellman

CORPORATE DIRECTORS

CRIMINAL CODES OF N.Y., ANNOTATED

HOW TO PROVE A PRIMA FACIE CASE
Revised Edition, 1939
Third Edition, 1954

HOW TO PROVE A PRIMA FACIE DEFENSE

CORPORATE SECRETARY'S MANUAL AND GUIDE
Revised Edition, 1949

SUCCESSFUL MANAGEMENT OF MATRIMONIAL CASES

MOTIONS DURING TRIAL

PREFACE

As every experienced trial lawyer knows, the most important part of any case is the presentation of direct evidence.

The ultimate aim of a litigant is to convince the fact finder (court or jury) that his cause is just and that, therefore, he should prevail. This can only be accomplished through the medium of positive proof. Although cross-examination, skilfully conducted, has its important function, the fact is that cross-examination rarely wins cases. The fact finder is more interested in what *did* happen than in what *did not* happen. Indeed, examination of records on appeal in many cases discloses that appellate courts have often reversed verdicts as against the weight of the evidence despite the fact that the winning side, below, had the benefit of brilliant and seemingly destructive cross-examination. The simple reason for reversal has been the lack of affirmative proof to sustain the verdict.

It is the astonishing fact that legal literature is relatively barren of discussion of the direct examination of witnesses. Except for a single monograph of 53 pages, a most casual mention of direct proof in some general books on trial tactics and indirect references, in an entirely different context, in treatises on the law of evidence, we search in vain for any in depth treatment in legal writings of either the importance, use, or legal principles governing the subject. To fill this inexplicable gap, the present volume has been conceived and written.

The art of presenting positive proof through direct examination involves the tripartite consideration of special preparation, precise knowledge of the legal principles involved and the techniques of actual questioning. It should not be assumed that general preparation of a case for trial encompasses the requisite special preparation of the witnesses to be called or that legal research on the substantive aspects of a case is sufficient to meet the question of

vii

the admissibility of each element of evidence sought to be presented. It is one thing to know the triable issues and to be prepared to meet them. It is an entirely different matter to work out
the actual presentation of the case and to be prepared to demonstrate legally the admissibility of every portion of one's proffered
proof. Finally, the technique of questioning individual witnesses
requires consideration and, sometimes, highly selective decision
long in advance of trial. This may involve such diverse elements
as the personality of witnesses, the use or deliberate non-use of
some available evidence and the determination whether expert
witnesses are to make tests or experiments in open court.

Over the years, certain practices have become almost standard
in the questioning of witnesses. Many counsel have utilized them
without any inquiry into their source, emergence, enlargement or
narrowing. No conscientious lawyer would dream of going to trial
without research into the applicable substantive law. Yet equally
important legal research as to the method of presentation is too
rarely undertaken. There is a tendency to go ahead on the general
assumption that the method of examination is static and unchang-
ing. This is not the fact. A lawyer so proceeding may lose valuable
opportunities to introduce proof, to short-cut his presentation or
to shut out adverse evidence. The changes in procedural provisions
directly connected with direct examination are constant by reason
of both legislative action and decisional law.

This book is designed as a practical working tool for lawyers. It
covers all aspects of direct examination of witnesses from the earliest interviews through preliminary and final preparation and then
considers, among many other things, the actual technique of examination, the use of documentary proof and depositions, the production of expert testimony and, finally, the problems and methods
of redirect examination and rebuttal evidence. As an important
adjunct to these considerations, there are included the citation,
analysis and discussion of applicable decisional and statutory law.
This should enable counsel, preparing for trial, not only to be advised of additional opportunities, but even to gain a knowledge of
the legal questions he should ask himself before propounding a
single factual question to any witness.

The author thanks the many judges and members of the bar who
have aided him through the media both of extended discussion
and the furnishing of records and briefs on appeal and in courts
of original jurisdiction. He hopes that this work will justify the

high measure of enthusiasm they expressed as they learned of its production.

Acknowledgement is gratefully made of the assistance of my secretary, Mrs. Ida Heller. She was much more than a mere amanuensis. It is no exaggeration to say that she was practically an editor of this work. Arthur Lionel Schatten, Esq., a member of the New York and New Jersey bars, was extremely helpful in doing statutory research.

My wife, who has now suffered through the production of several books written by me, again displayed her forbearance when writing or research kept me from home on many evenings and during innumerable weekends. Once again, she has been invaluable as a super proofreader and critic in going over the text of this volume. My measure of thanks to her should not be belittled by the difficulty of expressing it in words.

Howard Hilton Spellman

CONTENTS

CONTENTS

INDEX OF FORMS

Chapter I

NATURE AND SCOPE
OF DIRECT EXAMINATION

Sec. 1:1   Dual legal concepts of direct examination.

This volume is devoted to the *practical* (legal, strategic and tactical) aspects of direct examination of witnesses. It is concerned with the *method of presentation* and considers the application of principles of law as an adjunct to that concern.

By general acceptance, concepts of law governing the trial of an action are described as substantive and adjective. Substantive law consists of the principles governing the *right to recovery*. Adjective law consists of the principles governing the *method of presentation* of a cause, including such matters as pleading, pre-trial proceedings, the trial of the action and proceedings on appeal.

At first blush, it would seem that the only legal rules which need here be considered are those of adjective law. Technically, this assumption is correct. However, upon analysis, we must realize that the adjective law applicable to the direct examination of witnesses has two distinct subdivisions:

1. The law governing the production and examination of the witness, as such. This includes, among a vast number of others, such matters as the competency of the witness to testify, the permissible scope of direct examination,[1] the use of statutory presumptions in connection with testimony, the types of questions that may be asked of individual witnesses (as, for example, experts), and the right to impeach hostile witnesses. For convenience, this branch of the law may be denominated "the substantive law of direct examination."[2]

2. The law governing the right to engage in direct examination at various stages of the trial. This includes limitations on the right to put in one's direct case during the course of the opponent's case, particularly during the course of cross-examination. It rests upon the application to individual situations of statutes, court rules and decisions aimed at creating orderly procedure during the course of a trial. For convenience, this branch of the law may be denominated "the adjective law of direct examination."[3]

Illustrating a combination of the "substantive" and "adjective" law on direct examination, consider the following example.

In an action involving a written contract, the defendant has pleaded as a separate defense that, at the time he is alleged to have signed the contract, he was insane. He has also interposed a denial of knowledge or information sufficient to form a belief as to whether he signed the contract.

A plaintiff's witness, on direct examination during the course of the plaintiff's case, testifies that, on a certain day, he saw the defendant sign the contract.

On cross-examination, plaintiff's attorney asks this witness certain questions for the purpose of establishing the insanity of the defendant at the time the contract was signed and also asks the witness whether, in his opinion, defendant was sane at that time. Should objections to these questions be sustained?

---

[1] See section 1:4, *post*.

[2] In addition to the legal concepts here involved, this sub-division, as a practical matter, leads to consideration of subjects like preparation for direct examination, determination of issues, choice of witnesses, technique of examination, and the use of diagrams, tables and charts. See Chapters II, III, IV, V, VIII and XI, *post*.

[3] See section 1:6, *post*, wherein we review criticisms of the strict application of the rule limiting cross-examination.

Certainly, the witness can be interrogated about the general circumstances surrounding the signing of the contract, since the defendant has pleaded a denial of knowledge or information sufficient to form a belief as to whether he signed. Here, we have a question of adjective law, which is determined on the basis of the denial of an allegation of the complaint. The theory is that it is proper and consonant with orderly procedure of a trial for a witness, on cross-examination, to be asked questions related to his direct examination and bearing upon a subject as to which the party calling that witness has the burden of proof.

A related matter is presented by the questions of defendant's attorney, which seek to prove facts establishing that the defendant was insane at the time the contract was signed. Here, again, we have a question of adjective law. Is it consonant with the orderly process of a trial that a defendant be permitted, through the medium of cross-examination during plaintiff's case, to establish his pleaded separate defense? In a majority of American jurisdictions, objections to these questions would be sustained upon the ground that the defendant should reserve proof of matters upon which he has the burden of proof until plaintiff has rested and the defendant proceeds with his case.[4]

As to the question directed to plaintiff's witness concerning his opinion about the defendant's sanity at the time the contract was signed, we have, first, a question of substantive law. Assuming that the witness is not a physician, it is the law in most jurisdictions that he is not competent to state an opinion about sanity or lack thereof. An objection to the question would, therefore, be sustained on a substantive ground. In addition, as we have stated, above, it could also be sustained on the adjective ground that the defendant is trying to prove his separate defense through the medium of cross-examination during the course of plaintiff's case.

Sec. 1:2　Substantive definition of direct examination.

The substantive definition of the direct examination of a witness is the propounding of questions to him for the purpose of eliciting answers establishing the existence of facts favorable to the contentions of the questioner.

Ordinarily, the questions are directed to a witness in the course

---

[4] See section 1:6, *post.*

of a trial; but the definition is equally applicable to proceedings on the taking of depositions (whether through oral examination or the use of letters rogatory) and upon the use of written questions instead of oral examination (either by stipulation or pursuant to special court rule).

The employment of the word "propounding" in the definition is for the purpose of including not only a question asked by counsel, but also situations in which the actual questioning is done by some official appointed by the court, who reads to the witness written questions submitted by counsel.[5]

The key phrase of the substantive definition of direct examination is "establishing the existence of facts." Legally, it is axiomatic in our adversary system of jurisprudence that there can be no application of a principle of law unless a factual basis exists *in the record* for the utilization of that principle. Practically, one cannot expect to win a case unless convincing evidence is produced before the trier of the facts.

It is not an exception to this proposition that judgment may be rendered on the pleadings, or on written admissions, or summarily upon affidavits. In such situations the factual proof exists despite the circumstance that no witness is called to the stand in the course of a trial. But, in the vast majority of all litigations, the method of establishing the existence of facts is by question and answer. Indeed, in criminal prosecutions, due process and confrontation considerations require open trials. And in some jurisdictions in cases where, as a matter of public policy, it is considered desirable to subject *all* proof to the personal scrutiny of the trier of the facts, the nature of the evidence that may be introduced even in a non-criminal case by a method other than questioning in open court is significantly circumscribed.[6]

Facts sought to be established by direct examination are either positive or negative. Yet both types are proved by direct testimony. Such testimony will, as to positive facts, usually amount to a recital

---

[5] For example, New York C.P.L.R., Rule 3113(b) provides, in part: "In lieu of participating in an oral examination, any party served with notice of taking a deposition may transmit written questions to the officer, who shall propound them to the witness and record the answers."

[6] Compare, for example, New York C.P.L.R., Rule 3212(d), providing that, in a matrimonial action, a defendant's summary judgment motion (the plaintiff in such a case may not move for summary judgment) must be based upon "documentary evidence or official records which establish a defense to the cause of action."

of what the witness claims actually happened. As to negative facts, there may either be a recital of happenings differing from that of a prior witness, or a flat answer to the effect that, in the respects covered by the question, the statement of a previous witness was false. Thus, the substantive definition of direct examination should be enlarged to include as one of its purposes the eliciting of answers establishing the non-existence of claimed facts unfavorable to the contentions of the questioner.

This is not merely a philosophical distinction. It is essential, if possible, to prove the non-existence of unfavorable facts. Otherwise, unfavorable testimony remains uncontradicted. This leaves the record in a precarious position; because it is the general rule that, in the absence of inherent improbability, uncontradicted testimony is taken as true.[7] Indeed, "it has frequently been said that testimony which is not inherently improbable and is not impeached or contradicted by other evidence should be accepted as true by the trier of fact."[8] And another court has told us that "it is settled law that where a witness's testimony is not contradicted, a trier has no right to refuse to accept it."[9]

Sec. 1:3 Adjective definition of direct examination.

The adjective definition of the direct examination of a witness has been variously stated as follows:

> "The examination in chief of a witness by the party who called him to the stand."[10]
> "The examination in chief of a witness is called the direct examination."[11]

---

[7] *People v. Silver*, 87 Cal. App. 2d 337, 349; *People v. Taranto*, 2 Ill. 2d 476, 480–481; *Jenkins v. Gerber*, 336 Ill. App. 469, 471; *Hull v. Littauer*, 162 N.Y. 569, 572; *Kaye v. Donlon*, 281 App. Div. 617, 618, affd. 306 N.Y. 884; *People v. Richetti*, 109 N.Y.S. 2d 29, 41. But see, apparently superficially contra, *Matter of Nowakowski*, 2 N.Y. 2d 618, 622.

[8] *Gomez v. Cecena*, 15 Cal. 2d 363, 366, quoted with approval in *People v. Silver*, 87 Cal. App. 2d 337, 349. That there may be some further limitations on the requirement for full acceptance of uncontradicted testimony, see the cases cited in *People v. Richetti*, 109 N.Y.S. 2d 29, 41.

[9] *National Labor Relations Board v. Ray Smith Transport Co.*, 193 F. 2d 142, 146.

[10] Ballentine, *Law Dictionary* (2nd Ed., 1948), p. 377. Examination in chief is defined as the "first or direct examination of a witness by the party who has called him to testify." *Ibid.*, p. 457.

[11] *Bouvier's Law Dictionary* (3rd Revision, 1914), vol. I, p 867.

"The first examination of a witness in the orderly course, by the party calling him and upon the merits." [12]

"Under the usual order of proceeding at the trial, the plaintiff, who has the burden of establishing his claim, will first introduce the evidence to prove the facts necessary to enable him to recover, e. g., the making of the contract sued on, its breach, and the amount of damages. . . . During this stage each witness of the plaintiff will first be questioned by the plaintiff's counsel, upon direct examination, then cross-examined by opposing counsel, and these may be followed by re-direct and re-cross examinations." [13]

The purpose of the adjective definition of direct examination is to avoid confusion by establishing an orderly timetable for the trial. It is obvious that disorder would arise during the course of a trial if a defendant's attorney could interrupt with a question at any time during the direct examination of a plaintiff's witness and *vice versa*. Over the course of years, various suggestions have been made as to the order of examination. One school of thought is that a witness's testimony on a single subject should be completed and that he should then be cross-examined on *that* subject. Another group has suggested that there should be no cross-examination until one party has presented all of his witnesses on direct and that, thereafter, the other party should cross-examine all of these witnesses, *seriatim*. American courts have adopted the method above referred to—that is, the direct examination of each witness by the party calling him, followed by the cross-examination of that witness by his opponent and then re-direct and re-cross before the next witness is called.

Up to this point, we have discussed the timetable established for the examination of individual witnesses; but, either by usage, statute or court rule a further timetable exists. This defines the order of the trial as a whole, as distinguished from progression in the examination of individual witnesses. In general, the established order of trial is as follows (eliminating statutory requirements as to openings to the jury, summations and the charge of the court):

---

[12] *Webster's New International Dictionary, Unabridged* (2nd Ed., 1939), p. 738.

[13] McCormick, *Evidence* (1954), ch. I, §4, p. 6. The converse of this procedure comes into being during the course of defendant's case.

1. The plaintiff's main case (unless it is unnecessary for the plaintiff to produce evidence by reason of admissions in the pleadings);

2. The defendant's main case;

3. Plaintiff's rebuttal (ordinarily confined to the contradiction or explanation of facts brought out on defendant's main case);

4. Defendant's rebuttal (ordinarily confined to new matters brought out in plaintiff's rebuttal); and

5. In the discretion of the court, sur-rebuttal by either party.

In the timetable for the trial as a whole lurk hidden dangers for trial counsel. Despite statements in some decisions that the length to which counsel may go in producing evidence in support of his own case during the course of the opponent's case rests in the sound discretion of the trial court, reversible error may be created by proceeding in a manner that upsets the general timetable of the trial.[14]

This danger creates real problems *in planning the strategy of trial.*

For example, it is tactically advantageous for the defendant to bring to the attention of the jury, while the plaintiff is on the stand early in the trial, that the defendant has a perfectly sound defense and is *morally* right. Obviously, the sooner the jury gets this impression the better; because it will color the jurymen's reception of the evidence of all plaintiff's later witnesses, whose testimony will be taken with the proverbial grain of salt.

But plaintiff is entitled, in common justice, to present his case in an orderly manner, unprejudiced by distractions.[15] The defendant is not deprived of his right to make a full defense. All the law properly requires is that defendant bide his time and let plaintiff first attempt to prove his case. In due course, when defendant is on his own case, plaintiff will be prevented from introducing new issues until the time for rebuttal arrives. Thus, compelled mutual forbearance will permit each side a fair day in court. At least, this is

---

[14] This subject is covered in section 1:6, *post*, wherein we discuss the most usual breaches of the trial timetable (during cross-examination of an opponent's witness).

[15] Of course, cross-examination designed to impeach a party's general credibility will not be foreclosed merely because it may, incidentally, bring in new issues.

the philosophy in most American jurisdictions. Cogent contrary reasoning is discussed in section 1:6, *post.*

Counsel, in planning his strategy, would be well advised to consider the sanctions of the timetable before succumbing to the temptation of jumping the gun.

Sec. 1:4   Scope of direct examination.

When a party calls a witness on his own case, he may inquire of that witness as to *any* subject embraced within the pleadings. Examining counsel is now at the stage of the trial where he has the fullest chance to establish the justice of his cause. He should avidly grasp this opportunity.

It is insufficient advocacy merely to establish the bare bones of a *prima facie* case or defense. There are other matters as to which it may be profitable to ask questions so that the color of right as well as its technical existence will be brought to the attention of the triers of fact.[16] Trial counsel may decide that it will benefit his case to produce evidence on some matters not directly embraced in the issues on trial. How far one can go in this respect rests largely in the discretion of the trial court; but, short of creating the real possibility of reversible error, proper trial tactics dictate that substantial flesh be put on the skeleton of technical proof.

It should be noted that, in some cases, there is a significant difference between the original and *final* scope of direct examination by the plaintiff and by the defendant.

The plaintiff, primarily, produces evidence to establish his main case (plus such "color" material as he is permitted to prove). During the course of the plaintiff's case, however, it sometimes occurs that evidence is introduced which would appear to widen the issues. The defendant, of course, can make appropriate objection to the receipt of such evidence. However, the defendant's trial counsel may welcome the introduction of such extraneous material; because, in the circumstances of the particular action, the defendant is thus legitimately enabled to bring in further side issues redounding to his benefit

It is a familiar rule that, even though certain proof may not be strictly within the pleaded issues, the court will accept that proof

---

[16] See Chapter III, *post,* for a discussion of the advance determination of issues to be tried.

in the absence of objection. The case will ultimately be decided on the issues actually tried by the parties, who are deemed to have presented by implied consent additional issues not embraced in the pleadings. The principle is aptly stated in Rule 15(b) of the Federal Rules of Civil Procedure, as follows:

> "When issues not raised by the pleadings are tried by express or implied consent of the parties, they shall be treated in all respects as if they had been raised in the pleadings. Such amendment of the pleadings as may be necessary to cause them to conform to the evidence and to raise these issues may be made upon motion of any party at any time, even after judgment; but failure so to amend does not affect the result of the trial of these issues."

By desisting from objecting to a portion of the plaintiff's evidence, the defendant's attorney can widen the scope of his direct examination.[17] The ability thus created carries with it an appropriate warning: before introducing evidence outside of the pleaded issues, trial counsel should carefully consider whether he is extending the scope of the case to the advantage of his adversary.

Very often, particularly in cases tried to the court without a jury, the trial judge will announce that he will freely accept all proffered evidence, without immediately ruling on its materiality. This, again, widens the scope of permissible direct examination and, indeed, sometimes *requires* additional direct examination by the party against whom the proof is offered.[18]

The surprise testimony of a turncoat witness leads to a substantial extension of the permissible scope of direct examination. Practically, this extension amounts to the granting of permission to counsel calling a witness to cross-examine or impeach that witness, within reasonably well-defined limitations.

> "At common law, impeachment of a party's own witness whether by inconsistent statements or by an attack on character was forbidden. (McCormick, Evidence, ch. 5, §38, p. 70.) How-

---

[17] The same result flows from the court overruling an objection made by defendant's counsel, which ruling is sometimes accompanied by an on-the-spot amendment of the pleadings. Compare the last two sentences of Rule 15(b) F.R.C.P.

[18] See section 3:4, *post.*

ever, in order to 'correct the inequities occasioned by the fact that in many cases both sides were unfairly hampered by their inability to impeach unreliable witnesses upon whom they were compelled to rely', a limited statutory exception was adopted. . . . In addition, counsel has been permitted, since a time prior to the enactment of that section, to introduce this evidence [prior inconsistent statements in writing] under the accepted guise of refreshing the witness' recollection." [19]

The fallacy of the ancient (and now discredited) rule that a party calling a witness vouches for his credibility in all respects and cannot contradict him was recognized as early as the nineteenth century. As was stated in a leading opinion:

"The tendency of recent legislation, as well as of modern decisions, has been to relax somewhat the rules of evidence, so as to afford better opportunity for the development of truth. Modern experience has also shown that a party may sometimes be deceived in the character and animus of a witness whom he has called, as well as in the testimony he is expected to give; and he learns, after the witness begins to testify—a very inopportune time—that he has to encounter bitter and unscrupulous opposition where he had expected to receive only fair and honorable treatment. This may be evinced by reluctance or evasion on the part of the witness in answering questions, or by too great readiness in making or volunteering damaging statements contrary to his previous version of the matter. Under such circumstances, . . . in extreme cases, where it is apparent that a witness is giving testimony contrary to the reasonable expectation of the party calling him, such party should be allowed to cross-examine such witness, for the purpose of refreshing his recollection, with the view of modifying his testimony or of revealing his animus in the case, . . . and to ask him if he has not theretofore made other or different statements from those he has just given in evidence." [20]

Another court put it this way: [21]

---

[19] *People v. Freeman*, 9 N.Y. 2d 600, 603–604. Statutes authorizing introduction of prior inconsistent statements are cited in section 2:3, footnote 19, *post.*

[20] *Babcock v. People*, 13 Colo. 515, 519.

[21] *Crago v. State*, 28 Wyo. 215, 223–224.

"Thus the legal situation on this subject in the courts of the United States about the middle of the last century was that no party was permitted to discredit his own witness by showing that the latter had made statements out of court inconsistent with the statements made at the trial, unless the witness was one whom the party was compelled to call, as, for instance, a witness to a will; but a party was, in some instances, permitted to examine his witnesses in regard to such inconsistent statements for the purpose of refreshing his recollection. Further than that the courts would not go. Then came the era of legislation, where laws were enacted in some of the states similar to §5809 of our statute; and, perhaps mainly under the influence of such legislation, courts came to modify their views, permitting generally examination of the witness for the purpose of refreshing his recollection, and also permitting, under certain conditions and with certain limitations, proof of previous statements made out of court. We have twice held that a party's own witness could be examined, calling his attention to former statements made, for the purpose of refreshing his recollection: but we have not heretofore been called upon to decide whether the additional step could be taken of proving such former statements by other evidence. That is the question in this case. To this we now turn our attention.

"The purpose of impeaching one's own witness is to neutralize his testimony on the witness stand. But neither Courts nor Legislatures have permitted this to be done by attacking the general character of a witness. This character is, generally at least, known to a party just as well before as during a trial, and courts will not tolerate that he, vouching for the good character of a witness when producing him, should play fast and loose, get the advantage of the testimony if favorable, but repudiate it if unfavorable. Section 5809 of our statute recognizes this principle. But there are times when a party may be imposed upon; he may be deceived and surprised by a witness; the witness may be allured away from him, and from the path of truth. It would be harsh and unjust that a party should be put at the mercy of such witness or of an unscrupulous adversary tampering with him. But the Courts prior to the second half of the last century did not deem these facts of sufficient importance so as to lay aside the old established rule; and to meet this situation, and remedy the evils pointed out, the character of legislation mentioned was passed."

The right to impeach one's own witness, when counsel is taken by surprise, is akin to the familiar rule as to permissible interrogation of an unwilling or hostile witness. Many states have adopted statutes codifying prior decisions. Rule 43(b) of the Federal Rules of Civil Procedure is typical and reads as follows:

> "A party may interrogate any unwilling or hostile witness by leading questions. A party may call an adverse party or an officer, director, or managing agent of a public or private corporation or of a partnership or association which is an adverse party, and interrogate him by leading questions and contradict and impeach him in all respects as if he had been called by the adverse party, and the witness thus called may be contradicted and impeached by or on behalf of the adverse party also, and may be cross-examined by the adverse party only upon the subject matter of his examination in chief." [22]

A definite limitation still exists curtailing the rule of permissible impeachment of one's own witness. A party may not call a witness to the stand and then proceed to attack his *general* credibility. To this limited extent, the party calling the witness "vouches" for his credibility. Such a party is "not at liberty to impeach [the witness'] character for truth" but is "at liberty to dispute specific facts although sworn to by him".[23] Furthermore, although a witness may be confronted by a prior inconsistent statement for the purpose of impeaching his credibility or to show the witness that he is mistaken and induce him to correct his evidence and although proof of such prior inconsistent statement should not be excluded simply because it may result unfavorably to the general credibility of the witness, the prior inconsistent statement is hearsay (unless the witness happens to be a party to the action) and may not be used as proof of a fact on the issues at bar.[24] It has been said that the rule that such

---

[22] It should be noted that the last phrase of this Rule permits cross-examination by the adverse party "only upon the subject matter of [the] examination in chief." This is to prevent an adverse party from being able to utilize a hostile witness to establish his own direct case under the masquerade of cross-examination.

[23] *Cross v. Cross*, 108 N.Y. 628, 629.

[24] *People v. Purtell*, 243 N.Y. 273, 280, quoting with approval a succinct statement of the general rule from the opinion in *Bullard v. Pearsall*, 53 N.Y. 230. Statutory provisions covering prior statements are discussed in section 2:3, *post*.

prior statements have no substantial or independent testimonial value is "so firmly imbedded in the law of evidence that the citation of authority is scarcely required." [25]

The right to impeach one's own witness extends beyond merely confronting him with a prior inconsistent statement. The witness may be asked questions tending to prove his bias against the party calling him. The reasons for changing an earlier version of the facts may be inquired into; and, in this connection, the questioner may explore such matters as contacts between the witness and the opposing party or his lawyer, and even the question whether there has been actual corruption of the witness by reason of a bribe, payment for his testimony, or a promise of some future benefit (such as employment) proffered by the adversary. The interest of the witness in the result of the litigation, particularly where there has been some change in that interest, is a proper matter to be adduced.

The extent to which this type of interrogation may go is generally said to rest in the sound discretion of the trial court.[26] As in all cases where discretion is the controlling factor, the law is necessarily in a state of flux. It is of small benefit to the reader that citations of individual cases be furnished; because, even in the *same* jurisdiction, the rules constantly change due to the extension (or narrowing) of discretion in individual circumstances. When, in the course of preparation for trial, the question arises whether a specific inquiry will be permitted during the impeachment of a turncoat witness, the *latest* expression of the courts in the jurisdiction where the case is being tried should be investigated, or a standard work on the law of evidence should be consulted.[27]

If, during the course of a trial, counsel is genuinely surprised by the disclosure of hostility on the part of a witness he has called, the

---

[25] *People v. Kenda*, 3 A.D. 2d [New York] 80, 85, quoted with approval in *People v. Freeman*, 9 N.Y. 2d 600, 605. For an enlightening discussion as to when and under what circumstances a prior contradictory statement may be used see *Brown v. Western Union Tel.*, 26 A.D. 2d [New York] 316, 317–320.

[26] Compare: *Gant v. Gas Service Co.*, 156 Kan. 685, 687; *Moran v. Dumas*, 91 N.H. 336, 338; *State v. Todaro*, 131 N.J.L. 59, 60, affd. 131 N.J.L. 430, appeal dismissed, 323 U.S. 667; *Langley v. Wadsworth*, 99 N.Y. 61, 63–64; *State v. Stone*, 226 N.C. 97, 98–99; *McCauley v. Pacific Atlantic S.S. Co.*, 167 Or. 80, 98–100.

[27] The best collection of individual cases on this subject is found in *Wigmore on Evidence* (Third Edition, 1940, which is kept up to date with pocket parts) §§901–918. See, also, §900 to the effect that, even though a witness proves hostile, the party calling him may not introduce evidence as to the general bad moral character of that witness.

court should (and probably will) grant an adjournment or continuance to enable counsel to meet this eventuality. If the court refuses such respite, trial counsel should, *on the record,* indicate how he has been prejudiced, in order to lay the basis for an appeal upon the ground that discretion has been abused. In the last analysis, although broad discretion as to the scope of impeaching examination exists, an abuse of that discretion is reversible error.[28]

As has been indicated (footnote 26, *supra*), the impeachment of one's own witness is akin to cross-examination of a witness produced by the adverse party. Indeed, as a practical matter, impeachment of one's own witness and cross-examination of a witness called by the adversary are identical, *except that one may not attempt to establish the general bad moral character or lack of credibility of one's own witness.* It is of the utmost importance for counsel to note that a salutary rule of evidence is applicable in either event. This rule is that, although a party is not bound by testimony of his own witness on facts *material* to the issues on trial and may call other witnesses to contradict his own witness, he is *bound* by the testimony of his own witness on *collateral* matters (that is, as to matters which are *not* material as proof concerning the issues at bar). The word "bound" in this context is a word of art. It merely means that, as to a *collateral* matter, the questioner may not subsequently call other witnesses to prove that the statement made by the hostile witness is untrue.[29] What is a collateral matter depends upon the circum-

---

[28] *Fla. Coastal Theatres, Inc. v. Belflower,* 159 Fla. 741, 747; *Kelly v. Meyer,* 156 Kan. 429; *State v. Carns,* 136 Mont. 120, 136; *Davis v. State,* 186 Tenn. 545, 547; *Commercial Credit Plan, Inc. v. Beebe,* 123 Vt. 317. Conversely, there can be an abuse of discretion by allowing cross-examination to range too far. *State v. Bartell,* 15 N.J. Super. 450. A judge has stated that "[i]t is only where the cross-examination relates to contradiction on a collateral issue that there is discretion in the trial judge." *Commonwealth v. Rothman,* 168 Pa. 163, 166.

[29] *Martin v. United States,* 127 Fed. 2d 865; *Smith v. State,* 261 Ala. 270, 273; *Waterman v. State,* 202 Ark. 934, 935; *Davis v. Powder-Works,* 84 Cal. 617, 627; *Trujillo v. People,* 116 Colo. 157, 160–161; *Stewart v. State,* 42 Fla. 591, 594–595; *City of East Dubuque v. Burhyte,* 173 Ill. 553, 556–557; *State v. Blakesley,* 43 Kan. 250, 254; *State v. Washington,* 225 La. 1021, 1027–1028; *Commonwealth v. Farrell,* 322 Mass. 606, 623–624; *Patton v. State,* 209 Miss. 138, 141; *State v. Lynn,* 184 S.W. 2d 760, 765 (Mo. App.); *Ferguson v. State,* 72 Neb. 350, 354; *State v. Hatch,* 21 N.J. Super. 394, 399; *People v. Brown,* 265 App. Div. (New York) 153, 156; *State v. Hickman,* 77 Ohio App. 479, 486–487; *Zubrod v. Kuhn,* 357 Pa. 200, 203; *State v. Brock,* 130 S.C. 252, 254; *State v. Sheppard,* 49 W.Va. 582, 601. The same rule applies to limit calling witnesses on collateral matters to contradict testimony on cross-examination. *Peo. v. McCormick,* 303 N.Y 403, 404.

stances of each case. The prime guide is found in the pleadings. Sometimes, however, the pleaded issues are deemed enlarged through voluntary extension of issues by the express or implied consent of the parties.[30] The safest definition of a material matter is one concerning which the questioner would be permitted to propound questions on his own, direct case.[31]

Some statutes permit extrinsic contradiction on *specific* collateral matters of a witness called by an adversary. Typical of such statutes are those which permit record proof that the witness has been convicted of a crime, even though the witness denies that fact. However, since this goes to the question of the general credibility or moral character of a witness, it is not applicable to the impeachment of one's own witness.

Sec. 1:5   Cross-examination not a substitute for direct examination.

It is the recurring dream of the trial lawyer that, through the medium of brilliant cross-examination (sometimes buttressed by imaginative advance preparation), he will be able to "destroy" an adverse witness and thus win his case. Novels and plays have dramatized the destructive effect of cross-examination. Motion pictures, radio and television have done nothing to minimize its efficacy. However, the lawyer who believes that his successful cross-examination will necessarily win his case is enjoying a fantasy, the result of which may be to lull him into a sense of security that may ultimately result in defeat, through the medium of a simple motion by his adversary for a dismissal or directed verdict later in the case.

Even though cross-examination may prove that a witness is an absolute and deliberate liar, *it does not follow that the opposite of that testified to by the witness is the truth.* Because, where the examiner has the burden of proof as to a given fact, the record will be bare of such necessary proof unless the cross-examined witness testifies to the same as an independent fact, or other witnesses are produced to establish that fact. A judge's charge to the jury that they may take as established the opposite of the fact testified to by a witness when that witness is proved to be lying or mistaken is

---

[30] See Rule 15(b) F.R.C.P. and footnote 17 of this chapter, *supra.*
[31] *Cf., O'Neil v. Crampton,* 18 Wash. 2d 579, 585.

reversible error. A leading New York case illustrates this proposition: [32]

There, a defendant was charged with the crime of robbery and two eye witnesses identified him as the person who had committed the robbery on a given date between certain hours. The only defense witness was the mother of the defendant, who testified that the defendant had worked in her candy store between certain hours "every day." If her testimony was true, the defendant had a perfect alibi. On cross-examination, the mother conceded that defendant may have taken a week off to go somewhere. The court charged the jury that if they believed the defendant's alibi to be false, they could "take the falsity of the alibi on the question of the defendant's guilt." The court went on to charge "[t]hen, of course, if you reject the alibi, you naturally, logically, accept the testimony of the State's witnesses."

The defendant's conviction was reversed, the New York Court of Appeals stating with respect to the trial court's charge to the jury: [33]

> "Clearly this was error, and serious error. . . . Disbelief of the defendant's witnesses could not . . . be *corroboration* of the People's witnesses. Much less could it be, as the charge says here, that the rejection of defendant's proof spells acceptance of the People's proof. . . . The only real issue in this case was as to the accuracy of the identification testimony. When the jury were told that this issue might be decided by determining whether defendant's mother was falsifying or mistaken, the error was not one to be overlooked."

The courts are loath to permit a judgment to stand on the basis of cross-examination, alone, particularly where the cross-examination leaves the justice of the cause in doubt. Thus, in a case involving the value of property taken by the State in condemnation, the testimony of the claimant's expert, when subjected to cross-examination, established that his *method* of fixing value was not legally tenable. This left the record in a state where the only testimony as to value, which could be legally accepted, was that of the State's expert witness. There was nothing in the record to establish what value would

---

[32] *People v. Rabinowitz*, 290 N.Y. 386.
[33] 290 N.Y. at pp. 388–389.

have been found by the claimant's witness if he had applied proper methods of valuation. The lower courts had adopted the method of the claimant's witness, modified by the courts' own conclusions as to value, based on that method. New York's highest appellate court spoke as follows: [34]

> "We have concluded that the order should be reversed and a new trial granted for the reason that the theory of valuation advanced by claimant and adopted by the courts below is erroneous. This presents a question of law, and requires that the award be vacated and, under the circumstances here presented, a new opportunity afforded to claimant to prove its case. It would not be fair to reduce the award to the amount supported by the expert for the State. . . ."

Where, because of inaccuracies on the part of expert witnesses, the experts for one side are deemed insufficiently convincing, the other side is not helped unless there is independent evidence in the record supporting its contention.[35]

Although proof of deliberate fabrication by a *witness* cannot be accepted as evidence that the opposite of his testimony is true, a different rule comes into play when a *party* deliberately falsely testifies or causes another to testify falsely. This rule has been variously stated as follows:

> "The fabrication of evidence raises a presumption or, more properly, an inference that the truth, if disclosed, would be detrimental to the interest of the party who has been guilty of such an improper act. Such an inference is created whether the evidence fabricated is documentary or oral, including the exercise of improper influence on witnesses." [36]

> "An attempt to fabricate evidence is receivable as evidence of one's guilt of the main facts charged. Such fabrication is in the nature of an admission, for it will not be supposed that an innocent person would feel the necessity for fabricating evidence." [37]

---

[34] *Latham Holding Co. v. State of N.Y.*, 16 N.Y. 2d 41, 44. Cf., also, *Mtr. of Pepsi-Cola Co. v. Tax Comm.*, 19 A.D. 2d 56, 61–62 [New York].

[35] Compare *United States v. Aluminum Co. of America*, 44 F. Supp. 97, 120, reversed on other grounds 148 F. 2d 416, 432–434.

[36] 31 A *Corpus Juris Secundum*, Evidence, section 155, p. 391.

[37] 20 *American Jurisprudence*, Evidence, section 289.

"Such false testimony and such conduct are in the nature of admissions from which with other evidence liability could be inferred." [38]

It will be noted that the common denominator in the above statements of principle is either deliberately false testimony by the *party,* himself, or proof that the *party* caused another to fabricate. As has been stated by the Supreme Court of the United States:

"There was certainly no error in instructing the jury to disregard evidence that was found to be false, and the further charge that false testimony, knowingly and purposely invoked by defendant, might be used against him, is but another method of stating the principle that the fabrication of testimony raises a presumption against the party guilty of such practice. 1 Phillips, Ev. 448; *State* v. *Williams,* 27 Vt. 724; 3 Russell, Crimes, 6th ed. 358." [39]

Where it is claimed that a *witness* has deliberately falsely testified, the jury, before it can find that the opposite of his testimony is true, must have presented to it "independent proof of fabrication." [40]

Statutes in some jurisdictions permit a witness to be confronted with previous inconsistent statements made by him. These statutes vary considerably. Some permit the introduction of prior inconsistent statements only when made in writing subscribed by the witness or made under oath. Others have no such restriction. The practice with respect to the introduction of such statements also varies.

The general rule, in the absence of statute, is that before such a statement may be introduced as independent proof, the witness must be confronted with it and given an opportunity to explain it. [41]

---

[38] *Sheehan* v. *Goriansky,* 317 Mass. 10, 16, citing with approval *Boston* v. *Santosuosso,* 307 Mass. 302, 349.

[39] *Allen* v. *United States,* 164 U.S. 492, 500. Where an agent of a party falsely testifies, his act is imputable to the party. *Garippa* v. *Wisotsky,* 108 N.Y.S. 2d 67, 72–74, affd. 280 App. Div. 807, affd. 305 N.Y. 571.

[40] *People* v. *Russell,* 266 N.Y. 147, 154.

[41] Compare *State* v. *Reed,* 62 Me. 129, 146–147, wherein the court observed that "[the] force [of a contradictory statement] must depend very materially upon the circumstances under which it was made and the influences at the time bearing upon the witness. It would therefore seem to be self-evident that witnesses so situated should be permitted to make such explanation as might be in their power. . . . To refuse the opportunity to explain

The need for such prior confrontation seems, however, to have been eliminated by the text of some statutes. Typical of such statutes is the following:

> "In addition to impeachment in the manner permitted by common law, any party may introduce proof that any witness has made a prior statement inconsistent with his testimony if the statement was made in a writing subscribed by him or was made under oath." [42]

There can hardly be a better method of proving that the witness has testified falsely. But, as has been indicated hereinabove,[43] unless the witness happens to be a party, these previous inconsistent statements have *no* substantial independent testimonial value.[44] This proposition is a dramatic example of the principle, based on *logic*, that cross-examination of a witness cannot take the place of direct proof.

In addition to the legal considerations here involved, a practical strategic reason exists for submitting positive direct proof of facts, which might otherwise only rest upon inferences from cross-examination.

The trier of the facts (court or jury) is interested in determining what actually happened as the result of which the litigation was brought. The way this matter is determined is by a consideration of the evidence. Unless there is proof as to the actual happenings, there can be *no* basis for a determination. Thus, even though a given witness may be shown to have deliberately lied, there is not, in this showing alone, *any* basis upon which the trier of the facts can determine that the opposite of what that witness testified to is the truth.

This proposition is not one of law. It is based upon the common

---

would be in effect to condemn a party without a hearing, and without that information which in many cases would be material to a correct judgment." See, also, *Meadors v. Commonwealth*, 281 Ky. 622, 625–626; *Quartz v. Pittsburgh*, 340 Pa. 277, 279. Where one puts in a prior inconsistent statement, there is always the danger that the opponent can introduce the whole of that statement, which might be damaging to the party originally offering part. *Nitzel v. Austin Co.*, 249 Fed. 2d 710.

[42] New York C.P.L.R., Rule 4514.

[43] See section 1:4, footnote 25, *supra.*

[44] *People v. Freeman*, 9 N.Y. 2d 600, 605, quoting with approval *People v. Kenda*, 3 A.D. 2d (New York) 80, 85, wherein it was said that this rule is "so firmly imbedded in our law of evidence that the citation of authority is scarcely required."

experience of the human being (or the collection of human beings)
entrusted with the duty of determining what happened. We can well
envisage a discussion among jurymen in which one of them per-
suasively says: "I agree that the witness lied deliberately. But all
that proves to me is that this witness cannot be believed. I still don't
know what really happened. The judge told us that we could disbelieve the entire testimony of a witness whom we find to be a
deliberate liar. I agree that we should completely disbelieve this
witness. As far as I'm concerned, it's the same as though he never
testified. But where is the proof that something else is the truth? I
don't remember any and, therefore, I won't join in a verdict that
something else is the truth."

Any lawyer who has spoken to jurymen after a case is completed
and the verdict returned will probably remember that some member
of the jury plaintively asked: "Tell me, Mr. X, what *really* happened
to cause this mess?" This type of inquiry furnishes an appropriate
key to the thinking of finders of the fact. What they want to know
is what *did* happen, not what *did not* happen.

From this premise, we should draw an important conclusion about
trial tactics. Even though a key witness for the opposing party has
been proved to be untruthful, counsel should try to avoid resting
solely on that demonstration of falsity, even if it is coupled with an
admission by the witness, himself, that the fact is other than that to
which he originally testified. If there is any evidence available to
prove what the real facts were, this evidence should be produced.
It is not merely cumulative evidence. It is the positive proof of what
the fact *really is*.

It must be borne in mind that, if a witness is proved to have been
a deliberate liar, he may be *totally* disbelieved by the finder of the
facts.[45] Therefore, his admission favorable to the cross-examiner may
also be disbelieved by the fact-finder. If the only evidence as to the
true fact is contained in the admission made by this falsifying witness, the end result may be that the evidence, as a whole, is deemed
insufficient for a positive finding—and, as a matter of logic, only a
positive finding can determine a case.

Finally, trial counsel may be faced with the proposition that the
finder of the facts does not believe that the witness was deliberately
falsifying, but merely comes to the conclusion that he was honestly

---

[45] This is the basis for the legal maxim, *falsus in uno, falsus in omnibus.*

mistaken, or that his memory was not clear as to the whole subject under inquiry. In this contingency, the danger exists that the independent admission made by the witness is insufficient to prove a fact, either because the witness may again be honestly mistaken or because his memory is so clouded that his ultimate version of the fact cannot meet the test of proof by a preponderance of the evidence.

Sec. 1:6 Direct examination during cross-examination.

After opening statements by counsel (or, in a case tried to the court without a jury, after the trial judge has read the trial memoranda submitted in advance by counsel), the trial can be said to begin as far as the finders of the facts are concerned. No matter how impressive an opening may have been, the average juryman regards it with some suspicion. He realizes that counsel has put the case in the light most favorable to his client. The juryman takes a "show me" attitude. He wants to see whether the testimony will actually bear out what counsel has told him it is a party's intent to prove.

When the juryman hears the early testimony, his impression of the justice of the cause begins to take form, no matter how often the court may instruct him to reach no final opinion until *all* of the evidence has been presented on both sides. As a matter of clearly recognized psychology and common experience, first impressions are difficult to erase and are liable to persist.

For this reason, it is desirable and important for counsel to attempt, as early as possible in the course of the trial, to prevent unfavorable first impressions from coloring the ultimate attitude of the triers of the fact, or, at least, to alleviate the impact of such first impressions. Obviously, the best way to do this is to introduce evidence through the mouth of the adversary's witness, tending to equalize or reverse first impressions, at the first available minute. It may be possible to do this by bringing out on cross-examination additional facts, *on subjects concerning which the adversary's witness has not testified*. Since this type of cross-examination constitutes proof of facts favorable to the contentions of the examiner, it may properly be denominated "direct examination during cross-examination." [46]

---

[46] We are not here referring to cross-examination concerning the general credibility of the witness, his bias and possible corruption. This, of course

The result of this type of "direct" examination is that the *same* witness who was called by the adversary to testify *against* a party is employed to testify *for* him. The timeliness of the additional testimony as well as the source from which it springs give it additional practical weight.

Early decisions, although few in number, would appear to have established the rule that, upon cross-examination, a witness could be interrogated not only on the subjects to which he testified on direct examination but also "as to any matter embraced in the issue." The party against whom such witness was called could, on cross-examination, "establish his defense by him without calling any other witness." [47] However, as will presently be demonstrated, the earlier rule has been completely changed in most American jurisdictions and the rule now is that a *witness may only be cross-examined on subjects to which he testified on direct examination.* It is true that many decisions pay lip-service to the proposition that the extent of cross-examination rests within the sound discretion of the trial judge; but this discretion is so severely curtailed by the prevailing rule that allowing cross-examination on new subjects is often held to be reversible error.

At pages 2–3 (sec. 1:1) *supra,* we have given an example of the refusal of the courts to permit a defendant to establish a separately pleaded defense during the course of the cross-examination of a plaintiff's witness and have stated the reasons a majority of the courts in the United States would advance for their rulings in this respect. However, it must not be assumed from this example that the principle of curtailment of cross-examination applies solely to matters of defense, separately pleaded as such. The exclusionary rule is much broader. It concerns all cross-examination on matters not testified to on direct, even though such matters are within the pleaded issues of the case.

The main reason given by the courts for limiting cross-examination in this aspect of the cause is that such cross-examination would impede the "orderly progress" of the trial. Strict adherence to the timetable of trial is suggested as the easiest way to prevent confu-

---

is *always* allowed. (Compare matter accompanying footnotes 19–22 and 26–28, this chapter, *supra.*) Our present reference is to *new* testimony, within the issues framed by the pleadings, but not directed toward explanation or limitation of anything the witness testified to on direct.

[47] *Fulton Bank v. Stafford,* 2 Wend. 483, 485 [New York]; *State v. Allen,* 107 N.C. 805.

sion. However, it can be argued convincingly (and has been in some cases so maintained) that confusion can be *avoided* by permitting cross-examination to bring out *everything* the witness knows about the case within the issues on trial. Why should the *same* witness have to be recalled at a later stage in the case so that he can tell the balance of what he knows? Is it not better for the triers of the fact to gain their *total* impression of the matters within the knowledge of the witness at one time, instead of having to hear, piecemeal, the various things to which the witness is competent and able to testify?

Adherence to a timetable in conducting a trial is to be commended when it is a means to the end of doing justice in the cause. However, it is *only* a means and not an end in itself. If the doing of justice is impeded by following a predetermined timetable, such a practice should be abandoned. The timetable for a trial may be likened to the use of traffic signals, which have as their purpose an attempt to avoid congestion. Certainly, no one would suggest that the police should desist from capturing bank-robbers, because attempts to make an arrest would tie up traffic.

The requirement that a witness be recalled to complete his statement of knowledge of the facts may result, if he is not so recalled, in the absurd compulsion that the witness actually violate the oath he has taken when ascending the witness stand.

The conventional oath (or affirmation) taken by a witness is that he will tell "the truth, the whole truth, and nothing but the truth." Presumably, this undertaking is to the effect that the witness, *in responding to questions propounded to him*, will answer truthfully and hold nothing back. A proper corollary of this oath would appear to be that no impediment to the questioning of a witness should be forced upon the lawyer examining him, provided such questioning properly comes within the issues on trial.

Yet, it is an unfortunate anomaly of our law that, in a majority of American jurisdictions, a rule of procedure prevails, which effectively prevents counsel, during the course of cross-examination, from obtaining from the witness a full account of everything the witness knows about the case at bar. Thus, by restriction of permissible questioning, the law in many American jurisdictions actually *prevents* the witness from telling "the whole truth."

This type of restriction largely results from decisional law, although it is, in some cases, buttressed or codified by statutes. It is often called "the Federal rule," because it has been so firmly stated in decisions of our Federal courts and is often so referred to in decisions of the various states.

"The rule in Federal Court is that a witness can not be cross-examined except as to facts and circumstances connected with the matters covered in his direct examination." [48] How firmly this rule is imbedded in our jurisprudence is illustrated by the following quotation from the opinion in a leading case: [49]

"Of course it is the duty of the judge in a criminal case to allow full and free examination of the government's witnesses in order that all relevant facts may be disclosed; but in the federal courts for over a hundred years the rule has been that the scope of cross examination is limited to subject matter referred to during the examination in chief; and if a party wishes to examine a witness regarding other matters, he must do so by making the witness his own and by calling him as such in the subsequent progress of the trial. Philadelphia & Trenton R. R. Co. v. Stimpson, 14 Pet. 448, 461, 39 U.S. 448, 461, 10 L.Ed. 535; Moyer v. Aetna Life Ins. Co., 3 Cir., 126 F.2d 141, 143; Kincade v. Mikles, 8 Cir., 144 F.2d 784, 787; Wigmore on Evidence, (3d Ed.), §§1885–1888. See Hider v. Gelbach, 4 Cir., 135 F.2d 693, 695. This rule has been the subject of some attack; and an attempt was made by Advisory Committee when formulating the Rules of Civil Procedure in 1936 and 1937 to change the rule to allow cross examination upon all the material and pertinent issues of the action. The Supreme Court in rejecting these proposals and in adopting Rule 43(b) of the Federal Rules of Civil Procedure, 28 U.S.C.A. Rule 43(b), as it now stands, indicate that 'the historic limitation upon the scope of cross examination to the subject matter of the direct examination is still to be enforced in the federal courts.' Moyer v. Aetna Life Ins. Co., 3 Cir., 126 F.2d 141, 143; Wigmore on Evidence (3d Ed.) §1888. Nothing to the contrary appears in the Federal Rules of Criminal Procedure."

---

[48] *Kincade v. Mikles*, 144 Fed. 2d 784, 787. The principle has been described as "the familiar rule which limits cross-examination to the subject matter of the examination in chief." *United States v. Minuse*, 142 Fed. 2d 388, 389, adding that "[a]lthough the strict application of this rule is not always to be commended, this is a matter within the trial court's discretion."

[49] *Bell v. United States*, 185 Fed. 2d 302, 310–311.

The court's allusion to an attempt by the Advisory Committee to modify the Federal rule refers to the original draft of Rule 43, paragraph (b) of the Federal Rules of Civil Procedure. The rule in its finally adopted form is quoted in section 1:4, *supra*. The Advisory Committee, in its original draft, added to that text the following:

> "Except as stated in the last preceding sentence, any witness called by a party and examined as to any matter material to any issue may be cross-examined by the adverse party upon all matters material to every issue of the action."

This sentence was rejected by the Supreme Court of the United States and is not presently contained in the Federal Rules of Civil Procedure.

That the Federal rule leaves the door wide open for chicanery has been explicitly recognized in a leading Michigan decision criticizing the rule.[50] In that case, the matter in issue was confined to the single point whether a man named Wetmore had authority to make and indorse a paper sued upon. The court described what happened in the course of the trial and its conclusions with respect thereto as follows:

> "But although he [Wetmore] was the first witness called, and the case involved nothing but paper made or indorsed by himself, he was not asked respecting his signatures, and the notes were not offered in evidence while he was upon the stand. The reason for this was apparent as soon as the cross-examination commenced; for when the witness was asked any questions concerning the notes, the purpose of which was to show that he had signed or indorsed them without authority and in fraud of defendant, and that he had admitted that such was the fact, objection was at once interposed on behalf of the plaintiff; and the circuit judge, remarking that the witness had given no testimony in reference to the notes nor had any testimony been

---

[50] *New York Iron Mine v. Negaunee Bank*, 39 Mich. 644, 658–659. Michigan is one of the states which does not fully adhere to this rule, but leaves the matter entirely to the discretion of the trial court. Compare *Wilson v. Wagar*, 26 Mich. 452, 457, and *Malicke v. Milan*, 320 Mich. 65.

introduced by any other party in reference to them nor had the notes been put in evidence, sustained the objection. The questions on behalf of the plaintiff had been carefully restricted to that part of the facts which it was supposed would tend in its favor, and in respect to which a cross-examination could not be damaging, and were intended, instead of eliciting the whole truth, to conceal whatever would favor the defense. The witness, instead of being required, according to the obligation of his oath, to tell the whole truth, had been carefully limited to something less than the whole; and when questions were asked calculated to supply his omissions, they were ruled out because they did not relate to the precise circumstances which the plaintiff had thought it for his interest to call out. . . . For here was the principal actor in the transaction under investigation brought forward as a witness to support his own acts, but carefully examined in such a manner as to avoid having him utter a single word regarding the main fact—though it was peculiarly within his own knowledge,—and even his handwriting was left to be proved by another. In that manner he was made to conceal not merely a part of the transaction but a principal part, and made to tell, not the whole truth according to the obligation of his oath, but a small fraction only,—a fraction, too, that was important only as it bore upon the main fact which was so carefully kept out of sight while this witness was giving his evidence. It is true, the defense was at liberty to call the witness subsequently; but this is no answer; the defense was not compellable to give credit to the plaintiff's witness as its own for the purpose of an explanation of facts constituting the plaintiff's case and a part of which the plaintiff had put before the jury when examining him. One of the mischiefs of the rule . . . was that it encouraged a practice not favorable to justice, whereby a party was compelled to make an unfriendly witness his own, after the party calling him had managed to present a one-sided and essentially false account of the facts, by artfully aiding the witness to give such glimpses of the truth only as would favor his own side of the issue. What has been said on this point has in substance been said many times before. The necessity of repeating it is a singular illustration of the difficulty with which a mischievous but plausible precedent is sometimes got rid of."

Despite the foregoing and many other criticisms, the fact remains that the Federal rule is the one most generally applied in American courts.[51]

Sometimes, the state courts iterate the controlling rule in even stronger terms than do the Federal courts. For example, in a leading Illinois case, it was said that "it is never permissible to put one's own case on cross-examination." [52] And we find *dicta* in some cases that state the Federal rule, but nevertheless fail strictly to apply it by allowing wide discretion to the trial court.[53] Indeed, it may fairly be stated that whether or not the Federal rule is applied in a given jurisdiction (either by decisional law or by codifying statute), there seems to be a wide practice of entrusting the matter to the discretion of the trial court.[54]

Attempts may be seen in some jurisdictions, which generally apply the Federal rule or have enacted statutes codifying it, to avoid literal compliance with that rule by "construing" it. One court has told us that cross-examination "may extend to any other matters connected therewith which tend to limit, explain, qualify, or rebut any inference resulting from the direct examination." [55] Another decision, in a state not strictly applying the Federal rule, states that a party has a right "on cross-examination, not only to call out any fact which would contradict or qualify any particular facts stated on the examination in chief, but anything which would tend to rebut or modify any conclusion or inference resulting from the facts so stated." [56]

---

[51] *Austin v. State,* 14 Ark. 555, 563; *People v. Montgomery,* 47 Cal. App. 2d 1, 19; *Forest Preserve Dist. of Cook County v. Alton R. Co.,* 391 Ill. 230, 235; *State v. Musack,* 254 Iowa 104, 109–110; *State v. Emrich,* 361 Mo. 922, 929; *McCutcheon v. Larsen,* 134 Mont. 511, 514–515; *State v. Centalonza,* 18 N.J. Super. 154, 159; *Mevorah v. Goodman,* 79 N.D. 443, 455; *Lyday v. Holloway* [Oklahoma] 325 Pac. 2d 432, 433; *Tolomeo v. Harmony Short Line,* 349 Pa. 420, 423–424; *Vingi v. Trillo,* 77 R.I. 55, 59–60.

[52] *Homer v. Bell,* 336 Ill. App. 581, 588.

[53] *Neil v. Thorn,* 88 N.Y. 270, 275–276, which permits the trial court to extend, in its discretion, the scope of cross-examination, although the opinion indicates that it is "the general rule that a party cannot introduce his case to the jury by cross-examining the witness of his adversary."

[54] *State v. Ragona,* 232 Iowa 700; *Wrabek v. Suchomel,* 145 Minn. 468. See, also, the language of some of the decisions cited in footnote 51, this chapter, *supra.* Abuse of this discretion is reversible error. *Papa v. Youngstrom,* 146 Conn. 37. Compare *State v. Angelle,* 217 La. 852. A witness may be cross-examined to bring out further details of a circumstance to which he testified on direct examination. *Williams v. Graff,* 194 Md. 516. In this connection, compare *Wilson v. Wagar,* 26 Mich. 452, 457.

[55] *Maxwell v. Bolles,* 28 Ore. 1, 6–7.

[56] *Wilson v. Wagar,* 26 Mich. 452, 457.

Where a witness is a party to the action, a much wider latitude is given on cross-examination in jurisdictions which would otherwise adhere to the Federal rule.[57] And "[d]oubt respecting the limits to which cross-examination may go ought usually, if not always, to be resolved against the objection."[58]

In some jurisdictions, the courts flatly refuse to abide by the Federal rule. They adopt the so-called "English" or "orthodox" rule, which is that, upon cross-examination, there is no limitation to matters brought out on direct examination, but the cross-examination may extend to all matters within the issues on trial.[59] Elsewhere, the adoption of the orthodox rule is fortified by statute or court rule. For example, in an Arizona Rule it is provided that "A witness may be cross-examined on any matter material to the case."[60] In still other jurisdictions an ambivalent attitude exists, resulting in adherence to the Federal rule in some cases and to the English or orthodox rule in others. These cases usually refuse to admit a difference between two decisions, but base their findings on upholding or overruling the exercise of discretion by a trial court.[61]

It is very difficult, at times, for a trial court, to make an immediate decision as to whether a question on cross-examination relates directly to something that was explored on direct examination; particularly where the case is a long one and neither party has offered a transcript of the testimony to date to the trial judge. Thus, as appears in many of the cases cited in the foregoing footnotes, the appellate courts are willing to accept the determination of the trial judge as a matter of discretion. The same difficulty that confronts the trial judge is faced by counsel. Very often, no matter how care-

---

[57] *Jess v. McMurray*, 394 Pa. 526, 527; *In re Clogston's Estate*, 93 Vt. 46, 50; *Weadock v. Kennedy*, 80 Wis. 449, 453. Compare *State v. Shipman*, 354 Mo. 265, 269.

[58] *Cobban v. Hecklen*, 27 Mont. 245, 263.

[59] *Madden v. State*, 40 Ala. App. 271, 274; *Podol v. Jacobs*, 65 Ariz. 50; *Pride v. Pride* (Texas) 318 S.W. 2d 715, 719.

[60] A.R.S.; Rules Civ. Proc., rule 43(g). See, also, *Podol v. Jacobs* 65 Ariz. 50, commenting on the fact that the orthodox rule was established by the Arizona Code of 1939, section 21-922.

[61] For example, compare *Knapp v. State*, 139 Neb. 810, with *Griffith v. State*, 157 Neb. 448, and compare *Weadock v. Kennedy*, 80 Wis. 449, 452–453, with *Sullivan v. Collins*, 107 Wis. 291, 295. Note, also, *Mattice v. Allen*, 33 Barb. [New York] 543, 546, which seems to be self-contradictory in the *same* opinion, because it states that the orthodox rule "is the rule in this State" and then says that "a party has no right, before he has opened his case to the jury to introduce it and prove it on cross-examination of his adversary's witness."

fully he may have followed the direct testimony of a witness, counsel is not certain whether to object to a question on the ground that it is not within the scope of the direct examination. Thus, "in practice, such inquiries are often made on cross-examination without objection, and allowed by the Court as a matter of convenience." [62]

In planning his trial tactics, counsel should not abandon the strategy of trying to introduce evidence in support of his own contentions during the cross-examination of adverse witnesses even in states which apply the Federal rule.[63] Searching cross-examination about subjects testified to on direct examination or touching the credibility, bias or corruption of a witness is, as we have seen, permitted in all jurisdictions.[64] Such cross-examination is not limited to a mere categorical review of the matters testified to in the direct examination, but it may extend to any matter referred to on direct or within the fair purview of such examination.[65] Inquiry is permitted as to "all the facts and circumstances connected with the matters of the direct examination." [66] Cross-examination may relate to matters that were not even mentioned during direct examination if such cross-examination has, as its purpose, the production of facts bearing on the credibility of the witness.[67] A broad charter for cross-examination in states applying the Federal rule was iterated in a leading case, which tells us that although "cross-examination is proper only as to those matters brought out on direct examination" it may include "any question which reasonably tends to explain, contradict or discredit such testimony." [68] It has been held, for example, that a witness may be examined concerning his personal knowledge of matters to which he testified on direct examination.[69] And if, perchance, a witness for the plaintiff has testified during his direct examination to matters rebutting a prospective defense, the defendant may cross-examine on all matters which tend to establish his own case.[70]

---

[62] *State v. Green,* 35 Conn. 203, 208.

[63] In states wherein the orthodox or English rule is the law, no problem presents itself in this respect.

[64] Compare the cases cited in footnotes 26 and 28 of this chapter, *supra.*

[65] *State v. Shipman,* 354 Mo. 265, 269.

[66] *Williams v. State,* 32 Fla. 315, 317.

[67] *Dickey v. Wagoner,* 160 Kan. 216, 219–220.

[68] *Lyday v. Holloway,* [Oklahoma] 325 Pac. 2d 432, 433.

[69] *Carter Products, Inc. v. Federal Trade Commission,* 201 Fed. 2d 446, 450.

[70] *Kenny v. Walker,* 29 Ore. 41, 47.

Chapter II

GENERAL PREPARATION FOR DIRECT EXAMINATION

Sec. 2:1 Basic nature and functions of preparation for direct examination.

Although, in operation, the two subjects may interlock, there is a difference between the general preparation of a case and the specific preparation for direct examination.

General preparation for trial is concerned with such concepts as: (a) the determination of what type of cause of action or defense should be interposed; (b) what, if any, motions addressed to the pleadings should be made; (c) what provisional remedies or other interim relief should be sought, and the like. Preparation for direct examination rests upon the assumption that general preparation has been or will, in due course, be accomplished or undertaken. The function of preparation for direct examination is two-fold: (a) to have the evidence (whether through the medium of witnesses, documentary proof, depositions, or otherwise) in such shape that it is legally *and strategically* presentable; (b) to get the evidence into court (through the medium of subpoenaes, requisition of documents, the advance taking of depositions and the like).

The failure to recognize the difference between preparation for trial, in general, and specific preparation for direct examination can be disastrous. It is not enough for trial counsel to have carefully analyzed his case with resultant preparation of a trial memorandum, or to know, even in the greatest detail, what evidence he intends to introduce and in what order, or even to have carefully interviewed the party whom he represents and each of his proposed witnesses. Ultimately, the success or failure of a case depends upon the testimony *which is actually adduced.* Preparation for direct examination must include the meeting of every foreseeable contingency so that proof will not only be developed, but also that the proof will be *available for use on the trial.* Furthermore, such questions as the *selection* of evidence and of witnesses from a mass of available material and personnel requires careful consideration.

The present chapter is devoted to the broad facets of preparation for direct examination applicable to all cases. Individual problems are discussed elsewhere in this volume.[1]

Proof on direct examination consists of four main classes:

(a) Oral testimony of witnesses during the course of a trial;

(b) Depositions;[2]

(c) Documentary proof, including special exhibits;[3]

(d) Presumptions resulting from statutory aids to proof;[4] and

(e) The utilization of judicial notice.

Each of these classes of proof is dependent on separate techniques of preparation for its successful employment. In addition, prepara-

---

[1] For example: Chapter III (determination of issues, whether set forth in the pleadings, collateral to the pleadings or raised for the first time during the trial); Chapter IV (choice of witnesses, primarily in situations where more than one witness is available to prove a given fact or series of facts); Chapter VII (the use of depositions).

[2] See Chapter VII, *post.*

[3] See Chapters VI and VIII, *post.*

[4] See Chapter XI, *post*

tion for redirect and rebuttal testimony requires additional techniques of preparation.[5]

Although preparation for direct examination is, as has been indicated, something different from general preparation of a case, it must not be assumed that preparation for direct examination is in some sort of isolated pigeonhole. From the very first interview with a client until the trial has ended there should be constant awareness of the desirability of producing favorable evidence *in admissible form.* Alert counsel will grasp every opportunity to develop and prepare for presentation any new evidence that comes to his attention at any stage of preparation for trial or during the trial, itself. Indeed, this is his duty.[6]

Many lawyers refer to their work between court sessions as "repair jobs." This phrase, if it connotes only attempts to overcome disadvantageous occurrences during the trial, is not sufficiently inclusive. Either through a happening in court or the sudden recollection of a client not theretofore mentioned, counsel may learn for the first time of an opportunity to obtain and make available additional evidence not necessarily involved in the process of overcoming unfavorable proof. Or counsel may determine that, in the light of trial developments, he *now* finds it desirable to use some proof theretofore regarded as unimportant. He should, of course, obtain and use this proof.

Sec. 2:2   Availability of all data at trial.

It is wise for counsel to bring to court not only the material he knows will be needed for trial, but also other data in his possession, which may, no matter how remote the contingency, be used as evidence or as a lead to evidence. These data include *all* documents (letters, inter-office memoranda, statements or depositions of witnesses [whether or not it is intended to call a particular person as a witness] and every scrap of paper that may bear on the litigated dispute, directly or indirectly.) [7]

No matter how carefully a lawyer has prepared his case, certain

---

[5] See Chapter XII, *post.*

[6] Canon 15, par. 3 of the *Canons of Ethics* of the American Bar Association.

[7] See Chapter VI, *post,* on the preparation of documentary proof and section 2:3, *post,* on the tactical desirability of taking written statements from parties and witnesses. Chapter VII, *post,* discusses the use of depositions.

documents (particularly letters or casual memoranda) may seem to have practically no bearing on the issues at trial. However, during the actual trial, a situation often arises where a seemingly unimportant scrap of paper assumes a more respectable status. For example, an adverse witness may testify that he did not see or communicate with the client after a certain date. Despite this disclaimer, counsel may have in his possession a letter dated thereafter or an office memorandum concerning a conference subsequent to the date which the witness fixed as his last contact with the client. This letter or memorandum may have hitherto seemed unimportant, because it covered a subject not connected with the litigation. Confronting the witness with such a letter is obviously important. The memorandum may later be introduced as an entry made in the regular course of business.[8]

It is customary and advantageous for trial counsel to have his client at the counsel table during the course of trial. Very often, it is the client who remembers the "unimportant" letter which now turns out to have a significant bearing on the credibility of the adverse witness.

Incidentally, it should be noted that, particularly where a case is tried to a jury, it is unwise for the client to talk to trial counsel during the course of an examination. This subject is covered more fully in section 5:2, *post*. There, we demonstrate the practical and advantageous method of communication between a client and trial counsel in the courtroom during the course of direct examination.

Sec. 2:3   Taking statements of parties and witnesses.

Ordinarily, the first step in preparation for any litigation is an interview with the client. Here, the lawyer discovers the outline of the controversy, the client's version of the facts and, usually, what the client believes to be the position taken by the adversary.[9] As preparation advances, the client produces his proposed witnesses for interview.

Some lawyers make it a uniform rule to obtain written statements from clients and witnesses practically as a matter of course. This is a dangerous practice, particularly in situations where the client's

---

[8] See section 11:10, *post*.

[9] If the client is a defendant, the position of the adversary may be outlined in a complaint already served.

written statement is taken and subscribed at a very early stage in the course of preparation without consideration of the possibility that, when he is confronted by documents, the client may be impelled to change his version of the facts after his recollection has been refreshed.

By statute in most American jurisdictions, it is provided that, in addition to impeachment in the manner permitted by common law, any party may introduce proof that a witness has made a prior statement inconsistent with his testimony, particularly if the statement was made in writing subscribed by him or was made under oath. The precise terms of the statutes vary, but their meaning is uniform.[10] Thus, it is apparent that causing a client to write or subscribe a statement of the facts can subject him to a needless danger. Opposing counsel can demand the production of the client's statement and would not be loath to take advantage of the slightest variations between the prior written statement and the present testimony of a party. Therefore, with respect to a client, the better rule of thumb would be that statements made to the attorney should take the form of the attorney's own notes, which are protected by the rule of privilege-confidentiality. Another type of protection, when the client's statements become part of the attorney's notes and are not signed by the client, has to do with pre-trial discovery proceedings. Ordinarily, notes made by the attorney in preparation for litigation are not obtainable on pre-trial discovery.[11]

Statements of non-party witnesses are not in precisely the same

---

[10] FEDERAL: F.R.C.P., Rule 26(d)(1). ALABAMA: Code, Title 7, Equity Rule 50. ARKANSAS: Stat. Ann., §28-707. COLORADO: R.C.P., Rule 26(d). DELAWARE: 13 Code. Ann.; Super. Civ. Rule 26(d), Chan. Rule 26. FLORIDA: F.S.A. §90.09. GEORGIA: Code Ann., §38-1803. HAWAII: Rev. L. HAWAII 1955, §§222-24 and 222-25. IDAHO: Code R9-1210. ILLINOIS: Smith-Hurd ILL. St. Ch. 110, §60. INDIANA: Burns' Stat. §2-1727. IOWA: R.C.P., Rule 144. KANSAS: K.S.A. 60-462 and 60-422. KENTUCKY: R.C.P., Rules 43.07-43.08. LOUISIANA: LSA-R.S. 15:497. MAINE: R.C.P., Rule 26. MINNESOTA: R.C.P., Rule 26.04. MONTANA: Sec. 93-1901-12, Repl. Vol. 7, Revised Codes of MONTANA 1947. NEBRASKA: R.R.S. 1943, §25-1267.04. NEVADA: N.R.C.P., Rule 26(d). NEW JERSEY: N.J.S.A. 2A:84A, Rules of Evidence, Rule 63(1). NEW MEXICO: §20-2-1, N.M.S.A. 1953. NEW YORK: C.P.L.R. 4514. NORTH DAKOTA: R.C.P., Rule 26(d). OHIO: Page's Rev. Code Ann., §2319.45. OREGON: O.R.S. 45.590 and 45.610. PENNSYLVANIA: P.S. §327. TENNESSEE: T.C.A. §24-1208. UTAH: 9 Code Ann. 1953, R.C.P., Rule 26(d). VERMONT: 12 V.S.A. §1234. VIRGINIA: §8-293, Code 1953, 1957 Repl. Vol. WEST VIRGINIA: R.C.P., Rule 26(d). WISCONSIN: W.S.A. 326.06(6) and 326.12. WYOMING: R.C.P., Rule 26(d).

[11] *Puggiero v. Board of Education,* 49 Misc. 2d 532, 533 [N.Y.] and cases therein cited

class as those of parties. Counsel are often confronted by a witness who may appear friendly but who presents the danger that he will switch sides before trial. In such a case, it is desirable that the statements of such witnesses be taken in writing. Then, if the witness is a turncoat, he may be impeached by confronting him with his prior written statement, utilizing the statutes to which reference has just been made.[12] Incidentally, if such a witness makes an unfriendly written statement subsequent to the friendly written statement and thereafter again switches sides and testifies in a friendly manner, it is sometimes provided by statute that the earlier friendly statement may be introduced where there is an intimation of recent fabrication.[13]

A witness sometimes presents to interviewing counsel a memorandum which he has made of a past event. When this witness is called to the stand, he may be unwilling or unable to recall that past event. This very often happens when, in a courtroom, he is face-to-face with a party against whom he is embarrassed to testify. In such a case, the memorandum made by the witness can be received in evidence as part of his present testimony under the doctrine of "past recollection recorded."

> "The rule of past recollection recorded may be simply stated. When a witness is unable to testify concerning facts recited by or through him in a memorandum, the memorandum is admissible as evidence of the facts contained therein if he observed the matter recorded, it was made contemporaneously with the occurrence of the facts recited and the witness is able to swear that he believed the memorandum correct at the time made. (See 3 Wigmore, Evidence [3d ed.], §§745–754.) When admitted, the memorandum becomes part of the witness' present testimony." [14]

If there is any doubt about whether a witness is liable to change sides before trial, it is a proper precaution to take his statement. Preferably, the witness should be encouraged to write out the statement in his own handwriting. However, if the statement is dictated and transcribed, the witness should sign each page of the statement

---

[12] See, also, cases cited in footnotes 19–21 of Chapter I, *supra*.
[13] *Cf.*, California Evidence Code, sections 791 and 1235 (Deering's).
[14] *Peo. v. Caprio*, 25 A.D. 2d 145, 150, affd. 18 N.Y. 2d 617.

at the foot thereof and initial each correction. Furthermore, a statement has added veracity if the typed transcript thereof bears insertions in the witness' own handwriting indicating corrections or additions.

Sec. 2:4   Review of pre-trial proceedings.

No preparation for direct examination is complete without a thorough review of all pre-trial proceedings.

Of course, all depositions that have been taken in the case should be thoroughly examined.[15] But this is not enough. Every affidavit submitted by either side should be reviewed and any product of a discovery proceeding should be examined.

The purpose of this review and examination is two-fold: first, to obtain the advantage of any piece of evidence that may be helpful; second, *and vitally important,* to avoid any inconsistency between the proposed direct examination and statements previously made in a pleading, deposition or affidavit.

Sec. 2:5   Review of testimony on earlier trial of same case.

If there has been a previous trial of the same cause, the testimony on that trial should be thoroughly examined. Such examination may disclose the fact that, in the earlier trial, a party or witness was hurt on cross-examination through the establishment of unfavorable facts. After considering this situation, counsel may determine that, although the facts in question are unfavorable to his contention, they would have less impact on the trier of the facts if they were brought out in advance by his own witness. This technique sometimes pays off with happy consequences.[16]

The same observation applies to a situation in which a witness or party, who is to be called in the instant case, testified at an earlier time in another litigation, where facts reflecting on his credibility (for example, prior conviction of a crime) were brought out.

Sec. 2:6   Stipulations as to evidence or facts.

In order to save expense, experienced counsel are very often willing to stipulate either that certain facts may be deemed proved for

---

[15] See Chapter VII, *post.*
[16] See section 5:3, *post.*

the purposes of the present litigation or that a witness, if called, would testify in a certain manner.[17]

If such a stipulation can be obtained and if the case is to be tried to a jury, the stipulation should be so worded that a layman can readily understand it.

The phrase "experienced counsel" as herein employed has real significance. Unfortunately, inexperienced counsel are very often afraid to stipulate to *any* fact. Equally unfortunately, some counsel are so stubborn that they unreasonably refuse to stipulate to a fact. There is a remedy for this situation. In some jurisdictions, provision is made by statute or court rule, whereby either party may serve upon the other a request for admissions, which carries with it the sanction that, if the admission is unreasonably withheld, the cost of proving the fact can be charged against the party refusing the admission. The statutes and court rules covering this subject vary substantially in different jurisdictions. The broadest type of statute (which may be used as a guide for both statutory and decisional research) is section 3123 of the New York Civil Practice Law and Rules, which reads as follows:

"§3123. **Admissions as to matters of fact, papers, documents and photographs.**

(a) **Notice to admit; admission unless denied or denial excused.** At any time after service of the answer or after the expiration of twenty days from service of the summons, whichever is sooner, and not later than twenty days before the trial, a party may serve upon any other party a written request for admission by the latter of the genuineness of any papers or documents, or the correctness or fairness of representation of any photographs, described in and served with the request, or of the truth of any matters of fact set forth in the request, as to which the party requesting the admission reasonably believes there can be no substantial dispute at the trial and which are within the knowledge of such other party or can be ascertained by him upon reasonable inquiry. Copies of the papers, documents or photographs shall be served with the request unless copies have already been furnished. Each of the matters of which an admission is requested shall be deemed admitted

---

[17] The latter type of stipulation is sometimes made orally during the trial.

unless within twenty days after service thereof or within such further time as the court may allow, the party to whom the request is directed serves upon the party requesting the admission a sworn statement either denying specifically the matters of which an admission is requested or setting forth in detail the reasons why he cannot truthfully either admit or deny those matters. If the matters of which an admission is requested cannot be fairly admitted without some material qualification or explanation, or if the matters constitute a trade secret or such party would be privileged or disqualified from testifying as a witness concerning them, such party may, in lieu of a denial or statement, serve a sworn statement setting forth in detail his claim and, if the claim is that the matters cannot be fairly admitted without some material qualification or explanation, admitting the matters with such qualification or explanation.

(b) **Effect of admission.** Any admission made, or deemed to be made, by a party pursuant to a request made under this rule is for the purpose of the pending action only and does not constitute an admission by him for any other purpose nor may it be used against him in any other proceeding; and the court, at any time, may allow a party to amend or withdraw any admission on such terms as may be just. Any admission shall be subject to all pertinent objections to admissibility which may be interposed at the trial.

(c) **Penalty for unreasonable denial.** If a party, after being served with a request under subdivision (a) does not admit and if the party requesting the admission thereafter proves the genuineness of any such paper or document, or the correctness or fairness of representation of any such photograph, or the truth of any such matter of fact, he may move at or immediately following the trial for an order requiring the other party to pay him the reasonable expenses incurred in making such proof, including reasonable attorney's fees. Unless the court finds that there were good reasons for the denial or the refusal otherwise to admit or that the admissions sought were of no substantial importance, the order shall be made irrespective of the result of the action. Upon a trial by jury, the motion for such an order shall be determined by the court outside the presence of the jury.'

A somewhat narrower provision (which incorporates the assumption of admission if there is no denial) is found in Rule 36 of the Federal Rules of Civil Procedure, which reads:

> **"Rule 36. Admission of facts and of genuineness of documents**
>
> (a) **Request for admission.** After commencement of an action a party may serve upon any other party a written request for the admission by the latter of the genuineness of any relevant documents described in and exhibited with the request or of the truth of any relevant matters of fact set forth in the request. If a plaintiff desires to serve a request within 10 days after commencement of the action leave of court, granted with or without notice, must be obtained. Copies of the documents shall be served with the request unless copies have already been furnished. Each of the matters of which an admission is requested shall be deemed admitted unless, within a period designated in the request, not less than 10 days after service thereof or within such shorter or longer time as the court may allow on motion and notice, the party to whom the request is directed serves upon the party requesting the admission either (1) a sworn statement denying specifically the matters of which an admission is requested or setting forth in detail the reasons why he cannot truthfully admit or deny those matters or (2) written objections on the ground that some or all of the requested admissions are privileged or irrelevant or that the request is otherwise improper in whole or in part, together with a notice of hearing the objections at the earliest practicable time. If written objections to a part of the request are made, the remainder of the request shall be answered within the period designated in the request. A denial shall fairly meet the substance of the requested admission, and when good faith requires that a party deny only a part or a qualification of a matter of which an admission is requested, he shall specify so much of it as is true and deny only the remainder.
>
> (b) **Effect of admission.** Any admission made by a party pursuant to such request is for the purpose of the pending action only and neither constitutes an admission by him for any other purpose nor may be used against him in any other proceeding."

Sec. 2:7   Preparation for inviting judicial notice.

In one form or another, statutes and decisions require or empower trial courts to take judicial notice of the statutes (and, in some cases, the decisional law) of other jurisdictions. However, even where a court is *required* to take such judicial notice, it would be unreasonable to expect the trial judge to know, without assistance from counsel, what the foreign law is. Accordingly, preparation for trial should include the collation of material to render such assistance to the trial judge.[18]

Whether or not foreign law must be pleaded depends upon practice in individual jurisdictions. The present tendency is that foreign law need not be pleaded by reference to statutes or decisions. However, where a cause of action is, itself, the creature of a foreign statute, the statute probably should be pleaded, so that the defendant may have notice of the applicable law depended upon in order that available defenses may be discovered and pleaded.[19]

The simplest way to call the attention of the court to, or to prove, a foreign statute or decision is by producing a copy of that statute or decision, properly authenticated. This must be done in jurisdictions where foreign law is required to be pleaded and proved. In other jurisdictions, reference in a trial memorandum to the statute or decision, with the official (*and unofficial*) citation, is sufficient. As a further aid to the court, the trial memorandum should not only have a citation of the foreign statute, but should set forth its text. Decisions referred to by citation should be summarized and, if appropriate, quoted from.

In many jurisdictions and also pursuant to the amendment in October, 1965, of the Federal Rules of Civil Procedure, a distinction is drawn between the need to plead the law of a foreign country and the law of a state other than the state in which the case is being tried. A most comprehensive and enlightening discussion of the subject, in a case involving a demand for a bill of particulars reads, in applicable part, as follows: [20]

---

[18] As to the method of requesting the court to take judicial notice, see section 10:2, *post.*

[19] *Richards v. United States*, 285 F. 2d 521, 525, affd. 369 U.S. 1. *Cf., Johnson v. Phoenix Bridge Co.*, 197 N.Y. 316, 320–323; *Colozzi v. Bevko, Inc.*, 17 N.J. 194, 196.

[20] *Gevinson v. Kirkeby-Natus Corp.*, 26 A.D. 2d [New York] 71, 73–76.

"The analysis is best initiated by noting the sharp distinction that must be made between the requirements affecting reliance on foreign law, that is, the law of foreign countries, and that of sister States.

"Under the new practice, the court is obliged to accord notice to sister-State law whether pleaded or not, and whether advance notice is given or not (CPLR 4511, subd. [a]; 5 Weinstein-Korn-Miller, N.Y. Civ. Prac., par. 4511.03; cf. *Pfleuger v. Pfleuger*, 304 N.Y. 148, under Civ. Prac. Act, §344-a, holding that a pleading was not deficient for failure to plead Pennsylvania law, but suggesting corrective alternatives). Under the prior practice, it was still discretionary with the court whether it would take notice of the law of sister States (Civ. Prac. Act, §344-a; *Pfleuger v. Pfleuger, supra; Kipp v. International Harvester Co.*, 11 AD 2d 896).

"The law of foreign countries, on the other hand, should still be stated in substance in the pleading which relies upon it (CPLR 3016, subd. [e]; 4511, subd. [b]). But the court, even in this instance, retains discretion to apply the law of foreign countries, notwithstanding the absence of advance notice or request to do so (CPLR 4511, subd. [b]). In the event suitable notice is given of reliance on the law of foreign countries the statute provides that the court 'shall' take judicial notice, but the notice of reliance may be in the pleading, or prior to the presentation of evidence, or as the court may otherwise permit (*id.*).

"The Federal rules require advance notice only in the case of foreign law (Rules Civ. Proc., rule 44.1, as amd. at the Oct. 1965 Term of the Supreme Court of the United States). Prior to the new Federal rule, a Federal court had refused to permit interrogatories as to foreign law, and particularly, as to the names and citations of cases, on the ground that they called for legal conclusions (*Fishermen & Merchants Bank v. Burin*, 11 F.R.D. 142, 145). Of course, it would be almost unthinkable, especially in a diversity case, that the Federal courts would require advance notice or particularization of State law.

"The draftsmen of the CPLR were definite in the separation of the problems presented by foreign law and sister-State law, and the statute enacted leaves no room for failing to distinguish between the two (2d Preliminary Report of Advisory Committee on Practice and Procedure, N.Y. Legis. Doc., 1958, No.

13, pp. 258–260; 3 Weinstein-Korn-Miller, *op. cit.*, pars. 3016.13–3016.17 and 5 *id.*, 4511.05). Moreover, the separate treatment of the two kinds of law is now logically compelled. So long as the court is bound to notice sister-State law the failure to give prior notice to rely on such law, to particularize it, or to brief it, has no preclusive or limiting effect, the primary purpose of a bill of particulars (3 Weinstein-Korn-Miller, *op. cit.*, pars. 3041.03, 3041.07). With respect to foreign law the consequences are not the same, but even there, notice, of the very kind provided in the present complaint, is all that is required. Beyond that requirement, the advocate may have to make a calculated tactical decision on how to persuade the court to accord judicial notice to his contentions under foreign law, but generally that will be the office of briefing and argument, rather than of pleading, particularization, or even formal discovery (3 Weinstein-Korn-Miller, *op. cit.*, pars. 3041.05–3041.08; cf. *United States v. Selby*, 25 F.R.D. 12, 14).

"As a practical matter to treat sister-State law as if it were as strange to the adversary or the court as Afghanistan law is without basis. Moreover, in this connection, the entire court is agreed that to require more than citations to statutes and decisional law would be patent and futile harassment.

"This development with respect to the law of jurisdictions other than that of the forum is buttressed by the recognition today that nonforum law is not and never was a question of fact except in an artificial procedural sense. Today, all such nonforum law in this State and in most States is treated as if it were a question of law in the court of first instance and on appellate review (CPLR 4511, subds. [c] and [d]; Fed. Rules Civ. Pro., rule 44.1; Uniform Interstate and International Procedure Act, §§4.02, 4.03 [9B U.L.A., Pocket Part, 1965, incl. the Comrs.' Notes appended, pp. 99–101]; Uniform Judicial Notice of Foreign Law Act, §5[9A U.L.A. p. 569, including Comrs.' Note appended]). This is true as to foreign law, and it is, therefore, true *a fortiori* as to sister-State law.

"It is no longer logical, then, for the pleading or particularization of foreign or sister-State law to be analogized to the pleading or particularization of facts. Rather, all that may be required is notice. In the case of sister-State law there is no mandatory notice requirement, but judicious advocacy may suggest otherwise, as was the case in the instant complaint. If an advocate relies on keeping his legal bases secret from his adversary he may succeed, to his undoing, in keeping them secret from the court. In the case of foreign law, notice is required, if the court is to be compelled to accord it recognition, and the degree of notice will vary directly with the inaccessibility, strangeness, abstruseness, uncertainty, and other general difficulty in apprehending the foreign law. Notice as to the law of another common-law English-speaking country may be considerably less detailed than that required as to a non-English-speaking country with a civil or oriental jurisprudence. The law of Texas or any other sister State hardly presents comparable difficulties (see McKinney's Cons. Laws of N.Y., Book 7B, CPLR 4511 appended comment, p. 369: 'The law of other states is determinable almost as easily as the law of the United States and every lawyer should be capable of finding it.').

"Weinstein-Korn-Miller in their treatise suggest that particularization may still be utilized to provide details of foreign law, in which term they include sister-State law (*op. cit.*, vol. 3, par. 3016.17; vol. 5, par. 4511.05). Insofar as they discuss sister-State law they rely largely on cases arising under section 344-a of the Civil Practice Act. The discussion is not consistent in spirit with their strictures on the decline of function in bills of particulars (*op. cit.*, vol. 3, par. 3041.05). Moreover, the historical development clarifies the seeming confusion. The drafting of the Uniform Interstate and International Procedure Act occurred between the earlier and later drafting of CPLR drafts, and the later CPLR drafts influenced and were influenced by the Uniform Act drafts, the several draftsmen of both working in close co-operation at the Columbia University School of Law (see 9B U.L.A. [Pocket Part, 1965, pp. 80–81] Comrs.' Prefatory Note to the Uniform Act; see, also, Practice Commentary by Professor McLaughlin in McKinney's Cons. Laws of N.Y., Book 7B, CPLR, 1965 Pocket Part, appended to 4511, subd. [b] and reflecting his views of a 'confusion' in the several drafts of CPLR). In this context the Uniform Law Commissioners had this to say: 'Although a pleading requirement may be justified as a notice device, pleading is neither the only nor always the most desirable method of giving notice of the presence of an issue of foreign law. The shift in focus in many modern procedural systems from the pleading stage to other phases of pretrial was intended to eliminate much of the hypertechnicality of pleading and time-consuming and sterile motion practice that may polish the pleadings, but rarely disposes of the case on the merits. A requirement that notice of intent to rely on foreign law be given in the pleading only perpetuates prior notions and invites dilatory motions and amendments.' (Note to §4.01.)

"True, the Commissioners were speaking of pleadings and not bills of particulars, but this case illustrates the futility of particularization which is primarily an adjunct to pleading rather than a notice device (3 Weinstein-Korn-Miller, *op. cit.*, par. 3041.06).

"Some caveats are indicated

"It should be obvious that in a proper case, even one involving sister-State law, a court, in its discretion, may require an adversary to disclose the bases of his claim, if the bases in the statute and decisional law of another State are difficult of ascertainment, for whatever reason, by the usual legal research techniques, or, more important, if it is unclear whether the litigant is relying at all on nonforum law (e.g., a guest statute of another State). This requirement may, perhaps, be imposed in a particularization, or better yet, in one of the truly discovery or other pretrial procedures available to a litigant. The law of Puerto Rico, by way of example, might provide such a rare instance, for although Puerto Rico is not a State it is a commonwealth embraced within the national jurisdiction and therefore its laws are noticeable under CPLR 4511 (subd. [a]). But on no view, does the present case provide an appropriate instance for such particularization.

"If, however, a litigant should succeed in concealing the bases of his claim resting on sister-State law to the obvious prejudice of his adversary, a court in a proper case would have ample remedies. Even if the disclosure should not arise until the trial, the court would be justified, in aid of its own obligation to give judicial notice as well as to assist the adversary, to grant a continuance, impose conditions and, in a permissible case, withhold costs."

Sec 2:8 Prior testimony of unavailable witness.

Where, in a civil action, the testimony of a witness is not available because of privilege, death, physical or mental illness, absence beyond the jurisdiction of the court to compel attendance by its process, or absence because the proponent of his statement does not know and with diligence has been unable to ascertain his whereabouts, or because the witness is incompetent to testify by reason of other statutory provisions, numerous statutes provide that prior testimony of this absent witness and documents introduced in connection with it may be introduced in evidence by any party upon trial of the same subject-matter in the same or another action between the same parties or their representatives.[21]

In some jurisdictions, the statutes further provide that either party may cause the deposition of a witness to be taken for the purpose of perpetuating his testimony.[22]

As will be seen from examination of the appropriate statute in a given jurisdiction, there is often a provision that the testimony on a prior trial may not be used if the unavailability of the witness was procured by, or through the culpable neglect or wrongdoing of, the proponent of his statement. In some instances, the statute also provides that the original stenographic notes of testimony taken by a stenographer who has since died or become incompetent may be read in evidence by any person whose competence to read them accurately is established to the satisfaction of the court.

If the testimony of such a witness is to be used, proper preparation requires that a certified transcript of the prior testimony be obtained, whether the statute so requires or not. If the stenographer who took the testimony is dead or has become incompetent, the witness who will read his notes should be carefully interviewed by trial counsel and, as a matter of precaution, should be asked to transcribe the notes in advance of the trial. This will enable the transcribed notes to be introduced as an exhibit in the discretion

---

[21] ARKANSAS: Stat. Ann., §28-713. CALIFORNIA: Code Civ. Proc., §1870 (Deering's); Evidence Code §§1290–1292 (Deering's). CONNECTICUT: C.G.S.A. §52-160. FLORIDA: F.S.A. §92.22. GEORGIA: Code Ann., §38-314. IDAHO: Code, §9-206. ILLINOIS: Smith-Hurd Ill. St. Ch. 51, §24 *et seq.* IOWA: 43 Code Ann., §§622.97–622.102. KANSAS: K.S.A. 60–460. KENTUCKY: KRS 422.150. LOUISIANA: LSA-R.S. 13:4261. MASSACHUSETTS: Ann. L. Mass., c. 233, §80. MISSISSIPPI: 2 Code 1942 Ann., §1749. NEVADA: NRS 178.230. NEW JERSEY: N.J.S.A. 2A:84-14. NEW YORK: C.P.L.R. 4517. OHIO: Page's Rev. Code Ann., §2317.06. OREGON: ORS 41.900(8). RHODE ISLAND: Gen. Laws 1956, §9-19-15. SOUTH CAROLINA: Code 1962, §26-11. WISCONSIN: W.S.A. 325.31.

[22] ALABAMA: Code, Title 7, §§491–505. HAWAII: Rev. L. Hawaii 1955, §223-18. NORTH CAROLINA: Gen. Stat. §8-83. OKLAHOMA: 12 Okl. St. Ann. §447. PENNSYLVANIA: 28 P.S. §327. TENNESSEE: T.C.A. §24-1208. TEXAS: Vernon's Tex. Civ. Stat., Art. 3766.

of the court. It should be noted, however, that this may not always be possible, since opposing counsel has the right to object to any testimony previously given by the unavailable witness on the ground of inadmissibility (other than hearsay).[23]

Sec. 2:9 Subpoenaes.

Preparation for direct examination should include the drawing and service of subpoenaes.

Local statutes and court rules should be examined to determine whether the subpoena has to be issued by the court or whether the attorney of record may, himself, issue the subpoena, and the length of time before trial when a subpoena may be served.

In most jurisdictions, there is a provision that the subpoena may contain a requirement that the witness attend upon the stated day and upon any adjournment of the case. If such a statute exists, the subpoena should contain a *definite* statement that attendance is required not only on the appointed day but on each adjourned date.

It is usual for subpoena-statutes to require the payment or tendering of a fee to the proposed witness, which fee is ordinarily based on a flat sum plus mileage. In determining the amount of a fee plus mileage, it is wise to err in the direction of generosity so that there can be no claim that the proposed witness was underpaid. Where a statute permits a subpoena to require attendance not only on the appointed day but on subsequent trial dates, care should be taken to pay or tender to the witness sufficient additional fees to cover later appearances.

An affidavit of service of the subpoena should be prepared and verified immediately after service and should include the time of service, the place where made and a statement either that the subpoena fee (setting forth the precise amount) has been paid to the witness or that it was tendered to the witness and he refused to accept the same.

Sec. 2:10 Subpoena Duces Tecum.

The rules just above stated for subpoenaes apply, also, to subpoenaes duces tecum. In some instances, statutes or court rules provide a greater witness fee for a subpoena duces tecum other than for ordinary subpoenaes.

---

[23] *Cf.*, Rule 4517, New York C.P.L.R.

A subpoena duces tecum should, as nearly as possible, state precisely the documents and things that are required to be produced by the witness. A general statement in such a subpoena requiring the production of "all papers, documents and things relative to the subject-matter" of the case is often held to be so indefinite that it is practically meaningless. A witness could hardly be blamed for failing to judge, in advance, what documents or things he is being asked to bring to court. Furthermore, there may be a virtual carload of material covered by the general description. Certainly, in jurisdictions where provision is made for a protective order, any witness could obtain an order either cancelling the subpoena or requiring the service of a more definite and specific one.

In many jurisdictions, the service of a subpoena duces tecum does *not* require the appearance in court of the witness named therein. All he is bound to do is to cause to be produced the documents and things called for in the subpoena. Accordingly, if, in addition to the production of these documents and things, the testimony of the witness, himself, is needed, a personal subpoena should be served as well as a subpoena duces tecum.

In some jurisdictions, by statute or court rule, a public institution, such as a hospital, may cause subpoenaed records (or certified copies thereof) to be deposited with the clerk of the court. In such a situation, counsel may, ordinarily, examine the documents in the custody of the court clerk.

It is customary for banks and similar institutions to honor a subpoena by causing delivery of the documents (or copies thereof) directly to the attorney who issued the subpoena. This pleasant gesture may, sometimes, lead to unpleasant results when counsel seeks to introduce the documents in evidence, because the objection may then be made that there is no proper identification of the documents. Care should be taken to avoid this consequence, which avoidance may be accomplished by an appropriate stipulation or demand for admissions of genuineness.[24] If counsel does not desire to disclose to his adversary that certain documents have been subpoenaed, he will naturally avoid either a stipulation or demand for admissions, but will make sure that, upon the trial of the action, a proper identifying witness will be present or available immediately upon call.

---

[24] See section 2:6, *supra.*

Sec. 2:11   Stipulations covering appearances of witnesses.

By arrangement between counsel or by arrangement between a witness and counsel for one side, stipulations are sometimes entered into whereby a witness agrees to appear on a given date. It is advisable that, in addition to the signing of the stipulation by counsel, it also be signed by the witness. Under the terms of the stipulation, the witness may also waive the payment of witness fees.

In the case of a witness, particularly a professional man, who is too busy to appear in court and then wait until he is called, an arrangement may properly be made for the witness to hold himself available to attend upon telephone call. This may be accomplished by stipulation, which is often made after the witness has been subpoenaed. Where the witness is a friendly professional man (such as a physician or physician-expert) an understanding that he is to appear may be reached without the service of a subpoena. However, some professional witnesses request that they be served with subpoenaes for reasons of their own convenience.

Many witnesses, who willingly agree to appear, request that they be served with subpoenaes in order to avoid embarrassment when they testify against friends or acquaintances.

Sec. 2:12   Final collation of trial material.

One of the most important factors in preparation for direct examination is the collation, in convenient form to be used on the trial, of *all* data which is intended to be employed. In subsequent chapters, there is discussed the preparation and use of individual trial data.[25]

Unless it is absolutely necessary, counsel should not depend on gathering trial data after the trial is commenced. At the very least, he should bring with him to court at the opening of the trial and preserve thereafter the following:

(a) Marked pleadings (if required by law or court rule);
(b) An outline of the trial (see section 2:14, *post*, for the

---

[25] For example: Chapter IV (lining up of witnesses who are to be used with respect to individual facts at issue and outlining their testimony); Chapter VI (documentary proof); Chapter VII (depositions); Chapter VIII (diagrams, tables and charts); Chapter X (miscellaneous technical proof).

form of this outline), containing the names of witnesses and their addresses and telephone numbers, a notation of motions to be made, and a general order of proof (which is, of course, subject to change);

(c) A trial memorandum for the use of the court in advance of trial (a copy of which need *not* be served on the opponent); [26]

(d) An outline of the testimony of each witness intended to be called on direct examination and an outline of interviews with possible witnesses or persons who are not intended to be called;

(e) Copies of subpoenaes served on each witness with affidavits of service;

(f) Any signed statements of witnesses or parties;

(g) Depositions of witnesses and parties;

(h) All pre-trial proceedings, including affidavits;

(i) Testimony in all previous trials of the same cause or allied causes;

(j) Exhibits of all types;

(k) Other written data, which may or may not become exhibits.

In addition to bringing material to court or serving subpoenaes for the production of the same, it is sometimes necessary to requisition papers for use on the trial from another division of the court or from the office of the main court clerk. This should be done sufficiently in advance of trial to make sure that the papers will be available. Before the commencement of the trial, a check should be made to ascertain that the requisitioned papers have been produced.

The foregoing applies to the collation of material connected, or possibly connected, with the direct examination of witnesses. In addition, counsel should bring to court all similar data which he may desire to use or which may possibly be used by him on cross-examination.

---

[26] There is nothing unethical in presenting a trial memorandum to the court without serving one's opponent. Indeed, if the court refuses to receive such a memorandum unless it is served, most experienced counsel ask that it be returned to them, because a trial memorandum discloses many subjects for the convenience of the court, which it is not desired to make known to the opposition in advance of trial.

Sec. 2:13 Warnings to proposed witnesses.

In the last analysis, the trial of a case comes down to the question whether the story told by one side or the other is *believed* by the trier of the facts. No matter how great the skill of counsel, he is unlikely to be more persuasive than the evidence he presents. The question of belief rests upon the persuasiveness of the evidence. That measure of persuasion, in turn, depends upon whether the trier of the facts believes that a *witness* (or series of witnesses) is telling the truth.

As part of the general preparation for trial, counsel must not only make clear to his proposed witnesses what their function is, but should also make suggestions to them as to their *manner* of testifying and should warn them against the possibilities of traps into which they may be led through their own over-enthusiasm.

At a minimum, the following advice should be given to all witnesses:

(a) The function of a witness is to state, in his own words and to the best of his recollection, what happened on the occasions to which he is testifying. When being cross-examined, the witness should continue to state his best recollection of the *events* to which he is testifying. Some witnesses, when being cross-examined, have a tendency to frame their answers in the context of the discussions between the witness and trial counsel during preparation for trial. This is a grave error and can lead to confusion on the part of the witness. The witness should be reminded that he is to testify to his best recollection of the *events* as to which he is being questioned and that it is unnecessary for him to complicate his own memory-process by trying to remember what counsel may have indicated was the significance of those events.

(b) A witness should answer questions directly. He should not volunteer information. If the question asked of him seems to indicate that counsel may have forgotten some additional facts to which the witness is prepared to testify, the witness should *not*, by volunteering, try to assist counsel. A volunteering witness is often looked upon by the trier of the facts as a person so eager to help "his side" that his testimony must be taken with a grain of salt.

(c) The witness should avoid losing his temper or becoming irritated by cross-examining counsel. If he is able to keep his temper, the witness will make an excellent impression on the trier of the facts. If cross-examining counsel addresses unpleasant questions to the witness, such counsel, if the answers of the witness are returned in a dispassionate manner, will probably irritate the fact-finder.

(d) A witness should never memorize or learn by rote his testimony. Some witnesses have ruined a case by writing out, for their own convenience, what they intend to testify to and then memorizing this writing. Where a witness has committed material to memory, this fact becomes obvious during his recital on the witness stand. Indeed, it is a favorite gambit of cross-examining counsel to ask such a witness to repeat his prior testimony. When the witness repeats it, practically *verbatim*, it is obvious that the fact-finder will assume that the witness is merely reciting a set piece instead of his giving his best recollection of what happened.

(e) On cross-examination, a witness should do his best to answer "Yes" or "No" to the cross-examiner's question.

(f) On cross-examination, the witness should avoid the temptation of trying to explain an unfavorable answer necessarily given by him. It should be impressed upon a prospective witness that the easiest way to defeat cross-examination is by answering truthfully and simply, even though the answer may be damaging to the party calling the witness. Sometimes a simple yes or no answer to a cross-examiner's question may be harmful; but the witness should trust the counsel for the party calling him to explore the subject more fully on redirect examination and, thus, to minimize (or indeed, destroy) the apparently harmful effect of a simple affirmative or negative answer to a "trick" question.

(g) A witness should answer all questions he understands. He should not hedge, or stall, or argue with counsel questioning him. He should not give the impression of being so partisan that his testimony may not be fully believed.

(h) A witness should not try to outguess cross-examining counsel. The cross-examiner has the advantage of knowing where his question will lead. He has planned his tactics and strategy in advance. The witness cannot, in this aspect, be a match for him and should not try to be.

It is essential for trial counsel to explain to his prospective witnesses the procedure during a trial. It should be made clear to the witness that, after he has been cross-examined, counsel for the party calling him has the right to redirect examination. It should also be made clear to the witness that, if counsel calling him rises to object to a question, the witness should not answer the same until after the objection has been ruled upon.

Finally, it should be emphasized—and this cannot be done too strongly—that the witness is not the lawyer in the case and should not attempt to usurp any of the functions of trial counsel.

Sec. 2:14 Master outline for trial.

In section 2:12, *supra*, we have discussed the final collation of trial material. Therein has been mentioned the desirability of bringing into court a proposed outline of the trial. In subsequent portions of this volume, the method by which various parts of such an outline would come into being is considered.[27]

The master outline for trial is akin to a table of contents, with one important addition—that is the inclusion of addresses and telephone numbers of each proposed witness. It is essential to include addresses and telephone numbers of witnesses in a single place. The outline of the testimony of each witness will have similar notations,[28] but the master list is a ready reference and avoids the necessity for fumbling through other papers when an emergency arises and a witness has to be called quickly. If there are special facts concerning the non-availability of witnesses for a limited period during the trial, such facts should also be noted in the master outline.

The master outline should contain a statement of *every step* proposed to be taken during the trial, including necessary preliminary steps after the case reaches a ready calendar. So constructed, the master outline is an important check list for trial counsel. Form 1 is the suggested form of master outline.

---

[27] For example, Chapter IV (choice and order of witnesses), section 5:10 (tactical interruptions of dull testimony), Chapter VII (use of depositions), and, in general, Chapters X and XI (miscellaneous technical proof and statutory aids to proof).

[28] See Form 4, sec. 5:3, *post*.

Form 1.

Master Outline for Trial.

1. Marked pleadings to Court.
2. Trial memorandum to Judge.
3. Check on requisitioned files.
4. Check on subpoenaed data from institutions [hospitals, banks, governmental offices, etc.]
5. Motion to amend complaint [or answer].
6. Witnesses on direct case:
   a) William Smith, 201 East 90 St. (CA 4-3093)
   b) John Jones, 11 West 20 St. (DR 9-7061 [answering service])
   c) Helen Roberts, 132 Bryant Ave. (LO 9-2020 during business hours; PL 6-1234 in evenings)
   d) Read from depositions of Gladys Smith and of defendant
7. Witnesses for rebuttal: [29]
   a) Franklin Koss, 959 Broadway (GE 7-0491)
   b) George McNulty, 1112 Park Ave. (LO 9-3232)—*Not available*, Sept. 9–11 [in California, travelling, cannot be reached].
8. Motion to amend pleadings to conform to proof.
9. Motion for judgment [directed verdict, dismissal, etc.]
10. Summation or post-trial brief.

---

[29] This portion of the outline may have to be augmented during the trial. Space should be left for this purpose.

Chapter III

DETERMINATION OF ISSUES

Sec. 3:1 Scope of trial not necessarily limited by pleaded issues.

Presumptively, the pleadings in a case determine what issues are to be tried. However, as will be demonstrated in this chapter, this presumption may be overcome in the trial of a case by a number of factors to which reference will hereinafter be made in detail, and which factors may enlarge or narrow the issues.

As a matter of tactics, counsel should bear in mind that although the technical outcome of a case is often stated to be the resolution of pleaded issues, such resolution usually rests upon the method of proof and the impression which the *total* evidence leaves on the mind of the trier of the facts. Obviously, for example, an ultimate finding of fact may rest upon the subordinate determination concerning the credibility of a witness. In turn, this subordinate finding may have to be premised on proof completely *dehors* the pleading.

But there are more subtle questions which can be advantageously injected into the trial by skillful counsel without doing violence either to the rules of evidence or the Canons of Ethics. An example of such a side-issue is proof that a witness is a close friend or relative of a party against whom he is testifying. Except in rare instances, such proof is outside the pleaded issues, yet its effect upon the fact finder will probably loom large; because it will appear that one who is inclined toward a party is nevertheless compelled to utter truths damaging to that party.

In determining what issues he intends to try, counsel should never neglect the opportunity of bringing in profitable side-issues. On the other hand, he must avoid clearly objectionable matter, lest he be suspected of deliberately trying to becloud the merits of the case by creating prejudice, or (and even worse) lest he be permitted to make his proof with resultant reversible error.

In some instances, counsel who calls a witness should, as a matter of law and of tactics, attempt to demonstrate, at the outset, that this witness is unfriendly. He may be able to prove, for example, that the witness either avoided the service of a subpoena or, after being subpoenaed, refused to discuss the case with examining counsel or his client. Or, he may be able to prove, out of the mouth of the witness, himself, actual enmity between the witness and his client.

The technical justification for the introduction of this evidence is to lay the foundation for a ruling by the court that the witness is hostile and therefore subject to interrogation on broader lines than would be a normal, presumably friendly, witness. The tactical advantage of this proof goes much deeper. The fact-finder, at the very outset of the testimony of this witness, will be encouraged to lend greater credence to what he says in favor of his enemy than would otherwise be accorded to that testimony. If, upon cross-examination, this witness should give testimony unfavorable to the party who originally called him, his evidence would unquestionably be viewed by the fact-finder with a jaundiced eye.

The burden of determining which side-issues should be injected into the case falls more heavily upon plaintiff's counsel than on counsel for the defendant. The former has to run the twin risks of opening a veritable Pandora's box of dangerous material for unfriendly exploration and/or of boring the fact-finder with inconsequential matters. The latter has the advantage of knowing what the major issues are and whether he has proof to meet these major issues. He can avoid controversy as to minor or unimportant issues. He should not, of course, leave important issues uncontroverted; [1]

---

[1] The danger of permitting uncontradicted testimony to remain in the record is illustrated by the cases cited in footnotes 7, 8 and 9 in Chapter I, *supra.*

but he may, with comparative safety, refuse to cross-examine with respect to, or fail to adduce evidence to rebut, minor side-issues. Indeed, he may save any reference to these side-issues until his summation, when he can refer to them as obvious attempts to "draw a red herring across the trail."

Sec. 3:2 Narrowing trial of pleaded issues by nature of case.

Under most modern pleading statutes, a party is permitted to plead inconsistent causes of action or defenses. Where he has so pleaded, the party is usually required to elect which of the inconsistent causes of action or defenses he wishes to go to the fact-finders (particularly in jury trials).

There are some cases, however, where a party is not permitted to adduce *any* evidence as to an alternative cause of action because inconsistent proof during the trial precludes the introduction of such evidence. This is *not* a question of pleading. It involves the exclusion of prejudicial matter from the attention of the fact-finder.

The most familiar example of this narrowing of the issues permitted to be tried is the case where a plaintiff alleges, in one cause of action, a definite contract for the performance of services and alleges, in another cause of action, *quantum meruit* for services performed. The obvious purpose of the plaintiff, in such a situation, is to put before the fact-finder the enormous amount of work he did, even though that would have no bearing on the case where an existing contract, not rescinded, is proved.

It is well-established law that *quantum meruit* is premised upon a promise implied in law where no contract exists. A party cannot be bound by an implied promise, when he has made an express contract as to the same subject matter.[2] The law will not imply a promise as a substitute for, or an addition to, an express contract of the parties.[3] There can be no recovery upon an implied promise in the presence of a specific contract "for the implication is rebutted by the terms of offer and acceptance."[4]

Once the evidence has established that there is an express contract, proof of the value of the work done or material furnished in

---

[2] *Hawkins v. United States*, 96 U.S. 689, 24 L. Ed. 607, 610.
[3] *Aetna National Bank v. Fourth National Bank*, 46 N.Y. 82, 86.
[4] *Walton Water Co. v. Village of Walton*, 238 N.Y. 46, 52, citing with approval *Klebe v. U.S.*, 263 U.S. 188.

the performance of the job is immaterial and, if admitted, constitutes prejudicial and reversible error.[5]

From the foregoing, it may be observed that, in the peculiar circumstances of a particular case, the issues permitted to be tried can be narrowed to exclude certain issues that may have been pleaded in the alternative.

Sec. 3:3   Triable issues enlarged by proceedings during trial.

In section 1:4, *supra*, we have referred to the fact that, even though certain proof may not be strictly within the pleaded issues, the court ordinarily will accept that proof in the absence of objection. The case will ultimately be decided on the issues actually tried by the parties, who are deemed to have presented by implied consent additional issues not embraced in the pleadings.[6] Thus, by proceedings during the trial, the triable issues will be enlarged for all purposes. The same result is reached when the court overrules an objection made by counsel, which ruling is sometimes accompanied by an on-the-spot amendment of the pleadings. Even though the objection would have been good under the pleadings as originally drawn, the law of the case thereafter becomes that the admission of testimony as to a question to which objection was made enlarges the triable issues.[7]

The rule of extension of triable issues by express or implied consent has very wide application. Thus, where certain issues were originally pleaded but were enlarged by the admission of evidence without objection and the trier of the facts made findings only upon the basis of the originally pleaded issues, an appellate court, in a lengthy opinion, stated the actual issues as developed by the pleading *and* the proof and sent the case back to the trial court to make findings on the enlarged issues.[8]

The extension of triable issues by proceedings during the trial must result from *evidence* received. Due process is only met by a trial of issues. Colloquy between court and counsel cannot take the

---

[5] *Van Order v. Fox,* 32 App. Div. 173 [N.Y.]; *Abinet v. Mediavilla,* 5 A.D. 2d 679, 680 [N.Y.]. See, also, *Hoch Associates v. Western Newspaper Union,* 308 N.Y. 461, 463, holding that the admission of this evidence was so prejudicial that it could not be cured by a later charge of the court restricting its probative scope.

[6] Rule 15(b) F.R.C.P. specifically so provides.

[7] Compare last two sentences of Rule 15(b) F.R.C.P.

[8] *Falcone v. Falcone,* 24 A.D. 2d 50, 51, 52–53 [N.Y.].

place of such trial and cannot, in and of itself, enlarge the triable issues.[9]

Sec. 3:4 Acceptance of evidence subject to motion to strike.

In cases tried to a jury, the trial judge must necessarily rule practically immediately on whether he will permit the introduction of evidence to which timely objection has been made. The reception of objectionable evidence might lead to reversible error. Exclusion of acceptable evidence would have the same result unless the witness could be recalled conveniently. A trial judge can, if he so chooses, receive otherwise objectionable evidence "subject to connection," but this is a dangerous practice and the trial judge in a jury case usually prefers the procedure of having the instant witness temporarily excused so that the connecting evidence may be introduced out of turn.

Unfortunately, in cases tried without a jury, many judges state that they will take *all* proffered evidence, subject to a motion to strike. This attitude imposes an unwarranted, burdensome and unfair handicap upon the lawyer who interposes a timely and proper objection. He is faced by the immediate question whether the tentative ruling of the court has actually enlarged the issues on trial. He cannot possibly resolve this question unless the judge makes rulings as to the admissibility of the evidence before the witness has left the stand, or at the very latest, after his opponent has completed the presentation of his evidence.

Then comes the question whether proof should be introduced to rebut the evidence which is still subject to a motion to strike. If no rebuttal of such evidence is forthcoming and if the motion is later denied, the danger exists that uncontroverted evidence must be accepted by the trier of the facts. If, on the other hand, the motion to strike is later granted, the expense and effort entailed in controverting evidence no longer in the record is an exaggerated case of love's labor lost.

Particularly unfair is the judge who adopts the rule that he will "take everything subject to a motion to strike" and then criticizes counsel for wasting time when the latter is attempting to rebut evidence which clearly should not have been accepted in the first instance.

---

[9] *Matter of Gelrod v. Levine,* 24 A.D. 2d 756(4) [N.Y.].

Another cruel impediment is created by the "taking everything" practice. When counsel presents a post-trial memorandum or brief, he is obliged to consider all evidence that has not yet been struck from the record.[10] He thus must write, in effect, a multiple brief based on several versions of the record. First, he must assume, as to *each* piece of evidence that was received subject to motion, that the motion is granted and must, accordingly, treat the case as though it did not contain all or any part of this evidence. Second, he must assume that *none* of the evidence received subject to motion was struck from the record. Finally, he must treat each permutation and combination resulting from the striking of *some* of the proof and the retaining of *other proof.* If there have been *many* rulings receiving evidence subject to a motion to strike, the post-trial memorandum obviously will no longer be entitled to bear the name "Brief."

Sometimes, in the circumstances of a particular case, the reception of evidence subject to a motion to strike makes it almost impossible to continue with the trial. In such a situation, trial counsel should not hesitate to state that, with due respect to the court, he insists upon his right to a ruling as to the admissibility of the questionable evidence. If the court refuses the ruling, counsel should take an exception, particularizing as one of its grounds the disadvantages to his client resulting from the refusal of a ruling.

In all events, in order to preserve his original objection for the record and in order to indicate that he has not, by silence, acquiesced in prior rulings of the court, counsel should, at the end of the testimony of the witness *and* at the end of the presentation of his opponent's case *and* at the end of the entire case, make a specific motion to strike the portions of the testimony to which he has previously objected and which was taken by the court subject to a motion to strike. The motion should not be general in nature (such as "I move to strike all testimony heretofore received subject to my motion to strike"). The motion should specifically state precisely what testimony should be excluded and an appropriate exception should be taken (whether or not required by statute) to denial of the motion to strike.

---

[10] It is small comfort to counsel, who has been compelled to write an overlengthy post-trial memorandum to have the court finally rule, as it did in one case, that "[i]n so finding, the court has not considered any of the evidence which was received at the trial subject to a motion to strike and finds ample evidence to support the said findings from the evidence which was unconditionally received." *Johnson v. Johnson,* 47 Misc. 2d 805, 806 [N.Y.].

Chapter IV

CHOICE AND ORDER OF WITNESSES

Sec. 4:1 Criteria for choosing and calling witnesses.

Where more than one witness is available to prove a point, counsel may be enabled to choose which witness or which several witnesses he will call and, if he determines to call more than one, the order in which they will be brought to the stand.

There is not complete freedom of choice; because there are situations in which the failure to call an available witness may leave a bad impression. For example, if the available witness has been referred to as being present at an important conversation and it is known that that person is friendly to one of the parties, it may be legitimately inferred that the failure of that party to call him as a witness was because he might testify disadvantageously. Some decisions state that the failure to call an available, friendly witness leads to the legal inference that, if called, he would testify adversely to the party failing to call him. Others limit this doctrine and hold that the failure to call an available, friendly witness leads only to the inference that, if called, he would not rebut adverse testimony given by other witnesses. Whichever rule is prevalent in a given jurisdiction, the fact remains that the failure to call an available, friendly witness creates a bad *impression*, no matter what the technical legal result may be.[1]

After counsel's opening statements to the jury (or, in a case tried without a jury, after the presentation of a pre-trial memorandum to the court), the trial of a case assumes many of the aspects of a dramatic theatrical performance. The ultimate aim of counsel (a combination, in this context, of director and actor) is to make favorable points by the production of *proof*. Except for documentary evidence, this proof is established by dialogue between witness and examining counsel. Obviously, as is true in a play or motion picture, the points to be established are strengthened or weakened by the cast of characters (the witnesses) and the construction of the dramatic script (the order in which witnesses are called). The basic question confronting counsel in choosing witnesses and determining the order in which to call them is a simple one. He must ask himself: "What witnesses can I best choose and in what order can I best present them so as to create the ultimate impression that the *story* I am asking the triers of the fact to believe is the truth?" Note the emphasis on the word "story." This is the key to the whole situation. Counsel contends that certain things took place. He unfolds these facts through the mouths of his witnesses. In sum-total they amount to a connected story. He will succeed only if this story is *believed*. It makes no difference, in this context, whether the case is tried to a jury or only before a judge. Although the method of presentation may differ in these two classes of trials, the final aim is the same— that is the procurement of *belief* in a witness-stated *story*.

In determining which of several available witnesses to call,[2] counsel should consider as to each possible witness: (a) his personality; (b) the impression he is likely to make when testifying;[3] and (c) his ability to withstand cross-examination.

When the witnesses to be called have been selected, the criteria for determining the order in which they are to be brought to the

---

[1] Of course, if a witness is equally available to both sides and not particularly friendly to either, no adverse inference can be drawn from the failure to call him.

[2] See section 4:3, *post*.

[3] A witness with an excellent personality may, when testifying, create a bad impression. For example, he may speak hurriedly or in a manner indicating that he has memorized his story.

stand [4] include: (a) the manner in which it is best calculated to unfold the *entire* story; (b) the knowledge of each proposed witness as to the entire facts or only a small portion thereof; and (c) the desirability of sandwiching the testimony of weak but necessary witnesses between the testimony of strong witnesses.

Choosing which witnesses to call is the product of interviews with proposed witnesses. In addition to learning the facts of the case during such interviews, counsel should try to place himself in the position of the trier of the facts, so that he can reach subjective reaction as to the desirability of a given person as a witness. One *caveat* should be observed. When counsel has interviewed a proposed witness several times (or even during the course of a single protracted interview), he may develop a personal dislike for this proposed witness. This does *not* mean that the person being interviewed would necessarily make a bad witness. It should be borne in mind that counsel, during the course of witness-interviews, often covers many subjects that will never be brought to light during the trial. The reaction of the witness to one of *these* subjects may cause counsel to dislike him. Such personal dislike should *never*, in and of itself, be a reason for discarding a proposed witness. The determination whether to call a given individual should rest in major part on counsel's impression whether that witness would probably be *believed* when testifying.

In the foregoing discussion, we have been considering circumstances in which counsel has a choice whether or not to call a given person as a witness. In situations where a proposed witness is necessary to prove an important fact, the choice disappears.

Instances often arise where counsel cannot interview a witness in advance but must call him to establish a prima facie case or defense. Here, it is desirable to learn as much of the witness' background as possible and to try to gather material to contradict this necessary witness if he proves hostile. [5]

Sec. 4:2 Charting available witnesses.

As has been shown in Chapter III, *supra,* three types of issues can appear in a given case, to wit: (a) the issues framed by the pleadings or amendments thereof; (b) side-issues deliberately brought

---

[4] See section 4:4, *post.*
[5] Compare sections 1:5 and 1:6, *supra.*

into the trial as a matter of tactics; and (c) issues injected during the course of a trial and actually tried, although not originally encompassed within the pleadings.

The first two types (issues within the pleadings and deliberately introduced side-issues) are the main subjects of trial preparation. The last type (issues appearing in the trial although not originally pleaded or contemplated) can only be the subject of advance preparation in connection with counsel's *general* knowledge of the case and can rarely be prepared for prior to trial.

In arranging the presentation of his case, counsel must first analyze the pleadings. In many jurisdictions, there is a requirement that the attorney for the plaintiff must present to the court, in advance of trial, a copy of the pleadings, with an endorsement at the side of each pleaded paragraph indicating whether the allegations in that paragraph have been admitted or denied, or whether the answer (or reply to a counterclaim) has denied knowledge or information sufficient to form a belief as to the contents thereof. These are known as "marked pleadings." In such jurisdictions, counsel has a ready reference by which he may determine what issues remain to be tried. Even where neither statute nor court rule requires submission to the court of marked pleadings, it is wise for counsel to prepare such a set of papers for his own use.

With the pleadings duly marked as to admissions or denials, counsel can conveniently indicate for his own planning what witnesses are available to prove each litigated point. A much employed manner for plaintiff's counsel preliminarily to plan the calling of witnesses is to set up a chart, which recites each allegation of the complaint, indicates which portions thereof are admitted or denied and then lists the available witnesses to testify as to the denied portions. In jurisdictions where marked pleadings are required, a copy thereof may act as the chart and the available prospective witnesses can be listed in the margin of the marked pleading.

Defendant's counsel can follow the same practice, in converse, with respect to counterclaims and a similar practice involving his planned proof of denials of allegations of the complaint.

Where separate defenses are pleaded, but not as counterclaims, counsel for the defendant will list the witnesses available to prove his defenses. Counsel for the plaintiff can, conversely, list the witnesses available for disproof of the separate defenses.

For the purposes here under discussion, it makes no difference whether counsel lists all possible witnesses or only those whom he has chosen to testify. Indeed, it is probably better practice to list everyone available and to leave final determination until the better witnesses have been sifted out.

Typical plaintiff's preliminary witness-charts might read as in Form 2 and Form 3.[6]

Form 2.

Preliminary Witness-Chart Where Marked Pleadings Not Required.

ELEVENTH [the number of the allegation in the complaint]: On or about June 10, 1966, the defendant withdrew the sum of $7,000 from the aforesaid joint account of plaintiff and defendant without the knowledge or consent of plaintiff and against her express refusal to authorize such withdrawal.

(Denied except as underlined.)
WILLIAM SMITH
HELEN JONES
OSCAR WILLIS
PLAINTIFF

Form 3.

Preliminary Witness-Chart Where Marked Pleadings Required By Statute Or Court Rule.

(Denied except as underlined.)
WILLIAM SMITH
HELEN JONES
OSCAR WILLIS
PLAINTIFF

ELEVENTH [the number of the allegation in the complaint]: On or about June 10, 1966, the defendant withdrew the sum of $7,000 from the aforesaid joint account of plaintiff and defendant without the knowledge or consent of plaintiff and against her express refusal to authorize such withdrawal.

---

[6] Obviously this preliminary chart cannot be prepared finally until all witnesses have been interviewed and counsel knows to what they are prepared to testify, but some counsel prefer to start preparation of this chart at an early stage of preparation and to augment it as other witnesses come to light.

From the foregoing charts counsel learns the following: (a) that defendant admits having withdrawn the money from the joint account; (b) that defendant denies that such withdrawal was without the knowledge or consent of plaintiff and against her explicit refusal to authorize the withdrawal; (c) that, in addition to plaintiff, William Smith, Helen Jones and Oscar Willis are prepared to testify in favor of plaintiff as to the denied allegations; and (d) that plaintiff, herself, is prepared to testify that the withdrawal was without her knowledge.

In Forms 2 and 3, *supra*, we have considered only a single allegation of a complaint. There will be a like charting of witnesses with respect to the other allegations.[7] A complete chart covering all allegations very often discloses that a single witness will testify to several matters embraced in different portions of the complaint. Ultimately, charts should be prepared (as a guide to direct examination) covering the proposed testimony of each individual witness. This subject, including an example of such a chart, is covered in section 5:3, *post*.

Where "side-issues" are intended to be established (see section 3:1, *supra*), a reflection of the witnesses available for such proof may, at the option of counsel, be placed in the pleading-oriented charts (Forms 2 and 3, *supra*). However, it is better to reserve this indication for the individual witness chart (section 5:3, *post.*)

Sec. 4:3   Strong and weak witnesses.

As all experienced trial counsel know, there is danger in calling *any* witness. The fallibility of human memory combined with the appearance of a witness' unpleasant personality traits conspire to present the problem that even a completely honest witness will either be disbelieved or so disliked that his testimony can be a disadvantage to the party calling him. In addition, there is a subconscious tendency on the part of those hearing the case to identify the witness with a party. As a result, we may be faced with the unstated but existing danger that a verdict may be brought in against one of the parties because the fact-finder disliked a witness so much that he did not want the *witness* to have the satisfaction of "winning" the case.

---

[7] Where an entire allegation is either admitted or undenied, the use of witnesses as to that allegation is often unnecessary, although witnesses may be used, as a matter of tactics, even as to undenied matters.

No matter how grave the danger, the fact remains that we *must* call witnesses in order to prevail on a trial (unless, as attorneys for defendants, we are fortunate enough to obtain a dismissal at the close of the plaintiff's case).

One of the greatest responsibilities of an advocate is his determination as to what witnesses to call where several are available and, conversely, what available witnesses to discard. He must weigh the strong and weak points of each possible witness. If he is fortunate, he can choose the stronger witness. If unfortunate, he is compelled to choose the less weak witness. Indeed, where only several weak witnesses are available, counsel may be compelled to call all of them in the hope that they will, somehow, corroborate one another or that there can be an application of the non-legal axiom that "in numbers there is strength."

The ideal witness is one who gives the appearance that he is simply testifying to his best memory of the facts and that he is not over-eager for "his side" to win. Such a witness is a rare jewel. If he avoids seeming to take sides under the stress of a vigorous cross-examination, he is a jewel without price. A witness who exhibits these potentials should, of course, be called.

Let us now consider the types of persons who should *not* be brought to the witness stand if it is humanly possible to avoid that course.

It should be noted that it is too late after a witness is on the stand to determine that he is a weak witness. This judgment must be made while the witness is being interviewed in preparation for trial. In the course of such preparation, counsel should not only probe the memory of the witness as to the facts, but also should seek to uncover what weaknesses the witness may have *as a person.*

Here are a few (by no means all-encompassing) examples of weak witnesses:

> (a) *The exaggerating witness.*—This type of person is very often motivated by a strong desire to "win" the case for the party calling him. However, he may simply be one who has a born tendency for exaggeration. He is liable to testify untruthfully, where his falsity can be demonstrated. He can get himself into a position where he actually *believes* the falsehoods. This often leads to a cumulation of untruths which not only damages the witness' own credibility but may ruin the entire case. This type of witness, on cross-examination, can be led into self-

contradictions because, as the old saying goes, "a successful liar must have a good memory."

(b) *The self-centered witness.*—Here, we have the type of egoist who is anxious to demonstrate how sapient he is. Even without his saying so, he gives the impression that he feels that he knows more about the case than the parties, their lawyers, or the other witnesses. He is liable to respond to simple questions on direct examination by tossing in facts which he believes counsel may have forgotten. In so doing, he has the potentiality of destroying the entire strategy planned for trial. His attitude in general and his grimaces in particular can disgust the fact-finder. This type of "wise guy" can single-handedly cause a case to be lost, although we may be sure that, if such a disaster occurs, he will find others to blame for his own negative contribution. We may be equally sure that, prominent among such others, will be trial counsel.

(c) *The excessively apprehensive witness.*—Most fact-finders (particularly jurors) are inclined to be somewhat sympathetic to a witness who appears nervous. With rare exceptions, no person likes to be called as a witness. In the strange surroundings of a courtroom and in the unaccustomed position of being the cynosure of all eyes, an average citizen is uncomfortable and will probably exhibit some signs of nervousness. This is not the type of person we are presently discussing. Here, we are considering the *excessively* nervous witness. He is one whose outward manifestations of nervousness are so exaggerated that they can well lead to the impression that he is not telling the truth. Furthermore, a person of this type can be led, through skillful cross-examination, into damaging admissions, which may well be contrary to fact. For example, after such a witness has truthfully described the relative position of various persons at the scene of an accident, he may then be questioned in terms of the greatest precision as to where he was standing, who was standing next to him or in front of him, and his elevation with respect to the situs of the accident. As his apprehension mounts, the witness becomes an easy victim of the simple question: "From where you were standing, you really couldn't see the accident very well, could you?" There is at least a fifty percent chance that the witness will answer in the negative, thus destroying the effectiveness of his truthful description of the happening.

Where counsel is confronted by the *necessity* of calling a weak witness, he should try in advance of trial to prevent the weakness of this witness from too greatly damaging his case. This may have to be a laborious process, beginning with the first interview and going on practically to the date of trial. Counsel must make it his business to gain the full confidence of the witness and to appeal to his intelligence to overcome his faults.

In preparing for trial, counsel may be able to reassure a nervous witness. In some instances, in order to alleviate nervousness, trial counsel have deemed it wise to take the proposed witness to court to observe the surroundings and nature of court proceedings in cases with which the witness has no connection. Sometimes, the apprehension of a witness arises from the fact that he feels that cross-examination may be damaging to *him,* personally. A typical example of this type of fear is the witness who knows that he has been guilty of tax-evasion and worries that this fact will be brought out. Counsel can assure such a witness that it is not customary for a court, of its own motion, to refer such matters to the prosecuting authorities.

The exaggerating witness is a harder nut to crack. No matter how much he is warned against exaggeration, it is often impossible to overcome his life-long habits. The important thing is to go over the salient facts of the case, time and time again, and to impress upon the witness the undesirability of testifying to anything other than these salient facts.

The "wise guy" witness is, if possible, to be avoided like the plague. If he *must* be used, counsel should try to frame his questions in such manner as to call for a simple "yes" or "no" answer. However, this is easier said than done. In one instance, it was successfully accomplished (in a case where it was necessary to call the witness, even though he was a cumulative witness, because his absence could not be satisfactorily explained) by counsel asking: "Have you been in the courtroom while Mr. Jones and Mr. Smith were testifying?" The witness answered in the affirmative. He was then asked: "If you were asked the same questions, would you give the same answers?" Again, the witness answered affirmatively. Counsel then terminated his examination.

There are some types of witnesses who combine strength with weakness. For example, an extremely youthful witness is liable to excite the sympathy of the fact-finder. This is particularly true where the judge, before letting a child testify, inquires of him about his knowledge of the nature of an oath and the child acknowledges his belief in God and that he believes that testifying falsely will be a sin. Although most people have the impression that a very young child will probably tell the truth, many, on the other hand, believe that such a youngster is widely open to suggestion. Whether or not to call a child-witness *cannot* be the subject of a general principle. The question should be whether to call *this particular* youthful witness.

Sec. 4:4   Order of calling witnesses.

The order in which witnesses are to be presented is an important factor in planning trial strategy.

This order should be determined in advance of trial, but obviously need not be inflexibly followed. Developments during the taking of testimony may dictate that a change be made while the trial is in progress. For example, if the testimony of a witness is substantially damaged during cross-examination, it is often desirable immediately to call other available witnesses who can testify as to the same points, with the result that, if these other witnesses stand up under cross-examination, they will help blunt the weaknesses exhibited by their predecessor.

The first and last witnesses called by a party should be strong. In addition to the substance of the testimony that they will give, they should be selected upon the basis that, in all probability, they can withstand cross-examination.

The opening witness gives to the fact-finder (particularly in a jury trial) a "slant" which may well persist throughout the trial.[8] Furthermore, if the first witness is carefully selected, there can be developed through him the substantial outline of the entire case. Thus, his testimony will point up the significance of the evidence of subsequent witnesses. A later witness may testify to a miniscule fact, but a perceptive fact-finder will be enabled, through the testimony of the first witness, to see where that fact fits into the general picture of the cause.

The last witness can sometimes round out the entire picture and, if skilfully examined, can do so without appearing to be repetitious. This witness, particularly, should be chosen on the basis of his ability

---

[8] Despite the fact that jurors are charged at the close of each session of a trial that they must not make up their minds until all of the evidence is in, early impressions are hard to erase.

to withstand cross-examination. Obviously, the case ends on a sour note if the last witness called is substantially damaged by cross-examination. The impression can be created that the whole case was weak. Even worse, if the cross-examination of the last witness proves him to be a deliberate liar or a person of bad character, the entire case of the party calling him, in retrospect, is dirtied.

If there is some helpful dramatic point in the case, it is well to have testimony on this subject given by the final witness. Histrionics, as such, rarely win cases; but a dramatic point, testified to without visible emotion, can sometimes be all but decisive.

An example (although obviously an unusual one) is furnished by the testimony in a famous criminal case. There, two defendants were charged with systematic bribery of public officials. The last witness called by the prosecution testified that, on a certain evening and at a certain place, he had seen both defendants with one of the officials alleged to have been bribed. He was then asked whether, since he had been subpoenaed as a witness, he had received a communication from either of the defendants. He answered that, about a week before the trial, the defendants had met him in a restaurant where he was eating with his wife. He told how the defendants had asked to speak with him in the men's room of the restaurant. He then testified that, when they were there foregathered, the defendants had offered him the sum of $5,000 if he would testify that he was mistaken as to the time he was meant to have seen the defendants with the allegedly bribed official and that he was not sure that the person with the defendants was actually that official. The defendants were convicted, although the case against them was by no means a strong one. In the opinion of courtroom observers, the damaging testimony that the defendants had offered to bribe a witness was the final determinant in the minds of the jurors.

Ideally, witnesses should be called in an order which can develop the facts chronologically. If possible, as each witness leaves the stand, his testimony should have ended at a stage where the next witness picks up the story in point of time. Obviously, this ideal chronological presentation often cannot be utilized; because a single witness may be called to testify to disconnected series of facts as far as chronology is concerned and, under the order of trial adopted in most American jurisdictions, a witness must complete *all* of his direct testimony at one time.[9]

---

[9] See section 1:3, *supra.*

In determining the order of calling witnesses, one salutory rule should be followed: *Never,* unless it is absolutely unavoidable (for example, if a witness cannot be available at a later date), call a witness to a very late happening before the testimony of other witnesses has laid the foundation for the ability to give significance to that happening.

In conjunction with the attempt to establish a case chronologically, groups of witnesses should be so called that those who are to testify to a single incident are presented *seriatim* and without interruption. This permits the fact-finder to get a cumulative impression of that incident and to feel that he can now pass on to the next point in the case.

In section 4:3, *supra,* we have referred to "weak" witnesses. Where other witnesses can testify to some of the subjects covered by the weak witness it is wise to present their testimony *directly* before and after the testimony of the weak witness. Although this may have the result of temporarily disturbing chronology, such result is more than over-balanced by the corroborative effect of the testimony of these other witnesses. The strategy, here, is comparable to the calling of witnesses out of the predetermined order after a witness has been damaged on cross-examination.

Sec. 4:5   Cumulative witnesses.

As has been stated in section 4:3, *supra,* experienced counsel recognize that there is danger in calling *any* witness. This does not mean, however, that cumulative witnesses to the same incident should not be used, even where an earlier witness has testified well and has ably withstood cross-examination.

Where several "strong" witnesses are available, it is unwise to confine testimony on an *important* issue to but one witness. The key consideration, here, is whether the issue to which cumulative witnesses are presented to testify is *important.* There is a danger that the trier of the facts (particularly a jury) will be bored by the testimony of cumulative witnesses on *unimportant* matters; but if the matter in question is of great importance, the trier of the facts will be eager to hear any additional evidence that is offered on this subject.

If there is any danger that the failure to call an available, friendly witness can be the subject of adverse argument by an adversary or may lead to the inference that available and important proof is being withheld, witnesses should unquestionably be called, even though their testimony is cumulative. Here, the criterion is not whether the available witness is weak or strong. The dictate of calling him is one of necessity.

Sec. 4:6 Calling adverse party as witness.

It is sometimes tactically advantageous to call the adverse party as a witness. In addition to the element of surprise, there is also the thought that the early calling of an adverse party will prevent him from manufacturing a story to meet the evidence produced by one's own witnesses.

There is, of course, another side to the coin. If the adverse party proves to be a good witness in his own behalf, the case may get off to an unfortunate start and the good impression left by the adverse party may persist throughout the trial. Indeed, the trier of the facts may accept the adverse party's testimony very strongly and subconsciously require affirmative evidence of a substantial nature to overcome it.

An important advantage is lost by calling an adverse party as one's own witness. Although the party calling him is not "bound" by his testimony as to important points in issue and may call other witnesses to contradict the testimony of the adverse party, the opportunity is lost to impeach his *general* credibility, since one who calls a witness is "not at liberty to impeach [the witness'] character for truth." [10]

It sometimes occurs that the calling of the adverse party as the first (and even the *only*) witness permits the avoidance of subjecting one's own client to a cross-examination which he may not be able to withstand. An anchor to windward in such a situation is afforded by the fact that one can always call his own party if the adverse party's testimony proves unsatisfactory. The technique can be successfully employed, best, where the questioner has in his possession documents concerning which he can inquire of the

---

[10] *Cross v. Cross,* 108 N.Y. 628, 629. The principle here involved is analogous to that applicable to the interrogation of an unwilling or hostile witness. See discussion of the right to impeach one's own witness in section 1:4, *supra,* and the cases cited in footnotes 24, 25, 26 and 28 of that section. Compare, also, Rule 43(b) of the Federal Rules of Civil Procedure, codifying the decisional law on the right to interrogate an unwilling or hostile witness and to call in adverse party as a witness.

adverse party and which, together with the adverse party's practically formal testimony, can establish the point sought to be made.

An example of calling the adverse party as the only witness occurred in a case where a husband had sued out a writ of habeas corpus seeking permission to give him reasonable visitation with his children, who were living with his estranged wife. Obviously, a father has the right to see his children, unless it can be proved that he is an unfit person. The obligation of establishing that the father is unfit, or that his visitation would be harmful for the children, rests upon the person asserting that fact. Counsel for the father called as his first and only witness the mother of the children. He asked her whether she had refused to permit the father to visit the children. When her answers were equivocal, he confronted her with letters she had written to the father. On the basis of these letters, she was forced to admit that she had refused visitation to the father. At this point, counsel terminated his examination. When the mother was not cross-examined by her own attorney, counsel for the father rested his case. This put the mother's attorney at the disadvantage not only of having to go forward with the proof but also, if he called the father as *his* witness, of being deprived of the opportunity to impeach him generally, except insofar as such impeachment would have a direct bearing on the fitness of the father to visit with his children.

Sec. 4:7   Defendant's choice of witnesses and order of proof.

In some respects, the defendant has a distinct advantage in choosing his witnesses and determining the order in which they will be presented. By the time it is his turn to offer a direct case, the defendant has heard the plaintiff's testimony, is able within limits to assay its impression on the trier of the facts and can determine how full his own case should be.[11]

During the course of the plaintiff's case, defendant's counsel (preferably through an assistant) should make careful note of the testimony given by plaintiff's witnesses. Before undertaking his own presentation, defendant's counsel can perfectly properly ask for a

---

[11] Where a defendant substantially admits the facts but depends upon some cype of separate defense, such as the Statute of Limitations or the Statute of Frauds, he has the very simple task of limiting his presentation entirely to these technical matters and can do this in a concise, non-boring manner.

short recess in order to consider what witnesses he will call and in what order he will present them.[12]

Defendant's counsel should make certain not to leave the record in a situation where important facts remain uncontradicted. He should be sure, as to all *important* facts in the case, that his own witnesses, if they can truthfully do so, *specifically* deny the existence of these facts or offer an explanation. As to *unimportant* facts, this caveat need not be observed; but if there is any doubt in the mind of counsel as to whether a given fact is important or unimportant, it is best that the same be controverted or explained. It should be remembered that, not only in final argument to the fact-finder but also upon appeal, it will be advantageous to one's opponent to be able to point out that important testimony was neither contradicted nor explained. However, the contradiction need not take a lengthy form. A typical question and answer covering a mere contradiction without explanation would be as follows:

"**Q.** It has been testified that you told plaintiff that it was your fault that the accident took place and that you were driving your automobile at such a rate of speed that you could not control it. Did you make this statement or any similar statement to plaintiff? **A.** No."

It must not be assumed from the foregoing that it is proper merely to present categorical denials of testimony offered by the plaintiff. Where the defendant is in possession of good testimony having the effect of contradicting or explaining plaintiff's proof, he should present it at such reasonable length as will convince the trier of the facts. The plaintiff has told his story. The defendant must tell his. He must not only deny what plaintiff has presented but must affirmatively assert what he claims actually happened. In making such assertion, it is desirable to present something more than the defendant's own testimony. Witnesses who can buttress his story should be called. Documents which can support his oral testimony should be offered.

There are some types of affirmative defenses, which, although they admit certain facts pleaded and prima facie established by plaintiff require a full-dress defendant's presentation. For example,

---

[12] If the case lasts more than one day, some of this preparation should be done in the evening between court sessions.

where a plaintiff sues upon a promissory note, which has not been negotiated to an innocent third party, and the defendant claims that, when he signed the note, plaintiff assured him that it would not be presented for payment if defendant kept another promise made at the time he gave the note, the defendant will have to make a very strong showing. Here, the presentation of the defendant's case may require not only his own testimony but that of other witnesses. In such a situation, defendant's direct examination should follow all of the considerations generally employed in that of a plaintiff.

It is often true that, during the course of the plaintiff's case, evidence helpful to the defendant comes to light. It is unnecessary and usually undesirable to repeat proof on already established points during the course of defendant's case. What tactic to follow is a matter of judgment, depending upon counsel's determination whether the evidence in behalf of his client established during plaintiff's case is sufficiently strong that it need not be redeveloped. If a point has been made with sufficient strength, there is no sense in taking the risk of weakening it by having a witness allude to it and then, possibly, be damaged on cross-examination.

As a general rule, it may be stated that the defendant's counsel should develop uncontroverted facts only when it is necessary to reaffirm these facts as a framework for the full understanding of the testimony of a defendant's witness.

Although the order in which a defendant intends to call his witnesses is usually preliminarily set before the commencement of the trial, this order is much more liable to change than the order in which the plaintiff's counsel has determined to call his witnesses. For example, if the plaintiff has closed his case strongly on a particular point it is wise for the defendant to call his own strong witnesses controverting that point at the very beginning of the defendant's case. Chronology can here be sacrificed for the sake of tactical emphasis.

Chapter V

TECHNIQUE OF
DIRECT EXAMINATION

Sec. 5:1   Basic aim of all examination techniques.

The basic aim of all examination techniques, particularly those involved in the direct examination of witnesses, is to *grasp and hold the attention of the trier of the facts and to avoid any actions which would disturb the fact-finder's concentration.*

A paramount consideration in the direct examination of witnesses is, therefore, that the same should be conducted with a degree of smoothness and continuity, thus assuring, to the greatest degree possible, the attention and concentration of the fact-finder. This is particularly true in cases tried to a jury, but is also important when a judge or referee is the trier of the facts.

The personal habits, mannerisms and idiosyncrasies of individual

77

trial counsel are as varied as the differences between human beings. Trial counsel cannot be expected to remake himself merely because he is conducting a direct examination. It is a mistake for trial counsel to concentrate upon creating an "image" of himself, where the invention of such an image is a contradiction of his own normal personality.

Although advocacy is an art, trial counsel should avoid letting the utilization of that art become apparent. He must never permit it to appear that his skill is more important than the testimony of the witness. He may (and, ordinarily, should) let it be plain that he believes in the rectitude of his client's cause; but he should avoid any manifestation that it is his rather than his client's case which is on trial or that an important element in the trial is whether counsel can score a victory.

It is a great mistake for trial counsel to react with obvious pleasure or glee, whether by a change in his tone of voice or by a grin or other facial expression, to a favorable answer of his own (or, indeed, of his opponent's) witness. Such a reaction leaves the unfortunate impression that it is the lawyer and not the client who is benefited by the answer. *Never* should trial counsel by any act let the case degenerate into an obvious battle between attorneys. Counsel should so conduct himself that the trier of the facts is brought to realize that the issue at bar is the determination of who is right in the litigated controversy. A grimacing counsel is a detriment to his client's cause.

What has just been stated with regard to counsel's reaction to a favorable answer by a witness is conversely and even more importantly applicable to counsel's reaction to an unfavorable answer. He should not in any manner indicate that the testimony of a witness has been disappointing.

During the course of direct examination, the nature of the questions propounded by trial counsel and the answers given by witnesses emphasize the relative importance in the context of the entire case of particular facts. But exaggerated emphasis placed by counsel during direct examination on what testimony he conceives to be the highlights of his case is a mistake. Such emphasis should be reserved for summation. Repeated insistence during direct examination upon the importance of certain facts may lead to the denigration of other facts. The end result may well be that a fact deemed important, for example, by an individual juryman is, in effect, belittled by counsel's over-emphasis on other facts.

The sum-total impression on the mind of the fact-finder is what is important. Counsel should not deprive the fact-finder of his own ability to determine what is significant.

A common error of trial counsel, during direct examination, is to seek to emphasize particular testimony of a witness by summarizing that testimony in the form of a virtual repetition. It is wrong, for example, for trial counsel to follow a witness' satisfactory answer with a new question beginning with the phrase "In other words. . . ."[1] When the witness testified to this fact, the impression was that the *witness* remembered the happening in question. When counsel summarizes that testimony, it may lead to the impression that the witness is merely an automaton and that it is counsel, who was admittedly not present at the time of the happening being covered by the answer of the witness, who is spoon-feeding a subservient witness. This may destroy the effectiveness of the original satisfactory answer of the witness and can even wholly or partially destroy the general good impression created by other testimony of the same witness.

The safest technique for trial counsel to employ is one that leads the trier of the facts to believe that counsel is trying to act as an assistant to the fact-finder rather than an advocate intent upon winning a victory for his own aggrandizement. The proper attitude to be assumed by trial counsel is best summarized by the suggestion that he cast himself in the role of a "thirteenth juror."

Sec. 5:2   Communication in courtroom between trial counsel, his assistants and clients during trial.

If the direct examination is interrupted by oral conferences during its course between trial counsel, his assistant and client, the concentration of the trier of the facts may obviously be disturbed. A successful direct examination should have as its central figure *the witness*. Counsel's role is to bring forward, in its most convenient form, the testimony given by the witness.

If counsel constantly wanders over to his assistant or client, particularly when one of them beckons, the visual impact upon and psychological conclusions of the trier of the facts may be disastrous. As to visual impact, it is obvious that the trier of the facts will turn his attention from the witness, who is seated, and follow counsel,

---

[1] Indeed, such a summary-type question may be the subject of a successful objection by the opponent.

who is moving. As to psychological conclusions, the trier of the facts will certainly very humanly wonder what counsel, his assistants and clients are talking about. This may lead to the unfair conclusion that some sort of sinister plotting is being engaged in. It may also cause the trier of the facts to attach undue importance to the questions addressed to the witness directly following the oral courtroom conference, or to feel that the answer previously given by the witness was unsatisfactory or damaging.

It is, of course, essential for trial counsel to be in a position to accept suggestions from his client or assistant. This is best accomplished by the following method:

It is the usual and desirable practice for trial counsel to be seated at the end of the counsel table (in a jury trial at the end nearest to the jury). This assures him of greater mobility than if he were sandwiched in between an assistant and a client. Seated next to trial counsel should be his assistant. Next to the assistant should be the client.[2]

Both the assistant and the client should, if matters are believed by either of them to be worthy of calling to the attention of trial counsel, write their suggestions on slips of paper. The writing should be clearly legible and in *large* printing or script. This will enable trial counsel to pick up the slips of paper just before he has completed his direct examination. He can then consider the suggestions and utilize them if he sees fit. The notes to trial counsel should be very simply phrased. For example, the client may write: "He [the witness] wrote us a letter after June 19."

Some lawyers have considered it wise to leave one or two questions unpropounded when they return to the counsel table to pick up the suggestion notes. Thereafter, counsel can either use the suggestions or discard them, but he may return to his questioning posture and ask the last few questions which he had reserved for this purpose.

No matter how carefully counsel has prepared his case and questioned a witness on direct examination, it is possible that he may have forgotten or otherwise failed to bring out some important point. For this reason, it is wise for counsel, before he drops a witness, to

---

[2] In many cases, trial counsel does not have an assistant in the courtroom, although this may turn out to be extremely disadvantageous. In the roles assigned in the remainder of this section to an assistant and client, the client, himself, may be regarded, for this limited purpose, as an assistant, if, in fact, no assistant is present in the courtroom.

return to the counsel table and inquire of his assistant whether anything else remains to be asked. If the answer is in the negative, counsel can forthwith state that his examination is completed. The dramatic effect of such a conclusion leaves the impression that counsel is thoroughly satisfied with the witness' testimony and that the client and the assistant are also satisfied.

Sec. 5:3 Outline of testimony of individual witnesses.

In Forms 2 and 3 (section 4:2, *supra*) we have suggested a method of charting the available witnesses on the basis of their ability to give testimony on matters put in issue by the pleadings. When all available witnesses have been interviewed and their strengths and weaknesses assayed, a decision must be reached by trial counsel as to which witnesses he will actually call and in what order he will present their testimony.[3] At this stage of preparation, an outline should be made of the proposed testimony of each individual witness *as it will actually be presented on the trial.* This outline is a necessary aid to proper direct examination.

No matter how greatly counsel may pride himself on his memory, it is unsafe for him to go to trial without having prepared an outline of the testimony of each witness. This outline not only acts as a convenient reminder of the order in which questions should be asked, but also serves as a check-list by which counsel and his assistant can eliminate the possibility of failing to present the complete story of the witness.

Some lawyers have made it a practice to write out the full text of every question they intend to propound. This is a mistake for two major reasons: first, the reading of questions verbatim destroys the quality of spontaneity which is so important in holding the interest of the fact-finders; second, the reading of questions to a witness can create the unfortunate impression that the testimony of the witness is the result of a word-for-word rehearsal.

The best form of outline of the testimony of the individual witnesses is one which succinctly states (in a predetermined order) the subjects on which the witness is to be interrogated. As counsel covers each subject, he can check it off in his notes. Before he dismisses the witness, he can confer with his trial assistant (who,

---

[3] See sections 4:1, 4:3 and 4:4, *supra.*

presumably, has a copy of the outline and has similarly checked off the subjects covered) to make sure that nothing has been overlooked.

If, in connection with the testimony of a witness, exhibits are to be offered, the exhibits should be referred to in the outline at the point at which it is intended to offer them.

Although the order of propounding questions to the witness covering specific subjects is set forth in the outline, an unexpected answer from the witness, a query propounded by the court, an interruption in the course of testimony, or some other factor may cause trial counsel to change the order of questions. He might, for example, skip a few subjects intending to come back to them later. It is for this reason that he should check on his outline the subjects covered and then, before dismissing the witness, quickly determine what subjects have been omitted and ask questions concerning them. It is helpful for counsel's checkmarks to be very boldly made so that his ultimate review before the witness leaves the stand may be quickly undertaken.

It is helpful to have the outline of the testimony of each witness begin on a separate page of counsel's notes. Then, if he decides for any reason to switch the order of calling witnesses, he will not be plagued by having to rustle through his notes to find the beginning of the proposed testimony of a given witness.

A typical outline of the proposed testimony of an individual witness might read as in Form 4.

Form 4.

Outline Of Proposed Testimony Of Individual Witness.

WILLIAM SMITH, 22 Brook Avenue, Chicago, Illinois.

(a) Introduction of witness.[4]

(b) Conversation of June 1, 1967:
    1. Who was present at conversation and where it was held.
    2. Contents of conversation.

---

[4] See section 5:5, *post*, as to manner of introducing witness to fact-finders. Highlights of such introduction may appear in the outline of testimony. See section 9:6, *post*, as to method of introducing expert witnesses, including the establishment of their qualifications. Appropriate indications of this introduction and establishment should be set forth in the outline.

(c) Meeting of June 19, 1967:
    1. Who was present and where held.
    2. What, in substance, was said by each participant.
    3. Signing of contract.
    4. Introduce contract (our #22).[5]
    5. Read paragraphs 3, 21 and 22 of contract.

(d) Receipt of second installment of goods covered by contract on August 3, 1967:
    1. Examination of goods after receipt.
    2. Defects discovered in goods.

(e) Telephone conversation on morning of August 4, 1967.[6]

(f) Letter of August 4, 1967:
    1. Establish mailing of letter.[7]
    2. Request production of letter, pursuant to our notice to produce.[8]
    3. If original not produced, introduce in evidence our notice to produce (our #7).
    4. Read original or copy of letter.

(g) Receipt of reply to letter of August 4, dated August 13, 1967:
    1. Establish receipt of letter.
    2. Read letter.

(h) Meeting of August 19, 1967:
    1. Who attended meeting, where was it held and, in substance, what was said by each participant.

---

[5] Reference to "our #22" is for the convenience of counsel. A practical method of charting and numbering in advance proposed documentary proof is discussed in section 6:5, *post*.

[6] For method of establishing competency of telephone conversation see section 10:8, *post*.

[7] For method of proving mailing, see section 10:5, *post*. If the witness did not mail the letter, the court may be asked to receive the same subject to connection.

[8] Proof that the letter was mailed is unnecessary if, pursuant to a request for the production thereof, it is forthcoming. As part of pre-trial procedures, it is sometimes wise to demand admissions as to the genuineness of certain documents, such as letters. Practice varies in different jurisdictions; but, in general, if there is no denial of genuineness, a copy may be introduced without further ado except to put on the record the demand for admissions and the failure of denial. In some jurisdictions, the expense of proving the genuineness of a document or letter may be charged against the party unreasonably refusing the admission. In others, the mere failure to deny is insufficient to establish the genuineness of the document or letter accompanying the demand.

Sec. 5:4   Integration of counsel's opening statement with testimony of witnesses.

The opening statement of counsel and the testimony of the witnesses should, ideally, be an integrated whole. Therefore, not only should the opening statement unfold the story, but it should also be so constructed that it will act as an index to the testimony of the witnesses.

Counsel's opening statement (or, if the case is tried to the court without a jury, the trial memorandum presented to the court at or before the commencement of the trial) should enable the fact-finder to hear the whole story in advance. The phrase "whole story" is not intended to suggest that the opening should go into minute detail. Indeed, an opening which is too detailed may be disadvantageous because it could tip off the opposition as to individual elements of proof, which might otherwise come as a surprise. However, particularly in a complicated case, the opening statement should act as a means of informing the fact-finder *in advance* of the respects in which a witness' testimony as to minute details fits into the whole picture. For example, in a case involving the question whether a given person was present at a certain meeting, counsel may well state in his opening: "Not only will you hear the testimony of Mr. Smith that he was not even in New York at the time of the meeting, but you will also receive documentary proof that he was elsewhere."[9]

The opening statement of counsel has the advantage of presenting, in chronological order, the story which is to be unfolded by the testimony of witnesses. As has been noted elsewhere,[10] the order of calling witnesses, if possible, should be partly governed by the fact that the first witness can testify to the entire substance of the case in chronological order, but it is not always possible to present such a witness. The opening statement of counsel can, to some extent, remedy this deficiency. It can point out the times at

---

[9] Note the generality of this statement. The proof referred to may, for example, be an entry in a hotel register in another city showing that Smith was there on the date of the meeting, or a receipted hotel bill showing his presence elsewhere. There is no need to refer to this proposed proof in too great detail. Let the fact-finder be curious about the nature of the proof and, thus, be more attentive when it is introduced.

[10] See section 4:4, *supra.*

which things happened and may even afford the opportunity, without too dangerously tipping off the opponent, to tell the jury which witnesses will testify as to each step in the chronology.

Unless counsel is positive that he can produce a witness to prove a point, he should assiduously avoid referring to that point in his opening statement. Otherwise, he leaves the field wide open for his opponent, in summation, to tell the fact-finders that important proof (rendered important by counsel's reference to it in his opening) has been omitted.

Sec. 5:5 Introduction of the witness.

When a witness takes the stand, the fact-finders presumably do not know him and, unless he is a person of prominence, probably know nothing about him.

Before the witness testifies on the facts at issue, it is wise to "introduce" him to the fact-finders. In a few questions, his general background should be covered. Except in the case of an expert witness,[11] the introduction should be very brief.

One of the main functions of introducing a witness to the jury is, where the occasion arises, to deprive the opposition of the opportunity to bring out unfavorable facts on cross-examination. For example, if the witness is a relative or close friend of the party calling him, he should so testify. Similarly, if the witness has been convicted of crime, he should disclose this fact during the introduction.[12]

Occasions may arise where the bringing out of an unfavorable fact while the witness is being introduced can be transmuted into the creation of a generally favorable atmosphere. When such an opportunity is presented, it should be avidly grasped. The manner in which the subject is introduced requires extreme skill to avoid the thought that extraneous issues are being dragged in by the heels.

---

[11] See section 9:6, *post*.

[12] Where a witness has been previously convicted of crime, it is wise for counsel, when picking a jury, to ascertain that the prospective juror will not be so prejudiced against the witness by reason of a prior conviction that he will disbelieve the witness' testimony. Some counsel have adopted the practice of ascertaining this fact when picking a jury and making no reference to it during the course of introducing the witness to the jury. They go on the assumption that, if the conviction is brought out on cross-examination, it will have little effect.

An example of the use of this technique is illustrated by a case wherein an attack was being made in the New York courts on a Florida decree of divorce obtained by a husband against his wife. The wife's contention was that the husband had fled to Florida, deserting his wife and children in New York, and that he had, in Florida, retained skilled counsel to engineer a Florida decree, although the husband was actually a domiciliary of New York. To rebut this contention, the husband's New York lawyer called as a witness the husband's Florida attorney, presumably to prove the regularity of the Florida divorce action. The following questions and answers in the New York case exemplified a skillful approach aimed at overcoming the unfavorable inference that might be drawn because the witness was related to the husband:

> **Q.** Are you an attorney admitted to practice in the State of Florida and for how long have you been so admitted? **A.** Yes, I am a Florida lawyer and have been admitted to the bar for three years.
>
> **Q.** Did you represent Mr. X [the husband] in the Florida action to which reference has been made? **A.** Yes.
>
> **Q.** In the course of this representation, did you have conferences with any lawyer in Florida representing Mrs. X [the wife]? **A.** Yes, Senator Smathers discussed the matter with me on Mrs. X's behalf.
>
> **Q.** Where did Mr. X reside after he came to Florida? **A.** For the first two days he resided at my home and then he moved to the Floridian Hotel in Miami and then took an apartment on Collins Avenue in Miami Beach.
>
> **Q.** Was he living in that apartment at the time the Florida action was started? **A.** Yes and he still lives there.
>
> **Q.** You told us that when Mr. X first came to Florida he stayed at your home for a couple of days. How well did you know Mr. X? **A.** He is my cousin and I have known him since we were children.

The husband's counsel scored a bull's-eye by this facet of his introduction of the witness. He did not avoid the unfavorable fact that the witness was a cousin of the husband. However, he established that the witness was a neophyte at the bar and that the wife's lawyer was a United States Senator. Although not specifically stated, it would immediately become clear to the jury that the husband could hardly have engineered a "phony" divorce through some sort of political chicanery, when the wife was represented by a powerful Florida political office holder.

Sec. 5:6   Recital of entire story on direct examination.

The temptation sometimes arises to have a witness tell only part of the story during direct examination, holding back the remainder of his knowledge of the facts for redirect examination or on rebuttal. This is an extremely dangerous course and should only be employed when the nature of the case requires it as a matter of law.

It is true that an element of surprise may be advantageously utilized through the holding back of some part of the story during the main examination of a witness on direct. But it is equally and more generally true that, after a witness has been cross-examined, his redirect can look like an invention if there is no reasonable explanation for his failure to tell the whole story when he first had the opportunity to do so.

Furthermore, it is a general principle of law (subject, of course, to the exercise of discretion by the trial judge) that a witness will not be permitted to state anything during redirect examination which is not in direct rebuttal to matters brought out on cross.[13] Thus, the failure of the witness to tell the whole story during direct examination may result in the irreparable loss of advantageous testimony.

There are some instances where the nature of the case dictates, with good reason, that a witness need not and should not tell his entire story when he first takes the stand. Typical of such an instance is a suit by an original holder for value for non-payment of a negotiable promissory note, where the defendant pleads, as a separate defense, such matters as failure of consideration or fraud. There, the plaintiff need only testify to the delivery of the note for value, its presentation and refusal of payment. It is undesirable as a matter of strategy to anticipate the separately pleaded defenses, thus leaving the way open for cross-examination on subjects which it is the duty of the defense to bring forward in the

---

[13] The legal aspects of this subject are fully treated in section 12:1, *post,* wherein are also discussed the facets of the law applicable to recalling a witness in rebuttal.

first instance. Indeed, if an objection is made by the defendant, the testimony of the plaintiff in this respect would probably be bared for the very reason that it is anticipatory of a defense not yet offered through testimony.

Sec. 5:7   Realistic appraisal and handling of unfavorable factors.

In section 5:5, *supra,* we have discussed the desirability of alluding to the weaknesses of one's own witness when introducing him to the jury. The underlying strategic consideration is that it is better to have an unfavorable matter exposed through one's own witness than to let it appear either that an attempt was made to conceal that matter or that it was unknown to trial counsel because the witness was hiding it from him. A similar approach can be employed with regard to weaknesses in the case, itself.

During preparation, counsel very often is compelled to conclude that there are certain unfavorable factors, which, in all probability, will come to light during the trial and the existence of which cannot be successfully denied. These facts cannot be swept under the rug. They must be faced realistically and careful plans should be laid how best to mitigate their effectiveness.

Some unfavorable matters may be so unimportant when viewed against the entire background of the cause that emphasis placed upon them can only serve to enlarge their stature. It is wise either to treat these matters with skillful neglect, trusting to summation properly to belittle them, or not to mention them at all. This is a calculated risk. In a case tried to a jury, the plaintiff can afford this risk better than the defendant; because the plaintiff has the last chance to sum up and can gauge his treatment of the matter by the nature of the allusion to it in the defendant's summation. The technique here to be employed is to play up the unimportance of the unfavorable fact. This can be done by emphasizing important matters and then alluding to the miniscule impact on those matters of the unfavorable, although undenied, factors.

An example of this type of situation arose in a case where the plaintiff, an eminent author, sued to recover for the pirating of ideas (literary property) conceived by him. The plaintiff testified on direct examination that, several years before a motion picture studio had first undertaken the writing of a script utilizing his ideas, he had given these ideas to the person (one of the defendants) who sold them to the studio. On cross-examination, he was questioned in great detail about the dates of correspondence that he had had with the defendant who ultimately sold the story to the motion picture company. It was later proved, and the fact could not be denied, that the plaintiff's letters were dated more than a year after he had claimed that he presented the idea in the first instance. Plaintiff's counsel, recognizing that the letters offered in evidence were genuine, simply asked his client on redirect examination whether he now realized that he was mistaken about the dates of the letters. After the plaintiff had admitted this, his counsel asked him whether he had kept copies of the letters and he testified that he had not done so.

During summation, defendants' counsel laid great emphasis on what he described as the "deliberate lies" of plaintiff as to the dates of the letters. Plaintiff's counsel, when he summed up, alluded to the matter as follows:

> "Now, let us consider those letters which my client wrote to Mr. F and about which my opponent has made such a fuss in his summation. My client testified that he wrote the letters in June, 1947. When the letters were produced, it is clear that they were dated in April, 1948. My client frankly admitted to you that he was mistaken about the date. He didn't keep copies of the letters. He wasn't preparing for a law suit. In good faith, he was presenting ideas of his own conception in the hope that they would ultimately be incorporated in an epic motion picture.
>
> "My opponent claims that my client's mistaken testimony about the dates of the letters was a deliberate lie. But what motive could my client possibly have had for stating that he sent the letters a year earlier than he actually did? What possible importance could the difference in dates have? The really important thing is that the actual date of the letters is more than two years *before* the script of the motion picture was even commissioned to be written! The truly important thing is that, *whenever* the letters were dated, the ideas in them were stolen by the defendants. The *vitally* important thing is that the defendants should be compelled to pay the plaintiff for this theft. They should pay the value of what they stole and we have presented to you persuasive evidence of what the value was and is."

In the foregoing portion of his summation, plaintiff's counsel availed himself of the opportunity not only to point up the unimportance of the letter dates, but also to emphasize the basic justice of his cause, to wit, that plaintiff's original concepts had been stolen and that defendants stole them. He also used this opportunity to recall to the jury the fact that ample proof had been adduced as to the value of the stolen ideas and plaintiff's consequent entitlement to damages. *Immediately* after the portion of the summation which has just been quoted, plaintiff's counsel reviewed at length the testimony as to value and consequent damages. Thus, by placing the discussion of the dates of the letters in immediate juxtaposition to the review of proof of value and damages, he was enabled further to indicate, without directly saying so, that the false issue of the date of the letters was used by defendants in an effort to belittle the enormity of the wrong they had done to plaintiff.

Where counsel is faced by an *important* unfavorable factor, resulting from facts that cannot be denied or minimized but will be harmful if unexplained, it is nevertheless often desirable to bring out these facts through his own witnesses. Here, the strategic concept is *anticipation.* If the trier of the facts has already heard testimony about an unfavorable factor, he will be impatient if it is rehashed later in the case. Counsel to whose client the unfavorable facts will be damaging should try to bring them out in a somewhat casual way on direct examination, preferably interjected in the course of testimony helpful to his client.

An example of this technique occurred in a tort action resulting from an automobile accident. After plaintiff had testified to the fact that he was run down by defendant's automobile under circumstances clearly proving negligence, the following questions and answers occurred:

Q. When the policeman picked you up from the street, what happened? **A.** He helped me brush off my clothes and showed me the rip on my trousers and jacket. He asked me whether I wanted him to call an ambulance and I told him that I didn't think it was necessary. He called a taxi for me and I got into the cab and went home, where I took a shower and changed my clothes.

Q. What did you do then? **A.** I telephoned my secretary and told her I would be delayed getting to the office and, after about an hour, I went to my office.

Q. Did you feel any pain when the policeman helped you get up from the street where you were lying after you were hit by defendant's car? **A.** Not particularly, just a very slight pain.

Q. Did this pain continue when you got home? **A.** Only a slight bit, it was hardly noticeable.

Q. Did you feel any pain after you got to the office that day? **A.** The same pain. It wasn't much.

Q. When did you first consult a doctor? **A.** About five days later.

Q. Had you been going to your office regularly during the interim of five days? **A.** Yes, except the last day, when I called Dr. Morrison, I left my office early and went to his office.

Q. Did you feel pain before you called Dr. Morrison? **A.** Yes. For the first couple of days the pain was very slight. On the day I called Dr. Morrison, I was at my office. Suddenly, I felt stabbing pains in the middle and lower part of my back. They were excrutiating. As I got up from my office chair, I fell over on the floor and then I vomited and my secretary came into the room and helped me get up and she telephoned Dr. Morrison.[14] She and one of the office boys helped me into a taxicab and she accompanied me to Dr. Morrison's office.

After giving the foregoing testimony, the plaintiff testified to his visit to the doctor, the continuance of pain over a long period of time, the fact that he was hospitalized and the further fact that he still felt severe pains and that his movement was importantly limited.

By the interjection of the testimony quoted above, plaintiff's counsel practically deprived defendant of the effectiveness of proof

---

[14] Defendant's counsel could have objected to the plaintiff's testimony that his secretary telephoned Dr. Morrison. He wisely desisted from such an objection, since it was perfectly clear that the secretary could have been called as a witness to establish her telephoning Dr. Morrison.

that plaintiff attended at his office regularly for four or five days after the accident. This testimony had the advantage of establishing that plaintiff was not a person looking to bring a law suit, that he was willing to overlook slight pain, that he was not the sort of person who would make a fuss about such pain and call a doctor and that the onset of severe pain was postponed until several days after he was run down by an automobile. Subsequently, the treating physician and two specialists testified that the type of permanent disability and continuing pain which plaintiff suffered was very often not accompanied by severe pain until an appreciable period after the happening of the injury.

The *positioning* of the above-quoted testimony is significant. It came *immediately* after the plaintiff had testified to the negligent act which caused his damage. It was *immediately* followed by plaintiff's testimony about the severity of his pain, his subsequent hospitalization, treatment, continuing pain and disability. This positioning of the testimony could not help but create the impression that the mere fact that plaintiff went to his office for several days after the accident and felt very little pain during that period had no real significance and that plaintiff testified frankly on his own direct examination and without any desire to build up a case. Furthermore, it deprived defendant's attorney of the opportunity of creating an element of surprise by introducing these facts on cross-examination or through later proof by witnesses who had observed plaintiff attending at his office regularly for several days after the accident.

It must not be assumed from the foregoing that in every case counsel should bring out unfavorable facts during the direct examination of his own witnesses. In a great many instances, the damning facts are so important that, no matter when they come out, they will be vitally harmful. It makes no sense to help one's opponent by admitting these facts in advance. Indeed, the admission may create an atmosphere so unfavorable that the case may be lost during direct examination. If unfavorable facts can be met by explanatory favorable testimony, it is often wiser to reserve the explanation so that it will come as late as possible in the case. "Final impression" is a tactical advantage not to be easily surrendered. Also, it should be borne in mind that if an unfavorable fact is admitted during direct examination, the opportunity to cross-examine about that matter is irretrievably lost. In addition, there is always the possibility that, for one reason or another (for example, the failure of a witness to appear), one's opponent may be unable to prove the unfavorable fact.

Sec. 5:8 General principles of interrogation.

There is an ancient axiom in the field of journalism to the effect that an ideal newspaper story answers four questions: Who? Where? When? What? Nothing can better illustrate the correct general form of questions to be propounded on direct examination than the application of this 4W test.

Questions on direct examination should be as simple as possible. They should preferably cover single subjects but should be so connected that they *logically* lead from one answer to another.

The *answer* to a question should tell the story, *not* the question, itself. However, a question, without being leading, can and should preserve the continuity of the witness' story. For example, if a witness has testified to a particular conversation and then has given some disconnected details in answer to a question by the trial judge, the first query propounded thereafter by examining counsel should steer the case back into its chronological course. After such an interruption, the first question by counsel could well be: "What did you do after you had spoken to Mr. Jones on June 9?" This is obviously better than the question: "What happened on the afternoon of June 9?" The former query relates back to the conversation previously testified to. The latter leaves the subject in a vacuum unless the trier of the facts happens to remember that the conversation with Jones took place on June 9.

A very dangerous type of question is one which calls for the *text* of a conversation. Even though a witness, in fact, has a prodigious memory and can actually recall, word for word, what was said at a time in the past by another person or by himself, he may create the impression that he has memorized a story. It is an old trick to ask such a witness on cross-examination to repeat the conversation he has previously recounted. If, because of his truly excellent memory, the witness retells the conversation practically verbatim, his recital nevertheless has all the stigmata of a memorized script.

In asking a witness about a conversation, the first question regarding that conversation can be: "Tell us in substance what, if anything, was said by you and Mr. Jones and Mr. Smith when you met on June 9?" The witness will then begin his recital, *not* by repeating a conversation verbatim but by giving a summary of it. As the testimony progresses, counsel can well interject such questions as: "Did Mr. Jones say anything in answer to that?", or "Who said that, you or Mr. Jones?", or "Was it Mr. Jones or Mr. Smith who said that?" The use of such intermediate questions gives the testimony of the witness all the force that it would have if he were repeating a conversation verbatim but carries none of the danger of such a recital

In addition to keeping his examination on an even keel and, as far as possible, guiding a witness to a chronological exposition of the facts, counsel must make sure that each of his questions *has been answered*, even if he has to repeat them. Something more is involved here than a reminder to the witness that a nod of his head is no substitute for an oral answer. It is appaling how often a record on appeal is defective as to an important point because the witness did not answer a question due to an interruption followed by colloquy among counsel and the trial judge.

It should be remembered that an answer by counsel to a question propounded by the court is not testimony unless counsel is sworn as a witness. A statement by counsel is not a substitute for evidence, even though the opponent does not contradict it. Nothing short of a stipulation as to a fact (or that a witness, if called, would testify in a certain way) can take the place of evidence Colloquy, however extended, is *not* proof.[15]

Counsel, particularly when he has the burden of proof or of going forward with the proof, should try to simplify the issues by the nature of his questions. He should avoid the injection of details that may confuse the issues or divert the attention of the fact-finder from the question to be decided. However, he should not hesitate to prove, even in minute detail, facts which will support his primary contention.

The converse of the foregoing proposition must also be borne in mind. Counsel should avoid "over-proving" his case. Although the introduction of detailed proof is often desirable, there is no reason to repeat these details on numerous occasions, particularly where the details, themselves, are relatively unimportant. There are two dangers in such a repetitive performance: first, the fact-finder may be bored and become impatient; second, there is always the

---

[15] *Matter of Gelrod*, 24 A.D. 2d 756 [New York].

possibility that there may be a divergence between the witnesses as to the details.[16]

There is one important exception to the warning against "over-proof." Where a document is available to support some detail of the oral testimony, it is generally advantageous to offer that document in evidence. Although the matter involved may be relatively unimportant, documentary proof, which supports oral testimony, has a way of convincing the fact-finder that the witness who testified orally is probably a truthful person, in general.

The *method* of questioning is often as important as the content of the questions and answers. The interplay between counsel and witness, ideally employed, should give this total impression: The witness knows certain facts. Counsel knows that the witness knows these facts. Counsel, in his professional capacity, propounds questions as a guide to enable the witness to tell his story for the enlightenment of the fact-finder.

As far as possible, the questions and answers both should be in the nature of a conversation, without the injection of an element of mystery or of technical mumbo-jumbo.

The first requisite of a proper question is that the fact-finder should hear it. Counsel need not shout, but he certainly should not whisper or swallow his words. Soft tones do not mean unintelligible speech. If the trial judge tells a witness to "speak up," the sympathy of the jury may go to that witness; but if the trial judge is compelled to address the same remark to counsel, the jury has a right to be irritated and, if there is no jury, the irritation of the trial judge is clearly evidenced by his admonition.

Where a case is tried to a jury, it is advisable for counsel to station himself at the end of the jurybox farthest from the witness. Then, if the witness answers loudly enough for counsel to hear him, he will probably be heard by each juryman. In addition, when speaking directly to counsel so positioned, the witness will practically be facing the jury. Where the witness is an extremely nervous person and hence is likely to drop his voice, counsel can request him to speak louder so that *counsel* can hear him. The admonition coming from one friend to another, has a reassuring effect. It is certainly better for counsel to give this admonition than to wait until the trial judge or one of the jurymen has to do so.

---

[16] The criteria here involved are, in general, similar to those affecting the calling of cumulative witnesses. See section 4:5, *supra*.

Sec. 5:9 Leading questions.

It is a well-established principle of law that leading questions may not be asked on direct examination (except in the case of hostile or turncoat witnesses [17] or adverse parties); but this legal axiom is not the important reason for desisting from leading a witness on direct examination.

When counsel asks leading questions of his own witness the impression is created either that there has been a verbatim rehearsal of the testimony or that the witness is willing to affirm anything counsel suggests. Either assumption obviously destroys the efficacy of the witness' testimony.

Occasions sometimes arise where a witness has failed to mention something to which counsel knows the witness can testify. Here, a minimal type of leading question may be asked. For example, counsel may inquire: "You testified that Mr. Williams and Mr. Jones were present at the conference on June 29. Was anyone else there and, if so, please tell us their names?" Or, counsel may ask: "When I asked you, a moment ago, what you saw when your car turned the corner of 56th Street, you told us that you saw the defendant's car directly to your right. Maybe you didn't understand the full nature of my question. Did you see the plaintiff at that time and, if so, where was the plaintiff standing or walking?" The danger of asking a leading question in these circumstances is that counsel may appear to be prompting the witness. Therefore, the leading question should be so couched as to avoid suggesting its own answer.

The restriction against the use of leading questions does not apply to cross-examination. As a matter of strategy, it is sometimes wise to desist from calling a witness, even though he is believed to be friendly, so that he may be led on cross-examination. This tactic is best employed when it is known that one's opponent has subpoenaed this witness.

Sec. 5:10 Tactical interruptions of dull testimony.

In section 4:4, *supra*, reference has been made to the desirability of sandwiching the testimony of a "weak" witness between the

---

[17] See cases and other authorities cited in footnotes 26–28, Chapter I, *supra*.

testimony of "strong" witnesses who are able to buttress the testimony of the less secure witness in some substantial respects. A similar tactic, in converse, applies to the interruption of dull and relatively uninteresting testimony.

It is very often necessary to present undramatic but vital evidence at considerable length. For the fact-finder this can be a boring performance. For example, the production of statistical proof or massive documentary evidence, however important, can well have the effect of causing a juryman either to fall asleep or to hope that he could.

It is a wise tactic to interrupt the presentation of this type of evidence by introducing "spot" witnesses, who can testify to matters within their own knowledge and thus restore a human aspect to the case. If this can be accomplished without interrupting the basic chronology it is of particular value.

We are here discussing the interruption of massive technical evidence. If, during the normal course of telling his story, a witness' testimony can be strengthened by the use of letters, telegrams and the like or even by presenting to the fact-finder such technical documents as bills of lading, bank statements and receipts, there is no reason to hold back this documentary proof. Indeed, the best way to utilize it is to have it appear as part of the normal chronology of the witness' testimony. In such an instance, the maintenance of interest is assured by the story the witness is telling and the use of technical proof becomes part of the tale as a whole.

Chapter VI

DOCUMENTARY PROOF

Sec. 6:1 Classes of documentary proof.

Documentary proof is of five major types:

1. *Public records.* The production of these records, by reason of statutory aids to proof [1] act as proof (or, at least, as *prima facie* proof) of the facts therein contained. Examples of such records are certificates of public officers, certified copies of documents or instruments establishing the status of real property, marriage certificates, death certificates, Weather Bureau publications and official reports of population.

2. *Quasi-public records.* When a statute so provides, records of this type constitute *prima facie* evidence of the facts therein contained. Newspaper stock market reports are typical of this kind of record.[2] Physicians' and hospital reports, when covered by an appropriate statute, often fall into the same class as quasi-public records.

---

[1] See Chapter XI, *post*, wherein there is also discussed the method of authentication of public records.

[2] See section 11:17, *post*.

3. *Statutory proof of steps in a litigation.* Affidavits of service, affidavits of publication or posting of legal notices and certified copies of judgments or orders are in this class. The effect that they have is governed by the local statutes of the forum wherein the case is tried.[3]

4. *Business records and memoranda.* Under both common law rules and statutory provisions records or entries made in the regular course of business are admissible and such records act as proof of the matters therein stated.[4]

5. *Correspondence and miscellaneous proof.* In the normal litigation, this class of documentary proof is the one most often employed. Its function and nature may be subdivided and described as follows: first, to prove an essential element of a cause of action or defense (for example, a demand letter where demand is necessary to establish a cause of action, or a cancelled check or other voucher to establish a payment, or a bill of lading or receipt with endorsements to establish delivery); second, to establish an admission by an opposing party; third, to buttress the oral testimony of a witness (for example, a receipted hotel bill evidencing that the witness was at a certain place at a certain time); and fourth, to counteract opposing evidence (for example, a letter bearing a date subsequent to the date which an unfriendly witness has testified was the last time he communicated with a plaintiff).[5]

Irrespective of the class into which documentary proof falls, its important function is, to a large extent, to overcome strict application of the hearsay rule. When the contents of a document are used to prove the *facts* which the document recites, the effect is the same as though a witness, personally familiar with those facts, testified to their existence. Thus, for example, it might be impossible to produce a witness personally knowledgeable as to the date of birth of one of the parties. The birth certificate takes the place of such a witness. Of course, this does not mean that self-serving declarations of past events are admissible in evidence merely because they are contained in a letter or similar piece of documentary proof. Here, the written proof cannot take the place of a living witness, particularly if the letter was written after the

---

[3] See, for example, sections 11:5, 11:6, 11:7 and 11:8, *post.*

[4] This subject is covered in full in section 11:10, *post.* Private memoranda are often permitted to be used by a witness to refresh his recollection.

[5] Such a letter need not have any direct bearing on the issues being tried and may be introduced solely for the purpose of showing its date.

litigation was commenced or was in immediate contemplation.

Some documentary proof is admissible for a limited purpose. For example, a letter making a demand for payment can be received to establish the fact that a demand was made, but it is not always effective as proof of the facts concerning the indebtedness which may appear in the text of the letter.

It cannot be too strongly emphasized that the legal ability of documentary proof to act as *evidence* of the *facts* therein recited depends on both statutory provisions and common law principles. Where a statute is available, the extent of the legal operation of a document is easily ascertained; but care should be taken, in the absence of statute, to examine decisional law for the twin purposes: (a) of avoiding the danger that a given document may not be sufficient to establish a *fact;* and (b) of being able to take advantage of the contents of a document even though a specific statute does not cover the subject.

Sec. 6:2   Tactical use of documentary proof.

Where the facts proved by a document are necessary to establish a *prima facie* case or defense (for example, where the fact that a demand was made is proved by a document, or an accord and satisfaction or payment is similarly proved), no comment is needed as to why the document should be introduced in evidence.

A different situation arises where documentary proof is not absolutely necessary. Here, it is a tactical matter and not one born of necessity.

All experienced trial lawyers recognize the importance of documentary proof. It has been said, with good reason, that a single document is often worth more than the oral testimony of numerous witnesses. Nothing seems to impress a fact-finder (particularly a jury) more than a writing prepared and sent or exchanged before there was reason to believe that there would be litigation. Thus, as a matter of tactics, counsel should be eager to introduce such a document in evidence. He should not fail to do so merely because the proof thus afforded would be cumulative.

Where documentary evidence buttresses oral testimony it should be used, even though it has relatively minor bearing on the ultimate fact to be decided. A good example arises in a case where a witness accounts for his unavailability at a time when he is alleged to have been at a certain place. If this witness can produce a receipt from a hotel somewhat distant from the place where he is alleged to have been, showing that he was at this other place during the period in question, he will be strongly supported by a document not prepared by him. Even if the receipt shows that he was at this other place only a short period, it can be advantageously used if coupled with his further testimony that he thereafter went to other places but does not have receipts showing his presence there.

Statutory aids to proof sometimes provide that a given piece of documentary evidence acts as proof (or *prima facie* proof) of the facts therein stated.[6] However, such statutes are for the convenience of counsel. Very often it is wiser to make direct proof than to depend upon the aid afforded by statute to the presentation of a document.[7] In such a situation, common law proof should be made and, to buttress the same, documentary evidence may thereafter be offered.

The existence of unfavorable documentary proof, when known to counsel, should not be neglected. It may be assumed that one's opponent will have this proof or can obtain it. If it is possible to do so without ruining one's case, it is wise to introduce this evidence during the examination of one's own witness, coupling its introduction with such explanatory matter as may soften the effect of the document.[8] It must be realized, however, that the introduction of an unfavorable document can be extremely damaging. Sometimes, it is better to take the risk that one's opponent will not either have the document, or produce it, or offer it in evidence.

Sec. 6:3   Method of placing documents in evidence.

It is a fundamental rule that no reference may be made to the contents of a document until that document has been received in evidence. It is also a fundamental principle that a document may not be received in evidence until a proper foundation for its introduction has been laid. These matters are not mutually exclusive.

Before an attempt is made to introduce a document in evidence,

---

[6] See Chapter XI, *post.*

[7] For a full discussion of this subject see section 11:3, *post.*

[8] For a discussion of the realistic appraisal and handling of unfavorable matter, see section 5:7, *supra.*

it should be marked for identification. Such marking requires no special permission from the court. Counsel can simply hand the document to the court reporter and ask that it be marked for identification, but it is, in some jurisdictions, deemed a courtesy to the court to ask permission for this marking, which permission will uniformly be granted.[9] When counsel asks that a document be marked for identification, he is under no obligation to show it to his opponent. Such obligation only arises when the document is offered in evidence.

After the document has been marked for identification, counsel can proceed to lay the foundation for its receipt in evidence. He may, for example, ask the witness whether he has ever seen the document before and under what circumstances, whether he saw it signed or exchanged, what happened on the occasion when the document was exchanged, etc. After the foundation has been laid, counsel offers the document in evidence. He shows it to his opponent and to the court. After a ruling by the court, if the document is received, it is marked as an exhibit in evidence. If the court declines to receive it, an exception may be taken and the document is now sufficiently identified (through its having been marked for identification) so that, upon appeal, the ruling may be reviewed.

A different procedure is followed when the document is of a public nature and has been properly authenticated.[10] Here, all that is necessary is for counsel to offer the document in evidence. If the court refuses to receive it, it should then be marked for identification so that a proper record may be made for reviewing the refusal on appeal.

Where the admissibility of a document has been proved by the testimony of a witness, the document must be formally put in evidence before the close of the direct examination of the proving witness.[11] Otherwise, if the witness is permitted to depart, opposing counsel would be deprived of the opportunity to examine him about the contents of the document. This does not mean, however, that a document would be inadmissible if the witness, himself, were not

---

[9] In some jurisdictions, it is the custom, in advance of trial, for counsel to have the court reporter mark for identification all documents which he subsequently intends to offer in evidence. Even when so marked, counsel is under no obligation to offer the document as an exhibit. The whole process is merely a convenience for the court.

[10] For methods of authentication, see sections 11:4, 11:7, 11:8 and 11:9, post.

[11] *Wigmore on Evidence* (3rd edition, 1940), §1883, p. 530.

cognizant of the facts therein stated. Many statutes provide that an entry made in the regular course of business is admissible even though no witness is present who can do more than authenticate the entry, as such.[12] In such a situation, the entry may prove a fact and, indeed, may be the only evidence of that fact.

The order of introducing documentary proof is a matter of choice. The best method is to introduce the same at the time when it chronologically fits into the story as a whole.

Sec. 6:4 Reading documents to jury.

When a document has been introduced in evidence, the judge has presumably read it before ruling on its admissibility. However, the jury will know nothing about it unless they are informed as to its contents (nor will a judge, where the document was admitted without objection and the court had no reason to examine it prior to its admission). Therefore, once the document has been received in evidence, it should be read to the jury.

There is one exception to the rule that there should be an immediate reading of the document to the jury. This occurs in situations where a single document would be relatively meaningless until other documents have been received. In such a case, counsel should state to the court that he will read this document in connection with several others to be later introduced.

Sometimes it is not necessary to read the whole document. For example, if a form mortgage is introduced and the only questions involved are the amounts of payment required and the time for such payments, counsel may simply state to the jury that this is a mortgage and may set forth the dates of payment and the amounts thereof. Technically, counsel should obtain permission from his opponent or from the court to make this abbreviated statement, but such permission will rarely be refused.

Care should be taken when reading only a portion of an exhibit to a jury that nothing is hidden which the jury is entitled to hear or should properly have drawn to their attention. If the introducing counsel reads only a portion of the exhibit, opposing counsel has the right to read the balance immediately. He is not obliged to wait until cross-examination. He may, on the other hand, choose to hold

---

[12] For a number of such statutes, see Chapter XI, *post.*

back the reading of the balance and refer to it for the first time either on cross-examination or in summation. If it appears that counsel who originally read part of the document was withholding something, the result can, obviously, be disastrous.

Sec. 6:5   Assembling and charting documentary proof.

When counsel comes to court armed with documentary proof, he should be prepared to present that proof easily and expeditiously. Whether the case is tried to a court or a jury, the fact-finder will be irritated if counsel has to fumble through a mass of papers to extract the document he intends to present. Furthermore, when a witness is testifying and the introduction of documentary proof becomes an important part of his testimony, it is desirable that there be no hiatus between the oral and documentary evidence. The whole operation should be smooth and, to the greatest possible extent, uninterrupted.

In the course of preparation for trial, counsel should have obtained not only the documents which he ultimately intends to introduce, but also all writings that may have any bearing on the subject. Indeed, it is more than possible that the bearing on the case of some written proof will not become apparent until the trial has progressed for a certain period. In assembling documentary evidence in such manner that it will be readily and quickly available, counsel should also have at his immediate disposal all other written material.

There are two ways in which documentary data can be assembled: first, by isolating in a single place the proof on each subject which is intended to be introduced and keeping in another general folder the documents which, although not contemplated as exhibits, may become important; second, by arranging all documents, whether or not intended in the first instance as exhibits, in date order.

The first system can conveniently be used where there are but a few documents and the issues to be tried are simple. However, some documents may cover several subjects and if they are set aside in a folder relating to an individual subject, there may be a mad scramble when it is time to produce them in connection with another matter.

Where the issues are complicated, the documents numerous and a large mass of written material exists which it is not contemplated will be introduced in evidence, the wisest way to assemble the documents is by date. They should be placed in a single file (although this file may, because of the bulk of material involved, consist of a number of separate filing envelopes or even a file cabinet) *in date order*.[13] A chart should be prepared, which states very briefly the nature of each document and its date. A number should be assigned to each document and a blank should be left on the chart to indicate whether an individual document is received in evidence or marked for identification. Form 5 is a typical chart.

Form 5.

Chart of Documents.

Our number	*Exhibit number*	*Nature of Document*
1		Letter dated June 1, 1963 from plaintiff to defendant making offer to sell machinery.
2		Letter dated June 13, 1963 from defendant to plaintiff inquiring about horsepower of motors.
3		Memorandum dated June 15, 1963, of telephone conversation between Smith and Jones relating to separate motors for each class of machines.
4		Letter dated June 15, 1963 confirming conclusions of telephone conversation referred to in our number 3.
5		Letter dated June 29, 1963 from defendant to plaintiff accepting offer for sale of machinery.
6		Letter dated July 2, 1963 from plaintiff to defendant enclosing proposed contract.

It will be noted that, in the foregoing chart, the second column has been left blank. During the course of the trial, when and as any

---

[13] One of the advantages of assembling the material in date order is that, if the opponent should call for the introduction of a document not theretofore received in evidence or marked for identification, it can be readily located.

of the documents are received in evidence or marked for identification, an appropriate note of that fact should be written into the second column.

Once a document has been marked for identification or received in evidence, it should be placed in a separate folder. At the close of each day of the trial an additional chart should be drawn up, consisting of two columns, the first of which will contain the exhibit number and the second a description of the document. If the document was furnished by the opponent and returned to his custody after it was marked, this fact should be noted on the second chart.

The original chart of all documents can remain undisturbed during the trial. By looking at the second column of that chart, counsel can see whether a given document was received in evidence or marked for identification. If it has been so received or marked, counsel will know that it has been transferred to the exhibit file, or, if the document was furnished by the opponent, that it is in the possession of the latter.

It is important that, at the close of each day's session of a trial, counsel should check with his opponent to make sure that every document received in evidence or marked for identification on that day is present and accounted for, either by transfer to counsel's exhibit file or in the possession of his opponent. If, perchance, during the course of any day of the trial some documents were re-used (for example, during cross-examination) the check of documents at the end of that day should account for every piece of written material.

Sec. 6:6   Taking documents to jury room.

Under early law, it was the rule that writings under seal received in evidence or as part of the issue could be taken by the jury for further perusal upon their retirement to the jury room but that other writings could not be. This rule has long since been abandoned.[14]

The present rule varies in different jurisdictions and, in many instances, a rule once established has been overturned by later decisions or statutes. In main, court rulings can be divided into the following groups:

---

[14] *Wigmore on Evidence* (3rd edition, 1940) §1913.

1. In criminal cases, unless a statute specifically so provides, no exhibit may be taken into the jury room without the consent of the defendant. Even in the presence of a statute permitting the jury to take exhibits with them, a serious constitutional question exists as to whether this deprives a defendant of the right of confrontation.

2. Depositions, transcripts of testimony and the like are not permitted to be taken by the jury, whether the transcript or deposition was of the case on trial or of an earlier case.

3. Photographs, maps and diagrams drawn to scale may be taken by the jury to the jury room.

4. Correspondence, in general, may be taken by the jury to the jury room, but permission so to take them usually rests in the sound discretion of the trial court.

5. Where a statute so provides, the jury may take with them any writing used as evidence and, in the light of certain statutes, it is mandatory upon a trial judge, upon written motion, to send into the jury room any written instrument received in evidence.

6. Some cases hold that it is within the discretion of the trial court to permit or not to permit anything received in evidence to be taken by the jury to the jury room.

As a final matter, it should be noted that the decisions are unanimous that the jury is never permitted to take to the jury room any writing or other object which has not been received in evidence.

In some complicated cases and in criminal prosecutions where a jury may return one of several or many verdicts, certain courts have sent a "verdict chart" to the jury room, so that the jurors may know the various types of verdict they can bring in. Although the practice is not generally approved, the sending of such a verdict chart to the jury does not require reversal.[15]

---

[15] *Peo. v. Hudson,* 19 N.Y. 2d 137, 140.

Chapter VII

DEPOSITIONS

Sec. 7:1 Desirability of taking and using depositions.

There has been great debate among experienced trial counsel as to the desirability of taking depositions. It is suggested by some that depositions should be taken in every case. Others contend that, unless it is absolutely necessary, a deposition should never be taken.

A middle ground is that the nature of the case dictates the desirability of taking a deposition in given circumstances.

One thing is certain. That is that if it is decided to take a deposition, the method of taking the same should, as far as possible, avoid disclosing to the opponent the examiner's theory of the action. If the witness is tipped off as to what the examiner is seeking to establish, he can, with relative impunity, shift his testimony before the taking of the deposition has been completed.[1] Furthermore, it is common practice for a witness whose deposition is being taken to ask advice of his counsel and, upon the slightest excuse, to obtain adjournments of the examination, thus enabling him to tailor his testimony to the

---

[1] Statutes and court rules often provide that, before a witness signs a deposition, he can change it either by changing the text or by additions at the end.

exigency of the situation. Indeed, during these adjournments, the witness may read over the text of what he has said up to that point and thus be enabled to engage in a studied consideration of new explanations. Finally, it is perfectly clear that a witness' hesitations, facial expressions, obvious embarrassments and similar indicia of falsehood are things which cannot be conveyed to the fact-finder through a mere reading of the deposition.

An examiner who takes a deposition should be content if, in the process thereof, he can cause the witness completely to commit himself to a version of the facts (including, for example, such details as what was said, who was present, where and when an event took place and, in general, everything done by the witness or in his presence relating to the subject matter of the litigation).

When it comes to the question of whether a deposition should be used after it has been taken, two considerations are important: first, whether, under the law, the deposition can be used at a given point in the trial; and second, whether it is tactically wise to use the deposition instead of calling the witness or leaving the matter covered by the deposition untouched.

If the witness is personally available and can be called, the question whether to use his deposition *if he is friendly* depends upon what impression it is believed he will make upon the fact-finder if he personally testifies. Obviously, it is impossible for the cold words of the deposition to reveal more than *what* the witness said. The deposition cannot tell *how* he said it. Thus, if a witness' manner is impressive, it may be wiser to call him in person. If, on the other hand, he is the sort of human being who makes a poor impression, it is wise to use the deposition. These considerations should be modified by the thought that, in general, the impact of the testimony of the witness appearing in person is greater than that of one whose testimony is read.

In the case of *friendly* witnesses, there is, in general, little hope of improving on the contents of a deposition through personal testimony (except, of course, that personal testimony may be more complete than the contents of the deposition). The danger of calling a friendly witness whose deposition has been taken is that the deposition, itself, is available for impeachment. Therefore, if the witness enlarges upon the scope of his previous testimony, he may well be faced with the question why he had not, during the course of the taking of the deposition, recalled matters to which he now testifies.

In the case of an *unfriendly* witness whose testimony is essential to the establishing of a *prima facie* case or defense, counsel has a very narrow choice. If the witness is available (unless a statute or court rule prohibits it) counsel can use the deposition and thus be sure that he will not be taken by surprise as might be the case if the witness were personally called. However, there may only be a portion of the deposition helpful to counsel. The balance may be damaging. Under general rules of evidence, if one side reads a portion of a deposition the other side may read the balance. Thus, counsel using a deposition is faced by the danger that he may be opening the door to the reading of matter unfavorable to his cause. Of course, he is not bound by that matter as to any issue in the case; but this is small comfort if the fact-finder has been permitted to listen to it.

If an *unfriendly* witness is one who will make a poor impression and who can be easily led into admissions, it would appear wiser to call him in person than to depend on his deposition.

An *unfriendly* witness being obviously hostile may, with impunity, be confronted by his past contradictory statements.[2] If such statements are available (and they will be if his deposition has been taken) the danger that this witness will be damaging to one's cause is minimized.

Sec. 7:2   Federal and State rules on taking and use of depositions.

Under numerous statutes and court rules, the ability to take and use depositions during the course of a trial is limited. The most common limitation is that if the witness whose deposition has been taken is available in court (or within a stated distance from the courthouse) or subject to subpoena, his testimony by deposition, unless he is an adverse party, cannot be used.

The variations between statutes and court rules covering this subject are great. Some statutes are very broad, others go into the most minute detail. The subjects of which one must be aware are: (a) whose deposition may be taken; (b) how broad is the scope of examination permitted in the taking of a deposition; (c) before whom may a deposition be taken; (d) is there a difference between the taking of a deposition of an adverse party and of a mere

---

[2] Compare section 1:5, *supra.*

witness; (e) under what conditions can a deposition be changed by the person examined; (f) what formalities are required to authenticate the deposition; (g) under what conditions can the deposition be used on the trial.

Since statutes and court rules covering the taking and use of depositions are subject to constant change, counsel should carefully examine the law of the forum before he takes a deposition. In general, as has been stated above, some statutes are very broad while others are extremely detailed. The difference between the two types of statutes are well exemplified by the Federal statute and the New York State statute. For that reason, they are set forth in full, below.

Rule 26 of the Federal Rules of Civil Procedure covers both the question when a deposition may be taken and under what circumstances it may be used. The rule reads as follows: [3]

"Rule 26. Depositions pending action

(a) **When depositions may be taken.** Any party may take the testimony of any person, including a party, by deposition upon oral examination or written interrogatories for the purpose of discovery or for use as evidence in the action or for both purposes. After commencement of the action the deposition may be taken without leave of court, except that leave, granted with or without notice, must be obtained if notice of the taking is served by the plaintiff within 20 days after commencement of the action. The attendance of witnesses may be compelled by the use of subpoena as provided in Rule 45. Depositions shall be taken only in accordance with these rules. The deposition of a person confined in prison may be taken only by leave of court on such terms as the court prescribes.

(b) **Scope of examination.** Unless otherwise ordered by the court as provided by Rule 30(b) or (d), the deponent may be examined regarding any matter, not privileged, which is relevant to the subject matter involved in the pending action, whether it relates to the claim or defense of the examining party or to the claim or defense of any other party, including

---

[3] References in the quotation to other sections of the Federal Rules of Civil Procedure need not be regarded in the context of the present quotation.

the existence, description, nature, custody, condition and location of any books, documents, or other tangible things and the identity and location of persons having knowledge of relevant facts. It is not ground for objection that the testimony will be inadmissible at the trial if the testimony sought appears reasonably calculated to lead to the discovery of admissible evidence.

(c) Examination and cross-examination. Examination and cross-examination of deponents may proceed as permitted at the trial under the provisions of Rule 43(b).

(d) Use of depositions. At the trial or upon the hearing of a motion or an interlocutory proceeding, any part or all of a deposition, so far as admissible under the rules of evidence, may be used against any party who was present or represented at the taking of the deposition or who had due notice thereof, in accordance with any one of the following provisions:

(1) Any deposition may be used by any party for the purpose of contradicting or impeaching the testimony of deponent as a witness.

(2) The deposition of a party or of any one who at the time of taking the deposition was an officer, director, or managing agent of a public or private corporation, partnership, or association which is a party may be used by an adverse party for any purpose.

(3) The deposition of a witness, whether or not a party, may be used by any party for any purpose if the court finds: 1, that the witness is dead; or 2, that the witness is at a greater distance than 100 miles from the place of trial or hearing, or is out of the United States, unless it appears that the absence of the witness was procured by the party offering the deposition; or 3, that the witness is unable to attend or testify because of age, sickness, infirmity, or imprisonment; or 4, that the party offering the deposition has been unable to procure the attendance of the witness by subpoena; or 5, upon application and notice, that such exceptional circumstances exist as to make it desirable, in the interest of justice and with due regard to the importance of presenting the testimony of witnesses orally in open court, to allow the deposition to be used.

(4) If only part of a deposition is offered in evidence by

a party, an adverse party may require him to introduce all of it which is relevant to the part introduced, and any party may introduce any other parts.

Substitution of parties does not affect the right to use depositions previously taken; and, when an action in any court of the United States or of any state has been dismissed and another action involving the same subject matter is afterward brought between the same parties or their representatives or successors in interest, all depositions lawfully taken and duly filed in the former action may be used in the latter as if originally taken therefor.

(e) **Objections to admissibility.** Subject to the provisions of Rules 28(b) and 32(c), objection may be made at the trial or hearing to receiving in evidence any deposition or part thereof for any reason which would require the exclusion of the evidence if the witness were then present and testifying.

(f) **Effect of taking or using depositions.** A party shall not be deemed to make a person his own witness for any purpose by taking his deposition. The introduction in evidence of the deposition or any part thereof for any purpose other than that of contradicting or impeaching the deponent makes the deponent the witness of the party introducing the deposition, but this shall not apply to the use by an adverse party of a deposition as described in paragraph (2) of subdivision (d) of this rule. At the trial or hearing any party may rebut any relevant evidence contained in a deposition whether introduced by him or by any other party."

It is to be noted that Rule 26 of the Federal Rules of Civil Procedure covers more ground than is ordinarily provided for in statutes governing the taking of depositions. It is really a complete discovery proceeding. Thus, there is the provision (Rule 26, subdivision b) that inquiry may be made as to the location of persons having knowledge of relevant facts and that it is not a ground for objection that the testimony will be inadmissible at the trial if it appears reasonably calculated to lead to the discovery of admissible evidence. The further provision in the same subdivision of the statute that a deponent may be examined regarding matters upon which the examiner does not have the burden of proof is typical of modern practice. At one time there was a rule, which still persists in some jurisdictions, that a deposition could only be taken as to matters where the examining party had the burden of proof. This is no longer the general rule.

The New York statute, although in some respect similar to Federal Rule 26, is infinitely more detailed. Its major portions (contained in the New York Civil Practice Law and Rules) read as follows:

"§3102. Method of obtaining disclosure.

(a) Disclosure devices.   Information is obtainable by one or more of the following disclosure devices: deposition upon oral questions or without the state upon written questions, interrogatories, demands for addresses, discovery and inspection of documents or property, physical and mental examinations of persons, and requests for admission.

(b) Stipulation or notice normal method.   Unless otherwise provided by the civil practice law and rules or by the court, disclosure shall be obtained by stipulation or on notice without leave of the court.

(c) Before action commenced; real property actions.   Before an action is commenced, disclosure to aid in bringing an action, to preserve information or to aid in arbitration, may be obtained, but only by court order. The court may appoint a referee to take testimony. Where such disclosure is obtained for use in an action involving title to real property the deposition or other document obtained shall be promptly recorded in the office of the clerk of the county in which the real property is situated.

(d) After trial commenced.   Except as provided in section 5223, during and after trial, disclosure may be obtained only by order of the trial court on notice.

(e) Action pending in another jurisdiction. When under any mandate, writ or commission issued out of any court of record in any other state, territory, district or foreign jurisdiction, or whenever upon notice or agreement, it is required to take the testimony of a witness in the state, he may be compelled to appear and testify in the same manner and by the same process as may be employed for the purpose of taking testimony in actions pending in the state. The supreme court or a county court shall make any appropriate order in aid of taking such a deposition.

(f) **Action in court of claims.** In an action in the court of claims, disclosure may be obtained only by order of that court.

"§3103. Protective orders.

(a) **Prevention of abuse.** The court may at any time on its own initiative, or on motion of any party or witness, make a protective order denying, limiting, conditioning or regulating the use of any disclosure device. Such order shall be designed to prevent unreasonable annoyance, expense, embarrassment, disadvantage, or other prejudice to any person or the courts.

(b) **Suspension of disclosure pending application for protective order.** Service of a notice of motion for a protective order shall suspend disclosure of the particular matter in dispute.

(c) **Suppression of information improperly obtained.** If any disclosure under this article has been improperly or irregularly obtained so that a substantial right of a party is prejudiced, the court, on motion, may make an appropriate order, including an order that the information be suppressed."

"Rule 3106. Priority of depositions; witnesses; prisoners.

(a) **Normal priority.** After an action is commenced, any party may take the testimony of any person by deposition upon oral or written questions. Leave of the court, granted on motion, shall be obtained if notice of the taking of the deposition of a party is served by the plaintiff within twenty days after service of the complaint.

(b) **Witnesses.** Where the person to be examined is not a party or a person who at the time of taking the deposition is an officer, director, member or employee of a party, he shall be served with a subpoena. Unless the court orders otherwise, on motion with or without notice, such subpoena shall be served at least ten days before the examination. Where a motion for a protective order against such an examination is made, the witness shall be notified by the moving party that the examination is stayed.

(c) **Prisoners.** The deposition of a person confined under legal process may be taken only by leave of the court.

"Rule 3107. Notice of taking oral questions.

A party desiring to take the deposition of any person upon oral examination shall give to each party ten days' notice, unless the court orders otherwise. The notice shall be in writing, stating the time and place for taking the deposition, the name and address of each person to be examined, if known, and, if any name is not known, a general description sufficient to identify him or the particular class or group to which he belongs. The notice need not enumerate the matters upon which the person is to be examined. A party to be examined pursuant to notice served by another party may serve notice of at least five days for the examination of any other party, his agent or employee, such examination to be noticed for and to follow at the same time and place.

"Rule 3108. Written questions; when permitted.

A deposition may be taken on written questions when the examining party and the deponent so stipulate or when the testimony is to be taken without the state. A commission or letters rogatory may be issued where necessary or convenient for the taking of a deposition outside of the state.

"Rule 3109. Notice of taking deposition on written questions.

(a) **Notice of taking; service of questions and cross-questions.** A party desiring to take the deposition of any person upon written questions shall serve such questions upon each party together with a notice stating the name and address of the person to be examined, if known, and, if the name is not known, a general description sufficient to identify him or the particular class or group to which he belongs, and the name or descriptive title and address of the officer before whom the deposition is to be taken. Within ten days thereafter a party so served may serve written cross-questions upon each party. Within five days thereafter the original party may serve written redirect questions upon each party. Within three days after being served with written redirect questions, a party may serve written re-cross-questions upon each party.

(b) **Officer asking written questions.** A copy of the notice and copies of all written questions served shall be delivered by the party taking the deposition to the officer designated in the notice. The officer shall proceed promptly to take the testimony of the witness in response to the written questions and to pre-pare the deposition.

"Rule 3110. Where the deposition is to be taken within the state.

A deposition within the state on notice shall be taken:

1. when the person to be examined is a party or an officer, director, member or employee of a party, within the county in which he resides or has an office for the regular transaction of business in person or where the action is pending; or

2. when any other person to be examined is a resident, within the county in which he resides, is regularly employed or has an office for the regular transaction of business in person, or if he is not a resident, within the county in which he is served, is regularly employed or has an office for the regular transaction of business in person; or

3. when the party to be examined is a public corporation or any officer, agent or employee thereof, within the county in which the action is pending; the place of such examination shall be in the court in which the action is pending unless the parties stipulate otherwise.

For the purpose of this rule New York City shall be considered one county.

"Rule 3111. Production of things at the examination.

The notice or subpoena may require the production of books, papers and other things in the possession, custody or control of the person to be examined to be marked as exhibits, and used on the examination."

"Rule 3113. Conduct of the examination.

(a) **Persons before whom depositions may be taken.** Depositions may be taken before any of the following persons except an attorney, or employee of an attorney, for a party or prospective party and except a person who would be disqualified to act as a juror because of interest in the event or consanguinity or affinity to a party:

1. within the state, a person authorized by the laws of the state to administer oaths;

2. without the state but within the United States or within a territory or possession subject to the dominion of the United States, a person authorized to take acknowledgments of deeds outside of the state by the real property law of the state or to administer oaths by the laws of the United States or of the place where the deposition is taken; and

3. in a foreign country, any diplomatic or consular agent or representative of the United States, appointed or accredited to, and residing within, the country, or a person appointed by commission or under letters rogatory, or an officer of the armed forces authorized to take the acknowledgment of deeds.

Officers may be designated in notices or commissions either by name or descriptive title and letters rogatory may be addressed 'To the Appropriate Authority in (here name the state or country).'

(b) **Oath of witness; transcription of testimony; objections; continuous examination; written questions read by examining officer.** The officer before whom the deposition is to be taken shall put the witness on oath and shall personally, or by someone acting under his direction, record the testimony. The testimony shall be transcribed. All objections made at the time of the examination to the qualifications of the officer taking the deposition or the person recording it, or to the manner of taking it, or to the testimony presented, or to the conduct of any person, and any other objection to the proceedings, shall be noted by the officer upon the deposition and the deposition shall proceed subject to the right of a person to apply for a protective order. The deposition shall be taken continuously and without unreasonable adjournment, unless the court otherwise orders or the witness and parties present otherwise agree. In lieu of participating in an oral examination, any party served with notice of taking a deposition may transmit written questions to the officer, who shall propound them to the witness and record the answers.

(c) **Examination and cross-examination.** Examination and cross-examination of deponents shall proceed as permitted in the trial of actions in open court. When the deposition of a party is taken at the instance of an adverse party, the deponent may be cross-examined by his own attorney. Cross-examination need not be limited to the subject matter of the examination in chief."

"**Rule 3115. Objections to qualification of person taking deposition; competency; questions and answers.**

(a) **Objection when deposition offered in evidence.** Subject to the other provisions of this rule, objection may be made at the trial or hearing to receiving in evidence any deposition or part thereof for any reason which would require the exclusion of the evidence if the witness were then present and testifying.

(b) **Errors which might be obviated if made known promptly.** Errors and irregularities occurring at the oral examination in the manner of taking the deposition, in the form of the questions or answers, in the oath or affirmation, or in the conduct of persons, and errors of any kind which might be obviated or removed if objection were promptly presented, are waived unless reasonable objection thereto is made at the taking of the deposition.

(c) **Disqualification of person taking deposition.** Objection to the taking of a deposition because of disqualification of the person by whom it is to be taken is waived unless made before the taking of the deposition begins or as soon thereafter as the disqualification becomes known or could be discovered with reasonable diligence.

(d) **Competency of witnesses or admissibility of testimony.** Objections to the competency of a witness or to the admissibility of testimony are not waived by failure to make them before or during the taking of the deposition, unless the ground of the objection is one which might have been obviated or removed if objection had been made at that time.

(e) **Form of written questions.** Objections to the form of written questions are waived unless served in writing upon the party propounding the questions within the time allowed for serving succeeding questions or within three days after service.

"**Rule 3116. Signing deposition; physical preparation; copies.**

(a) **Signing.** The deposition shall be submitted to the witness for examination and shall be read to or by him, and any changes in form or substance which the witness desires to make shall be entered at the end of the deposition with a statement of the reasons given by the witness for making them. The deposition shall then be signed by the witness before any officer authorized to administer an oath. If the witness fails to sign the deposition, the officer before whom the deposition was taken shall sign it and state on the record the fact of the witness' failure or refusal to sign, together with any reason given. The deposition may then be used as fully as though signed.

(b) **Certification and filing by officer.** The officer before whom the deposition was taken shall certify on the deposition that the witness was duly sworn by him and that the deposition is a true record of the testimony given by the witness. He shall list all appearances by the parties and attorneys. If the deposition was taken on written questions, he shall attach to it the copy of the notice and written questions received by him. He shall then securely seal the deposition in an envelope endorsed with the title of the action and the index number of the action, if one has been assigned, and marked 'Deposition of (here insert name of witness)' and shall promptly file it with, or send it by registered or certified mail to the clerk of the court where the case is to be tried. The deposition shall always be open to the inspection of the parties, each of whom is entitled to make copies thereof. If a copy of the deposition is furnished to each party or if the parties stipulate to waive filing, the officer need not file the original but may deliver it to the party taking the deposition.

(c) **Exhibits.** Documentary evidence exhibited before the officer or exhibits marked for identification during the examination of the witness shall be annexed to and returned with the deposition. However, if requested by the party producing documentary evidence or on exhibit, the officer shall mark it for identification as an exhibit in the case, give each party an opportunity to copy or inspect it, and return it to the party offering it, and it may then be used in the same manner as if annexed to and returned with the deposition.

(d) **Expenses of taking.** Unless the court orders otherwise, the party taking the deposition shall bear the expense thereof.

(e) **Errors of officer or person transcribing.** Errors and irregularities of the officer or the person transcribing the deposition are waived unless a motion to suppress the deposition or some part thereof is made with reasonable promptness after such defect is, or with due diligence might have been, ascertained.

"Rule 3117. Use of depositions.

(a) **Impeachment of witnesses; parties; unavailable witnesses.** At the trial or upon the hearing of a motion or an interlocutory proceeding, any part or all of a deposition, so far as admissible under the rules of evidence, may be used in accordance with any of the following provisions:

1. any deposition may be used by any party for the purpose of contradicting or impeaching the testimony of the deponent as a witness;

2. the deposition of a party or of any one who at the time of taking the deposition was an officer, director, member, or

managing or authorized agent of a party, or the deposition of an employee of a party produced by that party, may be used for any purpose by any adversely interested party; and

3. the deposition of any person may be used by any party for any purpose against any other party who was present or represented at the taking of the deposition or who had the notice required under these rules, provided the court finds:

(i) that the witness is dead; or

(ii) that the witness is at a greater distance than one hundred miles from the place of trial or is out of the state, unless it appears that the absence of the witness was procured by the party offering the deposition; or

(iii) that the witness is unable to attend or testify because of age, sickness, infirmity, or imprisonment; or

(iv) that the party offering the deposition has been unable to procure the attendance of the witness by diligent efforts; or

(v) upon motion or notice, that such exceptional circumstances exist as to make its use desirable, in the interest of justice and with due regard to the importance of presenting the testimony of witnesses orally in open court.

(b) **Use of part of deposition.** If only part of a deposition is read at the trial by a party, any other party may read any other part of the deposition which ought in fairness to be considered in connection with the part read.

(c) **Substitution of parties; prior actions.** Substitution of parties does not affect the right to use depositions previously taken. When an action has been brought in any court of any state or of the United States and another action involving the same subject matter is afterward brought between the same parties or their representatives or successors in interest all depositions taken in the former action may be used in the latter as if taken therein.

(d) **Effect of using deposition.** A party shall not be deemed to make a person his own witness for any purpose by taking his deposition. The introduction in evidence of the deposition or any part thereof for any purpose other than that of contradicting or impeaching the deponent makes the deponent the witness of the party introducing the deposition, but this shall not apply to the use of a deposition as described in paragraph two of subdivision (a). At the trial, any party may rebut any relevant evidence contained in a deposition, whether introduced by him or by any other party."

It is customary for counsel to stipulate at the start of the taking of a deposition that filing of the same is waived, but that the party taking the deposition shall give to his opponent, without charge, a copy thereof.

It is also customary to stipulate that the deposition, when transcribed, may be sworn to before any notary public or other person entitled to take oaths. However, care should be taken as to this portion of the stipulation to provide that, if the witness refuses to sign the deposition, it can be verified by the oath of the person before whom it was taken.[4]

Where the deposition has been sworn to in a jurisdiction other than the forum, the authority of the person taking the oath should be authenticated by a proper certificate from that jurisdiction.[5]

It is a general requirement of most statutes involving the taking of depositions that the exhibits marked during the taking of the deposition be annexed thereto or filed therewith. If, in the course of taking depositions, documents are produced by the person being examined and marked for identification, there should either be photostats made of these documents and annexed to the deposition, or there should be a stipulation to the effect that the party being examined will produce the documents on the trial. In any event, these documents should be marked for identification by the person before whom the deposition is taken. If the person being examined is a witness and not a party to the action, stipulation between counsel in the case will not accomplish this purpose. In such an instance, copies should be made of the original documents if the witness is not willing to surrender them for filing and a stipulation between counsel should be entered on the record permitting these copies to be filed with the deposition or used upon the trial.

Occasions sometimes arise when a witness or party being examined becomes so obstreperous or difficult to handle that it is

---

[4] See Rule 3116(a) of New York Civil Practice Law and Rules, quoted above.

[5] As to the method of authentication of out-of-state oaths, see section 11:4 *post*.

necessary to obtain a referee before whom the deposition can be taken. This referee is ordinarily empowered to act as a judge for the purpose of taking the deposition, including the power to rule on objections. Statutes covering such a contingency vary. The New York statute (section 3104 of the New York Civil Practice Law and Rules) is typical and reads as follows:

"**§3104.   Supervision of disclosure.**

(a) **Motion for, and extent of, supervision of disclosure.** Upon the motion of any party or witness on notice to all parties or on its own initiative without notice, the court in which an action is pending may by one of its judges or a referee supervise all or part of any disclosure procedure.

(b) **Referee selected by stipulation.** All of the parties in an action may stipulate that a named attorney may act as a referee under this section. The stipulation shall provide for payment of his fees which shall, unless otherwise agreed, be taxed as disbursements.

(c) **Powers of referee; motions referred to persons supervising disclosure.** A referee under this section shall have all the powers of the court under this article except the power to relieve himself of his duties, to appoint a successor, or to adjudge any person guilty of contempt. All motions or applications made under this article shall be returnable before the judge or referee, designated under this section and after disposition, if requested by any party, his order shall be filed in the office of the clerk.

(d) **Review of order of referee.** Any party or witness may apply for review of an order made under this section by a referee. The application shall be by motion made in the court in which the action is pending within five days after the order is made. Service of a notice of motion for review shall suspend disclosure of the particular matter in dispute. If the question raised by the motion may affect the rights of a witness, notice shall be served on him personally or by mail at his last known address. It shall set forth succinctly the order complained of, the reason it is objectionable and the relief demanded.

(e) **Payment of expenses of referee.** The court may make an appropriate order for the payment of the reasonable expenses of the referee."

By decision and in a few instances by court rule, despite the broadness of statutes authorizing the taking of depositions, limitations are imposed depending upon the nature of the action. Typical of such limitations are:

(a) The proposition that, in a matrimonial action, there can be no general examination before trial;

(b) That, in a matrimonial action, an examination of the finances of the defendant will not be permitted until plaintiff has proved her right to matrimonial relief (divorce, separation or annulment); and

(c) That in an action for an accounting, the only examination before trial that will be permitted is that used for the purpose of establishing a right to an accounting and the examination as to the details of an account will be delayed until such right has been established.

In the light of these limitations, it is the practice in some jurisdictions to try the main case and, if the right to general relief has been established, to adjourn the case to permit interim examinations as to financial matters before the trial continues.

Most rules setting forth the limitations just described are accompanied by another rule, which permits examination at an earlier stage in the proceeding if necessity for the same can be shown by "special circumstances." As a practical matter, this means that the examination will only be permitted on motion instead of on mere notice.

Sec. 7:3 Preparing deposition for use.

Except in rare instances, counsel will not intend to use an entire deposition during the trial. He should, long in advance of the trial, carefully read all depositions, whether taken by him or his opponent, and make decisions as to what portions of each deposition he will use and under what circumstances.

If the depositions are lengthy, it is wise to prepare a detailed index of each of them. This index should cover the subject matter of every proposition encompassed within each deposition and an indication of the page on which such subject has been covered. The subject matter method of indexing the depositions is particularly helpful where an individual subject has been covered in several widely separated portions of a deposition. Some counsel have deemed it wise to prepare a major index of *all* the depositions so that, for convenient reference, counsel may quickly know where each subject was touched upon.

The purpose of indexing the depositions is not only to chart the portions of a deposition intended to be used by counsel,[6] but also to enable counsel, during the course of the trial if a deposition is used by his opponent, quickly to refer to his index in order to determine whether another portion of the same deposition should be utilized by him.

If depositions included exhibits, the index should show at what point the exhibits were introduced. If there are a great many exhibits, it may be wise to index them separately.

In preparing depositions for use upon the trial, care should be taken that each deposition has been properly authenticated.

Sec. 7:4   Charting portions of deposition to be used.

Before the start of the trial, counsel should prepare a chart of the portions of the depositions he intends to use. This chart should indicate the page of the deposition and the subject that this page covers.

It should be noted that the chart herein referred to differs from the index described in section 7:3, *supra.*

Form 6 is a typical chart.

Form 6.

Chart of Portions to be Read from Deposition.

Pages	Subject
3–7	Identification of Jones and organization of Company.
14	"Sparked" new idea.
25	No other reason for rejection than in letter of May 4, 1965.
26	In writing last paragraph of letter of May 4, did not have in mind that plaintiff should submit ideas gratuitously.

---

[6] See section 7:4, *post.*

Pages	Subject
26–28	Telephone calls and visit from plaintiff and then submission of report on beverages.
28–31, 41–42, 45–48	Business about the two exhibits re beverage and whether defendant retained the same.
	GET CONCESSION, at this point, that the first time that we ever got the original was in a conference between Mr. Williams [defendant's attorney], HHS and MF at our office on November 4, 1966.
66	When same beverages first on the market and similar products first on the market in 1958.
90–91	Beverage "brand new" and publicity in connection with it.
106, 107–108	"Important break" was getting away from synthetic flavors which presented the original problem.

The lawyer who intends to read from a deposition will, presumably, have two copies in his possession—the original and a carbon copy. It is advisable that, on the carbon copy, counsel should indicate by markings the precise portion he intends to read. He should *not* make any marks on the original.

Sec. 7:5 Method of reading deposition.

Reading a deposition has the same effect as if the witness whose deposition was taken is called to the stand and personally testifies. It is desirable, as nearly as possible, to enact a scene in which the witness is portrayed as personally testifying and the lawyer is portrayed as an actual questioner in open court.

To accomplish this end, it is customary for an assistant to the lawyer to be placed on the witness stand, taking with him the original of the deposition. The lawyer then reads from his copy of the deposition the questions which he intends to propound and the witness reads from the original of the deposition the answers given by the examined deponent. This process should be explained to the jury. It is not necessary to explain it to the court, where the case is tried without a jury, since judges are familiar with the method here outlined.

When the witness who is to read from the deposition takes the stand, he should be sworn as would any other witness. Thereupon, the following questions and answers are appropriate:

> **Q.** What is your business or occupation? **A.** I am an attorney at law and am assisting you in the trial of this case.
>
> **Q.** Do you have in your hand the original deposition of William Smith, a witness examined by me before trial? **A.** Yes.
>
> **Q.** Do you understand that it is your duty, when I read a question from this deposition to read the answer of William Smith, precisely as it was given when he was examined before trial? **A.** Yes.
>
> **Q.** Will you be good enough to follow that practice as I read questions to you and read me the answers precisely as they were given by William Smith? **A.** Yes.

The examination of the witness may now continue as though he were the person whose deposition was taken. If opposing counsel desires to object to a question, he may do so as soon as the question is read. The court can then rule on the objection. The notes of the court reporter will, of course, indicate this ruling.[7]

Although the use of a live witness to read back answers in the deposition will relieve boredom on the part of the fact-finder, that witness should not engage in dramatics. He can, of course, read the answers with expression, but there is no reason for him to be a Thespian. If opposing counsel uses the same witness to read back other portions of the deposition, the witness need not go out of his way to read these answers with too great expression.

It is inadvisable for counsel merely to read a deposition into the record without the use of a live witness, unless the deposition is very short or the questions to be propounded are few. Reading a long deposition is not only boring, but the fact-finder will probably lose the trend and will have no conception of the fact that, when the deposition was taken, a live witness was being questioned.

---

[7] It should be noted that, in the taking of the deposition, all objections except as to the form of the question have been reserved for the trial.

It is a great mistake for counsel merely to offer the deposition in evidence, even when the case is tried to the court without a jury.[8]

The tendency of some trial counsel to treat a deposition as an unimportant part of the case is a failure of their duty toward their clients. If the deposition was worth taking, it is worth careful reading to the fact-finder. This is true even though the deposition may merely cover a relatively unimportant point.

---

[8] If the case is tried to a jury, the jurymen are not permitted to take the deposition into the jury room with them while deliberating. See section 6:6, *supra.* If the court merely receives the deposition, there is no certainty that he will ever read it with great care.

Chapter VIII

VISUAL EVIDENCE

Sec. 8:1   Utility of visual evidence.

No matter how well a witness testifies, there are some situations in which, either because of the complexity of the issues or because some matters may be better understood by visualization than by description, it is advantageous to offer visual proof.

This type of evidence is admissible when, in the discretion of the court, it is deemed helpful to the fact-finder. Whether the evidence is received as a clarification of or supplemental to the testimony of the witness, the discretion of the trial court is rarely overruled. The types of visual evidence are numerous, among the more common being photographs, slides, motion pictures, x-rays, charts, diagrams, plans, maps and models.

Decisions in given situations are so largely confined to the immediate facts of the case in which the decision has been rendered that, in preparing to introduce visual evidence, counsel should try to be prepared with cases that, as nearly as possible, cover the precise factual problem presented to the court. Of course, if such decisions have been rendered in the jurisdiction of the forum, they are most advantageous. However, since decisions in this field are so closely premised upon the exact facts of a given case, counsel should not hesitate to use decisions from other jurisdictions.

Sec. 8:2 Classes of visual evidence.

Two main types of visual evidence are commonly utilized. They are: first, things prepared under the supervision of counsel to aid the jury in comprehending complex situations; and second, existing matters, not prepared specifically for use on the trial, which are better seen by a fact-finder than left to oral description.

From the point of view of admissibility, there is no distinction between these two classes of visual evidence. If the court rules, in its discretion, that a fact-finder will be helped by visual proof, such proof is admissible as a matter of law.

Whatever form of visual aid is used, it is requisite that it authentically portray that which it purports to show and that the conditions at the time the visual aid was prepared were the same as those prevailing at the legally significant time.[1]

At times, expert witnesses make demonstrations in open court.[2] There are, often, the introduction of exhibits which have a direct bearing on the requisite complete proof of the case.[3] These are not the type of visual evidence with which the present chapter is concerned. They are separately treated elsewhere in this volume.

Sec. 8:3 Diagrams and plans.

In cases where the location of objects or happenings, the method of ingress or egress from a given place, or other matters connected with the layout of premises are involved, it is sometimes difficult for a fact-finder to follow the testimony and keep in mind how the premises are constructed. In instances of this sort, it is common practice to introduce in evidence a diagram or plan of the premises.

A diagram or plan of this type must be drawn to scale and, where its contents are questioned or where there is an objection to its introduction in evidence, the person who prepared it must

---

[1] *Oklahoma City v. Lycan*, 193 Okl. 170; *Edelson v. Higgins*, 43 Cal. App. 2d 759.

[2] See section 9:5, *post*.

[3] For example, see section 9:11, *post*, dealing with fingerprints and other impressions.

be called as a witness to lay a foundation for its introduction. The witness is required to testify about exactly what method he used in preparing the diagram or plan, including a full statement of his taking of measurements. He should also be prepared to state the scale of the diagram or plan.

It is often the case, especially in large office or residential premises, for the renting or managing agent to have architectural plans, originally used in connection with renting operations. Such plans may have been drawn a long time before the case is brought to trial. The person who drew the plans is not a necessary witness if someone else testifies that he has compared the plans with the premises and has made measurements verifying the correctness of the plans. If it is intended to introduce a plan of this type, counsel should try to arrange with his opponent that there will be no objection to its introduction in evidence.

Diagrams of machines are very often used so that, during the course of testimony about such a machine, the fact-finder may be enabled visually to follow such testimony. Here, the basis for introduction of the diagram is similar to that used when a plan of premises is employed.

At times, in addition to a general diagram, additional diagrams of portions of machines are used. If the additional diagrams show internal portions of the machine, the supporting witness should be prepared to testify in the greatest detail how he was able to make the diagram. If different scales are used for a general diagram and partial diagrams this fact should be stated.

As in the case of plans of premises prepared by persons who are not called as witnesses, the supporting witness must testify that he compared the diagram sought to be introduced with the machine, itself. Manufacturers sometimes have diagrams of their machines produced in great quantity (for example, diagrams indicating the portions of an automobile to which lubrication is applied). In such instances, an arrangement may be able to be made between counsel and his opponent that these diagrams be introduced as exhibits.

Sec. 8:4   Charts.

In complicated litigations, it might be virtually impossible for a fact-finder to follow the testimony unless some overall guide to its content is supplied. For example, where analysis is required of complicated corporate structures or of ingenious devices which have been used to create confusion and cover up fraud, a fact-finder, who repetitively hears the names of corporations, partnerships and individuals, might be so confused that he could not determine the relationship of some of these names to each other.

To obviate this type of confusion, a properly prepared chart can be received in evidence. The test for its admissibility is whether it will be helpful to the fact-finders in analyzing the evidence. It is within the discretion of the trial court to determine whether such a chart should be received and the exercise of discretion, in this respect, is rarely overruled by an appellate court.

Different from plans, diagrams, photographs and models, such a chart does not purport to be a representation of anything living or dead. Its sole function is to relate various portions of the testimony to one another. Since it is necessary to have the chart before the fact-finder prior to the receipt of all the testimony, it is common practice for counsel to ask the court to receive the chart subject to connection. If the court refuses so to do, counsel will first have to put in his testimony, then produce the chart and then repeat a substantial portion of the testimony after the chart has been received.

A chart of this character (sometimes displayed on an easel or with copies of it in the hands of the individual fact-finders) can well prove to be the most important exhibit in a case. It serves as a constant reminder of the basic issues involved and as a perpetual check upon the testimony being offered. Being constantly in the sight of the fact-finder, who has heard evidence of the care with which it was prepared, the chart prevents digression from the issues.[4]

The use of charts in uncomplicated cases is, also, often very helpful. An outstanding example occurred in a suit against a large telegraph company to recover the fair value of an idea or plan for special telegraphic services to be offered to the public. The idea was for the creation of a special type of message to be known as a "tourate" message. The difficulty with proving the case arose from the fact that the value of the idea had to be established. Instead of throwing at the jury a vast mass of figures, counsel caused

---

[4] Many judges have stated that a well-prepared chart has not only aided them on rulings on the admissibility of testimony, but has been of inestimable help in framing a charge to the jury.

to be prepared a chart which visually showed the relationship of this type of special message to the other principal types of special messages used by the company. Thus, as witnesses testified to the number of other types of special messages in a given month, a bar on the chart colored red and drawn to scale visually showed the extent of these other types of special messages in each month under consideration. When witnesses testified to the number of "tourate" messages in each month, another bar on the chart, colored green, was placed next to the bar showing the volume of other types of special messages. In this manner, the jury was able to infer the relative proportions of each type of special message during each month.

There are other types of charts which may be introduced in evidence as part of entries made in the regular course of business.[5] For example, a hospital chart or the portions thereof showing the temperature of a patient at different hours on different days, or the portions of entries on charts kept in smeltering operations indicating the heat applied at various times, or charts maintained to show the pressures under which various operations were conducted. Charts of this nature are not prepared for purposes of litigation. They exist and, when properly authenticated, they are evidence of facts.

Sec. 8:5   Photographs and models.

Photographs are among the best examples of visual evidence. Properly authenticated, they are admissible in evidence.[6]

Different from charts, photographs are, in and of themselves, prime proof of *facts*. Their impression on fact-finders cannot be overestimated and, it should be particularly noted, when jurymen are permitted to take these photographs into the jury room with them during the course of their deliberations, the proof offered by the photographs is lasting and impressive up to the moment of verdict.

Models, whose construction is shown to be accurate, have a dual function. First, the model, itself, acts as proof of a fact. Second, the model can be employed as a guide to other testimony.

Before the model can be received in evidence, the person who

---

[5] See section 11:10, *post*.
[6] As to methods of authentication, see sections 9:12 and 10:7, *post*.

fabricated it must testify in detail about his manner of preparation. He should show the scale on which it was produced and the accuracy of each measurement when reduced to that scale.

Consider a prime example of a model which acts not only as proof of a fact but also as a guide to other testimony. In a law suit involving the accidental killing of a longshoreman, who was hit by a moving crane and thrown into the hold of a ship, the model is of the open hatch through which the longshoreman was thrown, the objects surrounding that hatch, the crane and the movement of the crane. The model having been introduced in evidence, witnesses testify to the tragic event. They point out on the model where the longshoreman was standing when he was hit by the crane. They then point to objects in the nearby vicinity, which prevented the longshoreman from seeing the crane in motion. By manipulation of the model, they describe how the crane swung around, and, before the longshoreman could duck, hit him and threw him into the open hatch. They then show where they were standing so that they could see the entire occurrence.

Sec. 8:6 Views.

In the discretion of the court, the fact-finder may be permitted to view certain premises, such as the situs of a crime or of an accident.

Certain precautions must be observed. No fact-finder may view premises independently. He is required, if part of a jury, to take his view with all of his fellow-jurors and in the presence of court officers (and, in some jurisdictions, of the judge). Nothing can be said to him during the view unless the court takes the official reporter with him and causes a notation to be made of every remark at the view site. If an individual juror views the premises, this is a basis for a mistrial or, if later discovered, for a new trial.

In one type of case, a view is permitted as an independent feature of research authorized by statute. This is in the case of commissioners or judges, who are required to view premises as part of their duty in fixing the value thereof in a land condemnation action or proceeding. Here, the examination of the premises is not regarded as a "view" in the ordinary sense. After an observation of this type, it is wise for the judge or commissioner to place in the record of the case a statement of what he observed and the consequences that, in his opinion, flow therefrom.

Chapter IX

EXPERT TESTIMONY

Sec. 9:1 Function of expert testimony.

Although, as will hereinafter appear, there are several classes of expert testimony,[1] and of "experts,"[2] the *sole* function of expert

---

[1] Section 9:2, *post.*
[2] Sections 9:2 and 9:7, *post.*

testimony is to assist the fact-finder in coming to a proper conclusion based on the evidence in situations where, without the assistance of an expert, the "common mind" is not "equal to the proper solution" of the problem presented.[3] Otherwise stated, it may be said that whenever the subject matter of a litigation is such that inexperienced persons are not capable of forming a correct judgment without expert assistance the opinions of experts are admissible.[4]

Whether the use of expert testimony is justified in a given case ordinarily rests in the sound discretion of the trial court, whose ruling in this respect will not be reversed unless it is based on an error of law, a mistake or an abuse of discretion.[5]

In cases involving the fixing of lawyers' fees, a situation is presented where the judge, as a fact-finder, may use his own experience in reaching a determination as to the reasonableness of compensation. Here, the fact-finder, himself, is an expert. If the facts about the attorneys' services are fully set forth in the record, even an appellate court may, initially, award judgment based on its own conclusions as to the value of professional services. Speaking of such a situation, the opinion of an appellate court in a leading case reads, in part: [6]

> "While his [plaintiff's expert witness] testimony was admissible and should be given due weight it is not conclusive on the court since the court is itself an expert on the question and may consider its own knowledge and experience concerning reasonable and proper fees and in the light of such knowledge and experience the court may form an independent judgment from the facts and evidence before it as to the nature and extent of the services rendered, make an appraisal of such services, and determine the reasonable value thereof. (*Matter of Sebring*, 238 App. Div. 281, 289, 290; 7 C.J.S., Attorney and Client, §191, subd. [d].)"

---

[3] *Finn v. Cassidy*, 165 N.Y. 584, 591–598, collating and discussing the standard arguments for and against the reception of expert testimony and citing numerous cases illustrating the desirability of the use of such testimony in specific circumstances.

[4] *Connecticut Mut. Life Ins. Co. v. Lathrop*, 111 U.S. 612; *American Bauxite Co. v. Dunn*, 120 Ark. 1; *Scott v. Astoria R. Co.*, 43 Ore. 26.

[5] *Commonwealth v. Spencer*, 212 Mass. 438; *Northern Supply Co. v. Wangard*, 123 Wis. 1.

[6] *McAvoy v. Harron*, 26 App. Div. 2d 452, 454 [New York].

In some cases where a trial court has fixed an attorney's fee, the appellate court modifies the determination. Common examples are the modification of an attorney's fee in matrimonial actions, stockholders' derivative suits, class or representative actions and decedent estate proceedings.

Sec. 9:2   Classes of expert testimony and methods of treating same.

There are two main types of expert testimony: (a) opinion evidence; and (b) demonstrative evidence.[7]

Both in preparation for trial and upon the trial, itself, the distinction between the types of expert testimony should be borne in mind. There is sufficient difference to justify separate treatment of each of the types. To a consideration of each of the types, separately, and their method of treatment, we now turn:

(a) Opinion Evidence

Opinion evidence (sometimes referred to as "pure opinion testimony") is, as its name implies, the statement by a duly qualified expert[8] of his *opinion* based upon testimony in the record. Evidence of this sort rests upon the presumption that the personal experience of the fact-finder (court or jury) will not enable him to make an informed judgment about the *ultimate result* of the operation of facts presented for his consideration. Therefore, the duly qualified expert presents his *opinion*, which the person calling him asks the fact-finder to accept.

A classic example of pure opinion testimony arises in actions for personal injury where the expert (a physician and, very often, a specialist) is asked whether a given state of facts are, *in his opinion*, the competent producing cause of an illness from which the victim of negligence suffers. Here, obviously, a lay fact-finder would be utterly incapable of reaching an informed conclusion without the guidance offered by the opinion of the expert. Indeed, in some types of cases a plaintiff cannot make a prima facie case without expert opinion evidence to support his contention. The

---

[7] As will hereinafter appear, in some situations there is a mixture of the two types.

[8] As to the establishment of qualifications of experts, see sections 9:7 through 9:17, *post*.

opinion of the expert is a vital and necessary connecting link between the record facts and the conclusion to be drawn from such
facts.

Where opinion evidence, as such, is involved, the ultimate question is *whether the fact-finder believes the expert.* It is unfortunately too often the case that opposing expert witnesses testify
to diametrically opposite conclusions on the same state of facts.
In such situations, a lay fact-finder may be practically compelled
to reach his verdict *solely* on the basis of determining which expert he believes. This presents a quandary which, except by coincidence, is remote from any concept of justice. The question at
bar should be what is the proper conclusion to be drawn from
record facts. By the nature of the case, no external criteria are
available to the fact-finder to enable him to work his way out of
the presented dilemma. Thus, strange as it may seem, the fact-
finder, as to this phase of the litigation, is basing his finding on a
conclusion as to *credibility.*

In preparing and presenting a case in which an important factor
is the opinion evidence of an expert witness, counsel must bear
in mind that, to an important degree, *the witness is on trial.*

The persuasiveness of an expert witness may rest upon his
method of presentation and his personality (or the appeal thereof
to the fact-finder). Thus, an important factor of preparation should
be the choice of an expert witness who has the ability to state his
conclusions and the reasons therefor simply and logically. Likewise,
it is desirable if possible to choose an expert who is not overbear-
ing, conceited or pontifical. Many a case has been lost because
the fact-finder (particularly when the case is tried to a jury) plain
and simply dislikes an expert witness.

The *weight* accorded to the opinion testimony of an expert is
often largely influenced by the fact-finder's assessment of the expert's ability. Therefore the introduction of this witness is of the
utmost importance. No effort should be spared at the very outset
of such a witness' testimony to establish his qualifications. This
should never be done in a cursory or purely formal manner. The
successful introduction of such a witness is fully accomplished only
when his qualifications are so fully laid out that the fact-finder is
led to the conclusion that this witness certainly must know what
he is talking about.

Where opposing experts testify to different conclusions, the acceptance of the opinion of one of them obviously requires a re-

jection of the opinion of the other. The choice, as far as surface manifestations are concerned, may be a difficult one. The fact-finder can well determine that both witnesses are conscientiously stating their true opinions. Such being the case, the choice to be made will rest upon the conclusion of the fact-finder as to which witness is better qualified to give an opinion.

It must be borne in mind that many persons have a tendency, in general, to distrust the opinion testimony of expert witnesses. Indeed, there is a school of thought which holds that no opinion of an expert can be trusted because the expert has been paid and will testify to any opinion which will best serve the interests of his employer. It is difficult to overcome this type of ingrained prejudice. However, if, in the course of an introduction, an expert witness is shown to be a person of high standing in his profession and in the community, the fact-finder may well come to the belief that such a person would not tailor his opinion for hire.

(b) Demonstrative Evidence

Certain types of expert witnesses perform a function apart from stating their opinions. These witnesses are called for the purpose of making demonstrations in open court from which the fact-finder can reach his *own* conclusion and base his decision upon his *own* opinion. It is true that witnesses of this type often render opinions and that these opinions may bear weight with the fact-finder; but the latter is at liberty to disregard the expert's opinion and to substitute therefor his own conclusion.[9]

The demonstrating expert witness must, at times, state a scientific opinion as an explanatory key to a demonstration. Let us consider, for example, the testimony of a ballistic expert: [10]

This expert will first testify to the scientific fact that bullets fired from the same gun will have the same characteristic markings caused by slight imperfections in or peculiarities of the barrel or firing pin of the gun from which the bullets are fired. Having established this premise, the witness will go on to his demonstration. He will first produce the bullet (properly identified by earlier testimony) taken from the body of a murdered man. He will show

---

[9] See *Boyd v. Gosser*, 82 S. 758 (Fla., 6 A.L.R. 500), quoted from and discussed in section 9:4, *post*. Compare, also, *Matter of Hopkins*, 172 N.Y. 363.

[10] A similar type of demonstrating expert is an examiner of questioned documents, commonly referred to as a handwriting expert. For a discussion of the type of evidence offered by such a witness, section 9:4, *post*.

enlarged pictures of this bullet (often taken with the aid of a microscope-lens) and will point out the peculiar markings on the same. He will then testify that he fired shots from the gun previously established to be the gun of the defendant and will produce the bullets so fired. Thereupon, with the aid of enlarged photographs of the test-fired bullet, he will show that the markings on it are identical with the markings on the bullet recovered from the body of the deceased victim.[11] From the demonstration thus made, the witness will state his opinion that the bullet found in the body of the deceased was fired from the defendant's gun.

In presenting the testimony of a demonstrating expert, it is proper, of course, to establish his qualifications. However, the important evidence consists of the demonstration, itself. Care should be taken to establish the scientific accuracy of the demonstration and the controlled conditions under which the original experiment was made. In some cases, it is possible to conduct an experiment in open court and to make the demonstration from that experiment in the presence of the fact-finder.[12] Obviously, such a procedure is highly persuasive.

In footnote number 7 of this section it was indicated that there are some situations in which there is a mixture of opinion evidence and demonstrative evidence. An example is the testimony of a "real estate expert" in cases involving the value of land and buildings for tax assessment purposes or upon condemnation for public use. Here, the expert testifies to such facts as the prices at which varying neighboring properties have been recently sold. He then gives his opinion that these recent sales are of properties so similar to the one under consideration that the sales price in a free and open market is an indication of the value of the subject property. He thereupon states his opinion of the value of the subject property. There are many variations of this type of testimony. For example, the expert may testify that a proper manner of fixing value is by appropriate capitalization of the net income of the property. He proceeds by indicating the capitalization figure used for similar properties, preferably in the same neighborhood. He then produces (or counsel calling him may cause to be produced)

---

[11] Sometimes, such an expert, using a machine constructed for that purpose, can actually super-impose the negatives of photographs taken of the two bullets and establish, beyond peradventure of doubt, the identity of the markings.

[12] Compare section 9:5, *post*.

the net rental income of the subject property and, by mathematically applying the capitalization component, states the resultant amount as his opinion of the value of the property. In connection with the testimony of a witness of this type, it should be borne in mind that, in addition to his opinion, the witness is testifying as to extraneous *facts* upon which that opinion is based.

A somewhat similar example of an expert testifying to *facts* is the so-called "expert on foreign law." Such a witness produces foreign statutes or the opinions of foreign courts.[13] Although the "expert" may venture an opinion of the state of the foreign law involved, his actual function is to produce *factual* proof of that law, from which the court can draw its own legal conclusions.

Sec. 9:3   Form of expert testimony.

Whether the expert is of the opinion or demonstrative class, it has been customary (and is still the rule in most American jurisdictions) that the interrogation is in the form of a hypothetical question. At the conclusion of the question, the witness is asked whether, on the basis of the facts he is asked to assume, he can express an opinion with reasonable certainty as to the conclusion to which he is being asked to testify. For example, the expert witness is asked: "Assuming that the plaintiff . . . ; can you, in your opinion, with reasonable certainty, say whether such an accident would be a competent producing cause of the injury you found him to be suffering from, which you have previously diagnosed as . . . ?" Before the witness can render an opinion, he must answer the foregoing qualifying question in the affirmative. His answer establishes that, within his professional competence, he can render an opinion. After he has given his affirmative answer, he is then asked the really important question, which enables him to state his professional opinion on the record. This question is a relatively simple one. For example: "Was it a competent producing cause?" The expert witness need merely reply, "Yes." This answer imbeds his opinion into the record and permits the finder of the facts to accept that opinion as evidence in the case.[14]

---

[13] This type of testimony may be in connection with a request that the court take judicial notice of some facet of foreign law. The subject is discussed in section 10:2, *post.*

[14] Of course, if the witness is testifying on the other side of the case, his answer will be "No."

The hypothetical question has been a great source of difficulty for trial counsel. It cannot be general in form, but must specifically state the facts that the expert is asked to assume.[15] It is fatal to a hypothetical question that any hypothesis assumed in the course of the question is not supported by the evidence.[16] "Hypothetical questions are allowed to be put to experts; but the hypothesis upon which they are examined must be based upon facts admitted or established by the evidence, or which, if controverted, the jury might legitimately find on weighing the evidence."[17] A hypothetical question must assume the truth of facts that the evidence tends to support, but it cannot call for inferences to be drawn from the testimony of witnesses in the case.[18]

In sum, the hypothetical question and the answer thereto must have the following characteristics: (a) The question must be based solely on evidence in the case, although it may be stated in terms most favorable to the questioner;[19] (b) The expert, having first been qualified (or his qualifications having been conceded by the opponent) must state affirmatively that, upon the basis of the facts set forth in the hypothetical question, he is in a position to give a professional opinion as to the conclusory facts sought to be established; and (c) he must state that opinion in precise and definite terms.[20]

---

[15] *Peo. v. McElvaine,* 121 N.Y. 250.

[16] *Cf., Hillard v. State of Texas,* 218 S.W. 1052 (Tex. Crim. Rep. 1920, 8 A.L.R. 1316).

[17] *Peo. v. Augsbury,* 97 N.Y. 501, 505–506, stating, also, that on cross-examination, abstract or theoretical questions not founded upon facts in the record may, within the discretion of the trial court, be put for the purpose of testing the knowledge or the expertise of the witness.

[18] *Prewitt v. State of Mississippi,* 106 Miss. 82.

[19] The finder of the fact (whether court or jury) must first make a preliminary finding as to whether the facts assumed by the question have been established either by a preponderance of the evidence in a civil case or beyond a reasonable doubt in a criminal case. Absent such an affirmative finding as to *each* fact, the conclusion of the expert becomes meaningless.

[20] *Lehigh & H.R. Ry. Co.,* (C.C.A., N.Y.) 84 Fed. 870; *Tucker v. Graves,* 17 Ala. App. 602; *Louisville & N.R. Co. v. Steel,* (Ala.) 59 So. (2d.) 664; *Hines v. Patterson,* 146 Ark. 367; *Gardner v. Willson,* (Ark.) 244 S.W. (2d.) 945; *In re Purcell's Estate,* 164 Cal. 300; *Norden v. Hartman,* (Cal.) 245 Pac. (2d.) 3; *Atlantic Coast Line R. Co. v. Dees,* 56 Fla. 127; *Brazell v. Hearn,* 33 Ga. App. 490; *Speirer v. Curtis,* 312 Ill. 512; *Blair v. Washington,* 77 Ind. App. 698; *Daniels v. Iowa City,* 191 Iowa 811; *Miller v. McCoy Truck Lines,* (Iowa) 52 N.W. (2d.) 62; *Hopson v. Union Traction Co.,* 101 Kan. 499; *Lechleitner v. Cummings,* 159 Kan. 171; *Bates & Rogers Const. Co. v. Fluharity's Guardian,* 179 Ky. 668; *Stein v. Louisville Water Co.,* (Ky.) 59 So. (2d.) 664; *In re Watson,* 31 La. Ann. 757; *In re Whiting,* 110 Me. 232; *Schiller v. Baltimore & O.R. Co.,* 137 Md. 235; *Langenfelder v. Thompson,*

In order to get away from the intricacies and dangers of the use of hypothetical questions, a few jurisdictions have statutes to the effect that, unless the trial court otherwise orders, questions calling for the opinion of an expert witness need not be in hypothetical form, but the witness may state his opinion and reasons without first specifying the data upon which the opinion is based.[21] A further provision of these statutes is that, upon cross-examination, the expert witness may be required to specify the data and other criteria supporting his opinion.

It will be noted that (with the possible exception of the Kansas statute), statutory authorization for the statement of expert opinion without the need of a hypothetical question is entirely *permissive*. The statute says that the witness "may" state his opinion without the propounding of a hypothetical question. However, in the circumstances of many cases, counsel examining the expert witness may prefer to use the hypothetical question. This enables counsel to bring before the trier of the facts, almost as though it were an advance summation, the basic contentions of his cause. If the hypothetical question is used, however, it is obvious that trial counsel must employ *extreme* caution to make certain that every hypothetical statement of fact encompassed in the question has been established by the proof.

---

179 Md. 502; *Neil v. Brackett*, 241 Mass. 534; *Dunwoody v. Royal Indemnity Co.*, 218 Mich. 358; *Hylaman v. Midland Ins. Co.*, 136 Minn. 132; *Erickson v. Northern Minn. Nat. Bank of Duluth*, (Minn.) 50 N.W. (2d.) 489; *Baldwin v. Kansas City Rys. Co.*, (Mo.) 231 S.W. 280; *Ambruster v. Sutton*, (Mo.) 244 S.W. (2d.) 945; *Murphy v. Nett*, 47 Mont. 38; *Albrecht v. Morris*, 91 Neb. 442; *Effinger v. Effinger*, 48 Nev. 205; *Olgiati v. New England Box Co.*, 80 N.H. 399; *Polgar v. Kantor*, (N.J.) 130 A. 732; *Schwartz v. Howard Sav. Inst.*, 117 N.J. Law 180; *Marion v. B. G. Coon Const. Co.*, 216 N.Y. 718; *Graham v. Sandhill Power Co.*, 189 N.C. 381; *Haynes v. Feldspar Producing Co.*, 222 N.C. 163; *Asch v. Washburn Lignite Coal Co.*, 48 N.D. 734; *Ross v. Stewart*, 15 Ohio App. 339; *Ft. Smith & W. Ry. Co. v. Hutchinson*, 71 Okl. 139; *Ada Coca-Cola Bottling Co. v. Asbury*, (Okl.) 242 Pac. (2d.) 417; *Yarbrough v. Carlson*, 102 Or. 422; *Shaver Forwarding Co. v. Eagle Star Ins. Co.*, 177 Or. 410; *Kelly v. Watson Coal Co.*, 272 Pa. 39; *Smoak v. Martin*, 108 S.C. 472; *Fetzer v. Aberdeen Clinic*, 48 S.D. 308; *Bateman v. Ryder*, 106 Tenn. 712; *Knights & Ladies of Security v. Shephard*, (Tex.) 221 S.W. 696; *Downing v. Wimble*, 97 Vt. 390; *Tinney v. Crosby*, 112 Vt. 95; *McComb v. Farrow*, 128 Va. 455; *Eddy v. Spelger & Hurlbut*, 117 Wash. 632; *Lopeman v. McGee*, (Wash.) 245 Pac. (2d.) 183; *Freeman v. Freeman*, 71 W.Va. 303; *Hazelrigs v. City of Huntington*, 116 W.Va. 757; *Casson v. Schoenfeld*, 166 Wis. 401.

[21] NEW JERSEY: N.J.S.A. 2A:84A, Rules of Evidence, Rule 58. NEW YORK: C.P.L.R. 4515. VERMONT: 12 V.S.A. §1643. In Kansas the rule is somewhat differently stated, being that the form of the question is within the discretion of the trial court. K.S.A. 60–458. This is a distinction without a difference.

Where several expert witnesses are called,[22] many counsel prefer to use a hypothetical question as to the first expert and merely call for the conclusions of the others without employing a hypothetical question. This will avoid boring the trier of the facts. However, if subsequent expert witnesses give opinions as to matters *in addition to* those rendered by prior experts, the subsequent experts should be subjected to a hypothetical question if it is necessary to include additional facts as a basis for their opinion.

Sec. 9:4 Handwriting experts as an example of "demonstrative experts."

A classic example of the "demonstrative expert" is an examiner of questioned documents, commonly referred to as a handwriting expert. In a way, the title "handwriting expert" is a misnomer. This type of witness is ordinarily employed to furnish aids to the triers of fact by which they are enabled, without any personal expertise, to reach conclusions as to the genuineness or lack thereof of a disputed writing. In the last analysis, however, the fact-finders have both the privilege and function of reaching their own conclusions as to the genuineness of documents and, even upon appeal, a court may disregard conclusions of the expert because of an unwillingness to accept a claim of expertise as to individual items.[23] The permissible field of operation of the handwriting expert is well illustrated in a leading opinion, reading in applicable part as follows: [24]

> "We stated in the opinion that there was much apparently credible positive evidence in the record to the effect that the signatures to the two documents involved were genuine. Both the rule and the statement of fact are correct, but the error in the conclusion arrived at upon the first hearing consisted in treating the testimony of the witness William J. Kinsley, the expert on handwriting, as merely opinion evidence.

---

[22] Wigmore tells us that it is "universally accepted" that "the trial Court in its discretion may limit the number of expert witnesses." VI *Wigmore on Evidence*, (Third Ed., 1940), §1908, p. 580 and 1964 Pocket Supplement, pp. 218 *et seq.*, citing numerous decisions, statutes and court rules.

[23] *Matter of Hopkins*, 172 N.Y. 363.

[24] *Boyd v. Gosser*, 82 S. 758 (Fla., 6 A.L.R. 500).

"It was something more than the mere opinion of the witness. It was a detailed statement of facts relating to the questioned signature of W. T. Boyd which was appended to the two documents; facts which were revealed by the use of mechanical instruments, and scientifically established to the degree of demonstration. These facts we deem to be wholly irreconcilable with the evidence of witnesses who testified to the genuineness of W. T. Boyd's signature, which testimony, although apparently credible, is not by any means indubitable when considered in the light of the facts established by the scientific investigations of the expert on handwriting. When so considered this 'apparently credible positive evidence' loses much, if not all, its character, and 'if the salt hath lost its savor, wherewith shall it be salted?'

"It was said in Re Gordon, 50 N.J. Eq. 397, 26 Atl. 268: 'Handwriting is an art concerning which correctness of opinion is susceptible of demonstration.'

"The learned judge writing the opinion said: 'I am fully convinced that the value of the opinion of every handwriting expert as evidence must depend upon the clearness with which the expert demonstrates its correctness.'

"The demonstration, when the signature of a person since deceased is attacked as a forgery, consists, as in this case, of an accumulation of a great mass of facts relating to the formation of letters; the field covered by both the admittedly genuine and questioned signatures; the spacing of the letters, both capitals and small letters; the angle on which they were formed; their relative positions in the signatures; their proportions, slant, alignment, and outline; the surface of the paper which, under the microscope, shows whether the line upon which the questioned signature rests was drawn before or after the name was written or before or after the paper was folded; the conformity in detail of two signatures, so that when superimposed they show no variation or divergence in a line or direction of a line. All these facts, when established, may confirm the testimony of apparently credible witnesses who testify to the genuineness of the questioned signatures, or establish to the degree of demonstration the falsity of it. In re Rice, 81 App. Div. 223, 81 N.Y. Supp. 68, affirmed in 176 N.Y. 570, 68 N.E. 1123, it appeared from the photographs and enlargements adduced by an expert that the four signatures to a will were absolutely identical, so that they could be super-imposed without showing the slightest divergence in the length or direction of a line. This, the court said, demonstrated conclusively that they were not genuine, but tracings. See also Osborn, Questioned Documents, p. 299; Green v. Terwilliger, (C.C.) 56 Fed. 384; Stitzel v. Miller, 250 Ill. 72, 34 L.R.A. (N.S.) 1004, 95 N.E. 53, Ann. Cas. 1912B, 412. In the note to the last-cited cases which appears in Ann. Cas. 1912B, 417, many cases are referred to as upholding the proposition that it is very improbable that two signatures written by a person in the ordinary course of business will be exactly alike so that one will cover the other when superimposed, and the fact that one signature is the facsimile of another is evidence that one was traced from the other, or both traced from a third. The cases cited are: McDonogh's Succession, 18 La. Ann. 419; Day v. Cole, 65 Mich. 129, 31 N.W. 823; Hunt v. Lawless, 7 Abb. N.C. 113; Re Rice, 81 App. Div. 223, 81 N.Y. Supp, 68; Re Burtis, 107 App. Div. 51, 94 N.Y. Supp. 961; Re Burtis, 43 Misc. 437, 89 N.Y. Supp. 441; Hanriot v. Sherwood, 82 Va. 1.

"In Re Burtis, 107 App. Div. 51, 94 N.Y. Supp. 961, it was said: 'Concededly, if one's signature conforms in every particular to another, one of them must be a forgery, because for all practical purposes no person can write his name twice exactly alike.'

"See also: 'The conclusion of a handwriting expert as to the genuineness of a signature, standing alone, would be of little or no value, but supported by sufficiently cogent reasons his testimony might amount almost to a demonstration.' Venuto v. Lizzo, 148 App. Div. 164, 132 N.Y. Supp. 1066."

Thus, the expert commonly furnishes enlarged photographs of an admittedly genuine piece of handwriting and, for comparison, enlarged photographs of the disputed document. He points out to the fact-finder similarities (or dissimilarities) between the two writings. He may, for example, demonstrate that in the admittedly genuine document the small letter "a" is commonly written with a closed top, whereas in the disputed document it is not closed. He may show that, in an admittedly genuine typing, one of the letters is customarily above the bottom margin of the other letters, whereas in the disputed document there is perfect alignment of this letter with the others.[25] He may show that, as to two documents presumably typed at the same time, the typing on one of them is much darker than the typing on the other and may state, as his conclusion, that they were typed at different times with ribbons of different freshness.

The handwriting expert must necessarily use as the basis for his entire testimony the existence of a *genuine* document. When such a document is presented *and* when there is independent proof (either by extraneous testimony, admissions in the pleadings or pre-trial discovery, or admissions during the trial) that the document is, indeed, a genuine example of the writing of the person sought to be charged with writing the disputed document, the expert may proceed to his demonstration and, within the limitations above suggested, give his opinion.[26]

Some statutes (in part merely repetitive of common law principles) provide specifically for the use of certain samples as bases for the rendition of expert opinions. For example, a common provision is that proof of the genuineness of a disputed writing may be made by comparison of that document with any writing proved to the satisfaction of the court to be the handwriting of the per-

---

[25] A properly qualified expert may testify as to comparison between two typewritten documents. *Cf., State v. Freshwater,* 30 Utah 442, 447.

[26] *Simonson v. Typer,* (C.C.A., Wyo.) 285 Fed. 240; *Qualls v. Qualls,* 196 Ala. 524; *Murphy v. Murphy,* 144 Ark. 429; *Hirshfeld v. Dana,* 193 Cal. 142; *Kauffman v. Meyberg,* 59 Cal. App. (2d.) 730; *National Fuel Co. v. Green,* 50 Colo. 307; *McGarry v. Healey,* 78 Conn. 365, 62 A. 671; *Marietta Fertilizer Co. v. Gary,* 2 Ga. App. 604; *Shinn v. Settle,* 222 Ill. App. 463; *Mueller v. Weiland,* 342 Ill. App. 240; *Plymouth Savings & Loan Ass'n No. 2 v. Kassing,* 72 Ind. App. 1; *State ex rel Winslow v. Fisher,* 109 Ind. App. 644; *Butman v. Christy,* 197 Iowa 661; *Baird v. Shaffer,* 101 Kan. 585; *Pioneer Coal Co. v. Polly,* 208 Ky. 548; *Martin v. Webb,* 300 Ky. 11; *Succession of Drysdale,* 127 La. 890; *Succession of Butterworth,* 195 La. 115; *Palmer v. Blanchard,* 113 Me. 380; *Councilman v. Towson Nat. Bank,* 103 Md. 469; *Haile v. Dinnis,* 184 Md. 144; *Noyes v. Noyes,* 224 Mass. 125; *Charvet v. Gildemeister,* 222 Mich. 286; *Weber v. Strobel,* (Mo.) 194 S.W. 272; *Hemonas v. Orphan,* (Mo.) 191 S.W. (2d.) 352; *Grosfield v. First Nat. Bank,* 73 Mont. 219; *In re O'Connor's Estate,* 105 Neb. 88, cert. denied, 256 U.S. 690; *In re Parvin's Estate,* 131 Neb. 853; *Davis v. Boston & M.R.R.,* 75 N.H. 467; *Wheeler & Wilson Manuf'g Co. v. Buckhout,* 60 N.J. Law 102; *Turner v. Breitung,* 195 App. Div. 200, aff'd, 233 N.Y. 649; *Broun v. Town of Hillsboro,* 185 N.C. 368; *Sutsman County Bank v. Jones,* 36 N.D. 531; *Baber v. Caples,* 71 Or. 212; *Seaman v. Husband,* 256 Pa. 571; *Campbell v. Campbell,* 146 Pa. Super. 58; *First Nat. Bank v. Goldman,* 46 R.I. 354; *Roberts v. Virginia-Carolina Chemical Co.,* 84 S.C. 283; *City Nat. Bank of Lincoln v. O'Leary,* 46 S.D. 101; *Campbell v. Campbell,* (Tex.) 215 S.W. 134; *Alexander v. State,* (Tex.) 115 S.W. (2d.) 1122; *In re Barron's Estate,* 92 Vt. 460; *Adams v. Ristine,* 138 Va. 273; *O'Brien v. McKelvey,* 66 Wash. 18; *Johnston v. Bee,* 84 W.Va. 532; *Young v. Wheby,* 126 W.Va. 741; *Alesch v. Haave,* 178 Wis. 19.

son claimed to have made the disputed writing.[27] It will be noted that this type of statute refers to a writing "proved to the satisfaction of the court" to be genuine. This does not necessarily mean that, where the trial is to a jury, the trial judge makes a final determination as to whether the sample is genuine. This is a fact to be determined like any other fact in the case. Unquestionably, in a jury trial, the trial court must determine whether there is prima facie proof that the sample is genuine; but the ultimate determination of the genuineness of the disputed document is for the jury.[28]

Very often, the genuineness of a sample is conceded. If there is no genuine sample at hand, the lawyer seeking to prove the genuineness of a disputed document may require a party, even called to the witness stand for this sole purpose, to submit a sample of his own handwriting. In such an instance, a continuance will often be granted to permit a comparison, by an expert, of the compelled sample with the disputed document. The tendency of modern practice is to prevent a situation where a genuine sample of handwriting may be unavailable.[29]

There is a distinction between proof of a writing for general, substantive purposes and proof of the genuineness of a disputed document. Under many statutes (for example, recording statutes and statutes referring to the formal requirements for proof of a testamentary document) it is essential that there be one or more subscribing witnesses. These statutes, except peripherally, have nothing to do with proof of the genuineness of a document. They are requirements of *substantive* law, whereby the document, even

---

[27] FEDERAL: 28 U.S.C.A. §1731. ALABAMA: Code, Title 7, §§420–421. ARIZONA: R.C.P. Rule 44(m). CALIFORNIA: Evidence Code §1417 (Deering's). COLORADO: CRS, §52-1-4. DELAWARE: 5 Code Ann.; Title 10, §4311. FLORIDA: F.S.A. §92.38. GEORGIA: Code Ann., §38-709. HAWAII: Rev. L. Hawaii 1955, §224-z. ILLINOIS: Smith-Hurd Ill. St. Ch. 51, §50. INDIANA: Burns' Stat. §2-1723. IOWA: 43 Code Ann., §622.25. KENTUCKY: KRS 422.120. LOUISIANA: LSA-R.S. 15:460–461; LSA-C.C. art. 2245. MARYLAND: Code, art. 35, §12. MICHIGAN: Stat. Ann., §27A.2144. MISSOURI: V.A.M.S. §490.640. NEBRASKA: R.R.S. 1943, §25-1220. NEW JERSEY: N.J.S.A. 2A:82-1. NEW MEXICO: §20-2-15, N.M.S.A. 1953. NEW YORK: C.P.L.R. 4536. NORTH CAROLINA: Gen. Stat. §8-40. NORTH DAKOTA: NDCC 31-08-02.1. OREGON: ORS 42.070. RHODE ISLAND: Gen. Laws 1956, §9-19-17. TENNESSEE: T.C.A. §24-708. TEXAS: Vernon's Tex. Civ. Stat., Art. 3737b. WEST VIRGINIA: Michies W.Va. Code 1961, §5722. WISCONSIN: W.S.A. 327.26.

[28] A Pennsylvania statute specifically so provides. 28 P.S. §§162–164.

[29] In Virginia, an interesting statute provides that unless the genuineness of a sample is denied by affidavit, no further proof of such genuineness is required. §8-114, Code 1950, 1957 Repl. Vol.

if genuine, is not legally valid because of the failure of the formal subscription required by statutes premised upon public policy. Where such subscription is not required to give *validity* to a document, it is a not unusual provision of law that the writing may be proved "as if there was no subscribing witness." [30]

Sec. 9:5   Demonstration in court to buttress testimony of expert witness.

In the foregoing section, we have discussed the function of an examiner of questioned documents as a "demonstrative expert." As has been therein noted, a demonstration in court (the production of photographs and enlargements of the questioned documents) amounts to *demonstrative evidence* which can be used as the basis for a finding of fact.

Where the expert witness is on such solid ground that he can make a demonstration to support his testimony *in the presence of the fact-finder*, counsel should not hesitate to have such a demonstration performed. Of course, the ability to employ this tactic necessarily rests upon the simplicity of the proposed demonstration. An excellent example of the use of a court demonstration after an expert witness has stated his opinion occurred in a case involving the legitimacy of a child.[31] There, the petitioner sued her husband for the support of three children. The respondent-husband admitted his liability for the support of two of those children, but claimed that the third was not his child. The history of the case as set forth in the following portions of the opinion covers both the matter of tests made at the office of the testifying doctor and those subsequently made during the trial, itself:

> "The respondent denied being responsible for the support of the said Vincent James Crouse, claiming that he was not

---

[30] ALABAMA: Code, Title 7, §416. GEORGIA: Code Ann., §38-706. IDAHO: Code, §9-405. MICHIGAN: Stat. Ann., §27A.2143. NEW YORK: C.P.L.R. 4537. NORTH CAROLINA: Gen. Stat. §8-38. NORTH DAKOTA: NDCC 31-08-02. RHODE ISLAND: Gen. Laws 1956, §9-19-16. TEXAS: Vernon's Tex. Civ. Stat., Art. 3734a. WEST VIRGINIA: Michies W.Va. Code 1961, §5723. WISCONSIN: W.S.A. 327.23. See, also, for variations of this type of statute, DELAWARE: 5 Code Ann.; Title 10, §4311. IOWA: 43 Code Ann., §622.24. KANSAS: K.S.A. 60-468. MASSACHUSETTS: Ann. L. Mass., c. 233, §68. NEW JERSEY: N.J.S.A. 2A:84A, Rules of Evidence, Rule 71. UTAH: 9 Code Ann. 1953, §78-25-10. WASHINGTON: RCWA 5.36.020.

[31] *Matter of Crouse v. Crouse,* 51 Misc. 2d 649, 649–653 [New York, Family Court, Nassau County].

the father of said minor child, and requested a blood grouping test pursuant to section 418 of the Family Court Act.
The said test was ordered by the court and the parties were
directed to appear at the office of Dr. Alexander S. Wiener
for the purpose of completing the said blood grouping test.
Blood tests were made of the petitioner and respondent at
Dr. Wiener's office on May 26, 1966, and of the child Paul on
May 27, 1966. The results of the blood grouping test indicated that the respondent was excluded as the father of the
child.

"The matter thereafter came on before the court for hearing on July 12, 1966. The attorney for the petitioner objected
to the introduction into evidence of Dr. Wiener's report unless he were given the opportunity to cross-examine Dr. Wiener
as to the accuracy of the report. The hearing was then adjourned to July 20 for the purpose of Dr. Wiener's testimony.

"The petitioner's attorney conceded the qualifications of Dr.
Wiener as one of the foremost serologists and hematologists
in the country and an expert in blood grouping tests. Dr.
Wiener is recommended by the Family Court to conduct such
tests because he is acknowledged as the discoverer of the
Rh-Hr blood types and the mechanism of their inheritance,
and a pioneer in the medicolegal application of blood tests
in cases of disputed parentage.

"An exclusion is convincing proof in questions of paternity
that the respondent is not the father of the child born out
of wedlock. But when a child is born in wedlock, the presumption of legitimacy of such child—which is one of the strongest
presumptions in law—calls for more than a fair preponderance
of the evidence in order to overcome said presumption. The
court must be entirely satisfied that the alleged father is not a
parent of the child.

"Dr. Wiener testified that the blood samples from Mr. and
Mrs. Crouse and Vincent James Crouse were taken in his presence by one of his assistants and the tests were performed
under his supervision. The blood samples of each person were
divided into four prelabeled tubes. Four tests were taken as
a matter of routine. The test was done and duplicated on one
day, then repeated on the following day, again in duplicate,
making a total of four tests for each individual. But when an
exclusion is found, as in this case, then two additional tests
are made to confirm the exclusion, so that actually in this

case the individual tests were done six times. When the tests were completed, Dr. Wiener interpreted the results and prepared a report, which was offered into evidence, to show the following results:

'Results:

Blood of	Group and Subgroup	M-N Type	Rh-Hr Type
1. Richard Crouse	A_1	MN	Rh_1Rh_1
2. Karen Crouse	O	MN	Rh_1rh
3. Vincent	B	N	Rh_1rh

'Interpretation:

'The results of the M-n and Rh-Hr tests in this case are not informative, but the A-B-O tests prove that Richard Crouse is not the father of Karen Crouse's baby, Vincent.

'Karen Crouse belongs to group O and her baby, Vincent, belongs to group B, so that Vincent's father must belong to group B or group AB, and cannot belong to group O or group A.

'Therefore, Richard Crouse, who belongs to group A, cannot be Vincent's father.'

"Dr. Wiener testified that the accuracy of the tests depends on the reliability of the worker and the interpretation of the said tests. He stated that there are 11 different serums for the A-B-O groups, and the type of blood is dependent upon the proper identification of the serum. The serum is identified by 'testing the serum against the blood whose types are known, and if the serum gives the proper reaction it reacts to the right blood and it does not react with other blood in conformity with the type of serum you use, and if the reactions are clear cut, that is a satisfactory serum. In other words, it must clump certain blood and it must fail to clump other bloods.'

"In order to confirm the exclusion indicated in the aforementioned report, Dr. Wiener then proceeded to perform the blood grouping tests of the parties involved in the courtroom. He stated 'this is the first time I am demonstrating this in a courtroom', and to his knowledge the first time it had been done in the world. Dr. Wiener stated: 'It is very brief and simple because we have a previous knowledge of the result. So that it is a self-controlled procedure because we know the three different types. Since I know what I am looking for I don't need blood from the vein. I can take a small sample from the finger and get directly to the point. Of course, this is not the way if I don't know. So I'm stating, it's not the way it's normally done. It's only possible because I know in advance what to look for. So it can be very simple for that reason.'

"Dr. Wiener recited the steps taken as he proceeded with the testing:

'I am now labeling the tubes in preparation. I have written Richard Crouse here. I have written Karen Crouse here, and here I am writing Vincent. Now I open one tube at a time so there is no chance of putting blood in the wrong tube. I am opening Richard's tube. So if Richard will step over I will take some blood. This is not the normal way to take a blood test. I will take it normally from the vein, but for the demonstration I am taking it from the finger. Prepare the finger with some alcohol. These are disposable needles. You use them only once.

'The skin is prepared with alcohol then punctured. Then the alcohol is wiped away and the blood is collected in a tube containing an anti-coagulant that prevents the blood from clotting.

(Blood samples were taken from Richard Crouse, Karen Crouse and Vincent James Crouse.)

'These are glass slides. There are three tests which I am going to do here. I am putting A serum and B serum . . . .

'Put a little blood on each side, here. That's number one. (Richard Crouse)

(Number two is Karen Crouse and number three Baby Vincent.)

'On the left side I put what is called anti-A serum against A.

'This test serum was tested yesterday to make sure it was active.

'I am now mixing the blood and the serum. Now, the reaction should be visible almost at once, and it is. Will you look at the first pair, Your Honor. You will see the blood has come together as clots on the right side, not on the left. It reacts with the A serum. That makes it A. In the second pair there was no reaction. That is group O. The third pair, the reaction is on the B side which makes it B. If you wait a few minutes it becomes sharp.

Q. 'To clarify the results, as are visible to the Court and the Counsel and all parties, Richard Crouse's blood is determined to be Type A? **A.** That's correct. That is seen very clearly. The reaction is only with the A serum.

Q. 'And Karen Crouse's blood is determined to be? **A.** Group O.

Q. 'And Vincent's blood is determined to be? **A.** 'Group B. It only reacts to anti-b serum.

Q. Now, then, it is a fact, in your expert opinion, if Vincent's blood is B and Karen's is O and Richard's is A, that Richard is excluded as the father of Vincent? **A.** 'Yes, because if the child has B it must come either from the mother or father or both. That completes the demonstration. This will make the seventh time the test has been done in this case.' "

Another method of buttressing the conclusions of an expert is by showing, through the expert, himself, that his conclusions are in accord with authoritative text-book statements on the matter at issue.[32] However, in the absence of a statute permitting the introduction of text-book material, a text book, as such, is not admissible in evidence, since this would be an obvious violation of the hearsay rule.[33]

A Massachusetts statute [34] provides that in medical malpractice cases, a "statement of fact or opinion on a subject of science or art contained in a published treatise, periodical, book or pamphlet shall, in the discretion of the court, and if the court finds that it is relevant and that the writer of such statement is recognized in his profession or calling as an expert on the subject, be admissible."

---

[32] *State v. Baldwin*, 36 Kan. 1; *Peo. v. Vanderhoff*, 71 Mich. 158.
[33] *Thompson v. Ammona*, 160 Ga. 886; *Foggett v. Fischer*, 23 App. Div. 297 [New York.] Contra: *Staudenheimer v. Williams*, 29 Ala. 558.
[34] Mass. Gen. Laws Ann., ch. 233, sec. 79C (1959).

Nevada has a practically identical statute.[35] The purpose of these statutes was to prevent dismissal of actions against physicians because of the reluctance of other physicians to furnish expert testimony in malpractice cases. However, such a statute has been of little practical help, because of the requirement that the writer of the text must be proved to be an established expert. Physicians who, themselves, are reluctant to give testimony are equally reluctant to certify to the expertise of a text writer whose writings may be used in a suit against a fellow-physician.[36]

The subject of the unwilling or reluctant expert witness is more fully covered in section 9:9, *post*.

Sec. 9:6 Special preparation for direct examination of expert witnesses.

In Chapter II, *supra*, there has been discussed the preparation for direct examination of witnesses, in general. All of the factors therein described are applicable to preparation for the direct examination of expert witnesses. However, there are additional matters of a special nature which should be covered before an expert witness is called to the stand.

The first thing to be considered is whether the specific problems posed in a given litigation are appropriate for the aid of expert testimony. As part of this problem, the question arises whether there are any experts or classes of experts who can furnish the requisite aid.

The function of expert testimony has been described in section 9:1, *supra;* but the general principles therein enunciated are not always easy of application in a given case. For example, there can be no question that a properly qualified physician can be called as an expert with respect to the permanency of injuries sustained in an accident. Many similarly obvious uses of experts come to mind. Less obvious, though also fairly common, is the use of an experienced builder or building contractor to render his opinion whether a certain construction or renovation was accomplished with due care. In other classes of cases, we may have experts who testify as to the "reasonableness" of professional services or the

---

[35] Nev. Rev. Stat., tit. 1, ch. 51.040 (1959).

[36] Kehoe, *Massachusetts Malpractice Evidentiary Statute—Success or Failure?*, 44 B.U.L. Rev. 10, 28–29.

"reasonable value" of merchandise or of real property and its improvements.

If a statute or court rule provides that expert witnesses can be used in stated circumstances no problem arises. Likewise, there is practically no difficulty where long and accepted usage has dictated the utilization of expert witnesses. However, in marginal or unique situations, trial counsel may have an uphill battle in persuading the court to permit the introduction of expert testimony. Not only should trial counsel carefully examine decisional law before he calls an expert but, if there are no cases in his own jurisdiction directly in point, he should not hesitate to cite cases from other jurisdictions. If he is able to find no decisions directly in point, counsel should be prepared to argue by analogy from reported cases, wherever found. As a last resort (or as an accompaniment to his discussion of analogous cases), counsel should indicate that an advance in general, scientific or social knowledge and the development of expertise in new fields justify the use of expert testimony not theretofore employed.

Wherever there is a serious question of the right to use expert witnesses, counsel should hand a memorandum to the court (usually as part of his trial memorandum), in advance of the trial, specifically covering this point. In such a memorandum there should be included the legal argument *plus a description of the experience and qualifications of proposed expert witnesses* and a complete exposition of the state of the art and its development which should have the effect of persuading the court that the fact-finder (court or jury) can be materially aided by the proposed expert testimony.

The next matter to be considered is the choice of the expert witness. At first blush, it might seem axiomatic that, where there are several available experts, the person to be chosen is the one who has the greatest knowledge of the subject. This is not, however, a rule of thumb mechanically to be followed. The *personality* of the expert is sometimes as important as the depth of his knowledge. Particularly is this true where the expert is called for the purpose of rendering his opinion (as distinguished from a demonstrating expert).[37] Here, the finder of the facts, where there is conflicting expert testimony, must decide which expert he believes. In a broad

---

[37] As to the difference between opinion and demonstrating experts see section 9:3, *supra.*

sense, it is the expert who is on trial. The manner in which the expert testifies may be almost as important as the substance of his testimony; because, particularly where a jury is involved, there is much less likelihood of an analytical consideration of the quality of the expert testimony than of a striving by the fact-finder to resolve the simple question—"Which of these expert witnesses do I believe is telling the truth?"

The ideal expert witness is one who can state his opinion and the hypotheses upon which it is based in simple language, comprehensible to the layman. Whether the case is tried to a jury or to a court without a jury, the witness who uses technical terms without explanation of their meaning is, obviously, at a great disadvantage if the opposing expert talks simply and in clearly understandable terms. A fact-finder is loath to depend upon an opinion (or the description of an experiment) which he cannot understand.

A pompous, conceited, or patently self-satisfied expert should, if possible, be avoided. No fact-finder likes to be patronized. If the expert gives the impression that he knows so much about the subject that it is beneath his dignity even to try to explain his conclusions to a court or jury he may build up a resentment that could be fatal to the case. On the other hand, where the expert appears to be genuinely interested in assisting the fact-finder, this expert is a great asset and may even, by his attitude, overcome the reluctance of many jurymen to give credence to expert testimony, in general.

Other things being equal, the demonstrable qualifications of a proposed expert are important in choosing which expert to call. By "demonstrable qualifications" is meant the type of qualifications that will appear obvious to a fact-finder. For example, the fact that the witness has written books or a substantial number of articles covering the subject on which he is testifying is impressive. The practical experience of the expert is an appealing factor. The offices held by the expert in scientific societies are noteworthy as is the fact that the expert has been a professor teaching the subject on which he is testifying.[38]

That the expert has, on numerous prior occasions, given expert

---

[38] For the practical method of establishing the qualifications of an expert and the principles upon which such establishment depends, see section 9:7, *post.*

testimony on the subject presently in litigation is, presumably, a plus factor. However, some experienced trial lawyers believe that, where a case is tried to a jury, this matter should not be referred to lest the impression be conveyed that the witness is a "professional expert," willing to sell a favorable opinion to the highest bidder. Where there is no jury, prior testimonial experience of the witness is valuable to convey to the court that this expert's testimony has been accepted by fellow-jurists.

Where several expert witnesses are available, it may be wise to interview all of them, even if there is a charge for such consultation, before making a final choice.

After the expert witness has been chosen (and, sometimes, during the course of the process of making a choice) *intensive* consultation should be had with the expert. Properly conducted, such interviews may result in mutual education of the lawyer and the expert.

Trial counsel starts with the basic assumption that he would like his expert witness to testify to a specific favorable opinion (or to conduct a demonstration in court leading to a satisfactory conclusion). However, the expertise of the proposed witness may enable him to suggest a broadening of the field. He may disclose that, in addition to the opinion originally solicited, he can express opinions on other matters which will be helpful. For example, an expert who is called upon to testify about the permanency of an injury can very often go much further and state his opinion about deleterious side-effects not presently apparent but scientifically prognosticatable.

Conversely, counsel, due to his past experience in cases similar to the one being prepared for trial, is often in a position to indicate to the expert additional subjects for opinion, or additional methods of making a court demonstration, or a reason for conducting specific experiments prior to rendering an opinion, or the existence of facts to fortify the opinion of the expert and to add new dimensions to the question of liability. Thus, in a case based upon secondary product liability, although the expert is ordinarily prepared to give an opinion about the improper design of a mechanical contrivance or vehicle, he may never have had occasion to investigate whether similar contrivances or vehicles, identically manufactured by a defendant, have proved so dangerous or defective that they had to be recalled from the market. Counsel can, with the greatest propriety, furnish to the expert the facts known to him on this subject and suggest that the expert conduct an investigation so that he can testify about such facts and state the dimensions of his investigation.

Preparation conferences with the expert should include an exploration of available scientific literature, which will not only explain but also buttress the expert's opinion. Here, again, in addition to the treatises and articles known to the expert, counsel can fortify his witness by suggesting further published material.

If the expert witness has, himself, written books or articles encompassed within the zone of his testimony, these should be carefully read.

It is as important to consider published material which tends to contradict the expert's opinion as it is to be prepared with material supporting it. Particularly is this true where the expert has written on the subject and where an earlier opinion contained in his writings suggests a conclusion different from the one he will render on the witness stand. There is more to such a study than preparing the witness for cross-examination. A change in opinion with the passage of time can be used advantageously. The expert witness should frankly testify about his prior contradictory opinion. He can then tell the fact-finder about progress in the scientific field covered by his testimony and show how the improvement in technology led to a new opinion. This has the advantage of causing the witness to transmute unfavorable proof into the establishment of the fact that the witness, as an individual concerned with a particular scientific discipline, has maintained an open mind in the best scientific tradition and has not hesitated to alter his conclusion when the alteration is based on the progress of science. It has the further advantage of getting in as part of the direct testimony of the witness material that would be damaging if first brought out by the opposition.[39]

Through his conferences with an expert witness (and the conferences are very often numerous and lengthy), trial counsel must attempt to become more than generally familiar with the scientific field to be covered by the expert testimony. It cannot, of course, be anticipated that counsel, himself, will become an expert; but

---

[39] In section 5:7, *supra*, there is treated the general manner of handling unfavorable evidence by presenting it as part of direct testimony instead of affording an opportunity to the opponent to bring it out as new matter on cross-examination.

he owes it to his client to understand *completely* not only the nature of the expert's testimony but also the scientific data on which it is premised. If the expert witness conducts experiments to establish a factual basis for his opinion, counsel should put himself in a position to visualize and understand every feature of the experiment.

There is a distinction between experiments and demonstrations. The methods of preparing for them and presenting them should be separately considered.

An experiment is conducted by the expert outside of the courtroom for the purpose of establishing an ultimate factual or factual-scientific basis for his opinion.[40] If physical experiments are conducted, counsel should try to be present during the conduct of the same, since he will thus be better prepared not only to suggest to the witness how the experiment should be described to the jury but also to conduct the examination of the witness. An example of the advantage of counsel being present during the conducting of an experiment is found in a case where a witness will ultimately give his opinion that stains found on a garment are blood stains and, in part, of the same type of blood as that of a defendant. Here, as counsel watches the experiment, he learns how it is done, what chemical reagents are used and why the use of such reagents scientifically establishes the facts as to which an opinion will be rendered.

A demonstration in open court is, by its nature, seen by counsel. Thus, when an examiner of questioned documents (a handwriting expert) produces enlarged photographs of admitted and contested specimens of handwriting, counsel is there and introduces the photographs in evidence. However, counsel should learn from the witness, well in advance of his testimony, the method by which the witness makes deductions from the demonstration. Here, again, there is the twin advantage of being able to suggest to the witness how and in what order he should present his exhibits and opinion and of preparing to ask questions and elicit answers easily understandable by a lay finder of the facts. It should be remembered that, even in connection with a simple demon-

---

[40] The experiment is not necessarily of a physical nature. For example, although it may seem strange to apply the term "experiment" to reading done by the expert, the concept is thoroughly applicable where the expert consults data such as stock exchange reports, consumer and price indexes and the like.

stration, the witness should testify about the *exact* method of preparing his exhibits in order to indicate that there is no possibility of error or distortion.

One of the most important considerations in the preparation of expert testimony is anticipation of requirements for *redirect examination*. A substantial part of this portion of preparation very often necessarily takes place *during the trial*.

When an expert testifies in a complicated scientific field, questions may be addressed to him on cross-examination which tend to becloud the issue, cast doubt on the expert's testimonial conclusions, introduce contrary opinions in the published works of other experts, or confuse the fact-finder by the use of highly technical terms.

As has been previously stated, it cannot be expected that counsel, through conferences with his expert witness, will, himself, become an expert in the scientific discipline within which the expert's opinion is given. Let us assume that careful advance preparation has included: reading by the lawyer of the applicable scientific literature; an explanation of that literature by the expert; the building up of a glossary of scientific terms which may come to light during the trial; a reasonably detailed explanation of the scientific principles underlying the expert's conclusions; the nature, function and details of experiments conducted by the expert and used as a basis for his opinion; and questions which may arise with respect to the validity of court-made demonstrations. Despite such exhaustive advance preparation, the very real possibility (indeed, probability) exists that substantial questions raised during the cross-examination of the expert witness can leave even a carefully prepared lawyer in a morass of doubt. Indeed, it often happens that the lawyer may not even recognize the danger to his case which some portions of the cross-examination present.

It follows, practically and logically, that counsel should not attempt redirect examination of an expert witness without consulting that witness *after* he has been cross-examined. A judge, whether or not the case is being tried to a jury, will certainly allow counsel a short recess to prepare for redirect examination of the expert. Where the cross-examination has been completed late in the trial day, a court may recess the case until the next morning for this purpose. If the cross-examination has been lengthy, the court may permit counsel to suspend with the expert, reserving the right to recall him at a future session of the trial for redirect examination.

Counsel's conference with the expert, after cross-examination in preparation for redirect, should include at least the following:

(a) Learning from the witness in what respects *he* feels the cross-examination may have been damaging;

(b) Stating to the witness the portions of the cross-examination that *counsel* regards either as harmful or requiring clarification;

(c) Obtaining from the witness his suggestions for remedying damage and also the meaning of technical terms, unfamiliar to counsel, which have been used during the cross-examination;

(d) Outlining what subjects should be covered on redirect examination;

(e) Preparing the actual redirect examination (including, if time permits, the text of questions to be asked and, where applicable, the introduction of additional printed material covering scientific theories); and

(f) Anticipation of what may arise on re-cross-examination.

In the last analysis, it is the responsibility of counsel to decide what the scope of redirect examination will be. Although the expert may perceive that the cross-examination has led to scientific doubts, counsel must bear in mind that super-technical matters, if reopened, can place undue emphasis on a subject which otherwise would have little effect on the fact-finder. Within the ambit of a scientific doctrine, counsel is a layman. So is the judge and so are the jurymen. Therefore, counsel is in a better position than the expert finally to determine what material will forward his cause and what subjects or portions of subjects should be treated with skillful neglect—that is, not touched upon on redirect examination. If counsel determines not to advert on redirect examination to some technical considerations raised by the expert, he must avoid creating antagonism on the expert's part. Also, after fully explaining to the expert why certain subjects will not be pursued on redirect examination, he should warn the expert to avoid bringing up such subjects by embellishing his answers to questions not directly concerning them.

The final step in the preparation of expert testimony is laying out the *text* of the questions to be propounded.[41] The interplay of the testimonial conversation between counsel and the witness is at its best when both questions and answers appear spontaneous.[42] Ordinarily, it is unwise for counsel to write out the text of his questions and read them to the witness. However, where the witness is called as an expert, it is safer that the text of the questions be prepared in advance and that the expert participate in wording the questions. This avoids the danger that a question, by its very terms, may give rise to an opening for cross-examination or leave an unplugged hole, the existence of which can be of advantage to one's opponent (either in later calling his own expert witness or for use in summation).

A fact-finder, who might be bored or might have the reaction that the testimony of a witness arises from advance rehearsal and is trumped-up when a lawyer reads questions to a lay witness, would not have the same reaction about questions read to an expert. It is obvious, even to inexperienced jurymen, that there would have had to be extensive pretrial preparation before an expert was called to the stand.

The fee of the expert should be agreed upon in advance of the trial. If possible, the expert should be paid in full before he testifies. The fact that the expert is being paid should be stated by him early in his testimony. Unless other factors dictate its omission, the amount paid should also be disclosed. The expert witness should, clearly and unequivocally, testify that he has no personal interest in the litigation and that no part of his fee is contingent on the success of the party calling him.

Insuring the attendance of an expert witness in court at the time his testimony is needed presents special problems. For example, although the witness should, as far as it is practicable, be told the general period within which the case is likely to be reached, it may transpire that during this general period the expert will have an extended professional engagement, or the general period may be at a time when the expert customarily takes a vacation. Counsel would be well advised to arrange for adjournments or continuances beyond this general period. Meeting the convenience

---

[41] As to direct examination this is done in advance of the trial. Questions for redirect should be framed during trial after cross-examination.

[42] Compare sections 5:8 and 5:9, *supra*.

of an expert witness and letting him know that changes were made in a trial date for that purpose pays dividends in assuring the friendly co-operation of the witness.

In many jurisdictions where there are large trial calendars, it is almost impossible to let the expert know in advance the precise day and time he will be needed. In such situations, the best that can be done is to ask the witness to hold himself available within reasonable limits. As an adjunct to this availability, counsel must make sure that he can reach the witness practically immediately. At the very least, there should be given to counsel all telephone numbers through which the witness can be called and this should include both office and home telephones.

For the convenience of expert witnesses (particularly physicians) a court will often permit the witness to be called to the stand immediately upon his arrival in court, even though this may cause the temporary withdrawal of another witness whose testimony is in the process of being taken. The court should be informed in advance, preferably at the beginning of the trial and again on the day when the expert is expected to arrive, about this contingency. If the court, when first apprized of the situation, should indicate that he will not permit an interruption of testimony, the arrangement with the expert witness must be that he will appear on a certain date and be asked to await a call to the witness stand.

This inconvenience can be partially alleviated by counsel's assurance to the witness that, if he remains "on call," he will not be telephoned to until it is reasonably certain that he can testify shortly after he gets to court.

It is not customary to serve a subpoena on an expert witness unless he so requests. However, if the witness is balky, it may be necessary to do so. In some jurisdictions, there is a statutory provision or court rule to the effect that a witness served with a subpoena may, by his written stipulation on the face of the original subpoena, agree to hold himself subject to telephone call and to appear immediately upon receipt of such call. Where such a statute or court rule exists, some experienced attorneys have adopted the uniform practice of serving the expert witness with a subpoena and having him sign the agreement to appear when telephoned to.

In some cases, it is desirable to arrange with the expert witness (upon appropriate payment for the time involved) to be present during the trial considerably in advance of his being called to the stand. There are two prime examples of this type of situation:

(a) An expert witness called by the opponent may testify prior to the testimony of one's own expert. This is usually true where counsel represents a defendant. The plaintiff, during the course of his main case, will probably present expert testimony. Counsel should have his own expert in court to assist him in preparing his cross-examination of the opponent's expert.[43]

(b) In jurisdictions where an expert witness is permitted to render an opinion without the posing of a hypothetical question,[44] it is appropriate for the expert to be in court during all of the testimony prior to his own, so that he can testify that he has heard the prior testimony and has used the same as a partial basis for his opinion. In a long case, where it would be an imposition on the expert to be present during the whole trial prior to his testimony or where it would be too expensive to have him do so, the expert can be given a transcript of earlier testimony and can attend the trial only on the day when he is to be called. In such an instance, the expert will be in a position to testify that his opinion has been based partially on the reading of the transcript of earlier testimony plus his hearing the later testimony.

Sec. 9:7 Establishing qualifications of expert witnesses.

As has been stated in section 9:1, *supra,* the sole function of expert testimony is to assist the fact-finder in coming to a proper conclusion based on the evidence in situations where, without the assistance of an expert, the "common mind" is not "equal to the proper solution" of the problem presented. This succinct exposition of the legal justification for introducing expert testimony suggests one of the most important problems confronting counsel

---

[43] The court will ordinarily grant a short recess after the direct examination of the opponent's expert has been completed, in order to permit consultation for the purpose of framing cross-examination. The willingness of a court to grant such a recess will be increased if counsel states that, through consultation with his own expert, he can probably foreshorten cross-examination.

[44] See section 9:3, footnote 21, *supra.*

who call expert witnesses. The court may rule, *as a matter of law*, that the case is a proper one for the utilization of expert testimony; but this is a far cry from convincing the fact-finder (whether court or jury) that the expert's testimony should be relied upon.

It is a great mistake for counsel to establish the qualifications of an expert in a perfunctory or off-hand manner. The fact-finder must be impressed at the very outset that the expert is of sufficient skill to be able to render a reliable opinion and the expert's testimony should establish that he has enough familarity with the facts of the case at bar to make his opinion of real importance.

It is not uncommon, when an expert is called to the stand, for the opponent to state that he will concede the expert's qualifications. Except in rare instances (for example, where the case is tried to the court without a jury and the expert is a well-known figure), *it is a mistake to accept this concession.* Particularly where the case is tried to a jury, an expert witness whose qualifications are conceded remains a stranger who has never demonstrated that he knows what he is talking about. The offer of concession is very often preceded by such a phrase as: "In order to save time, I will concede. . . ." Counsel calling the witness need not fear that the fact-finder will be prejudiced by his apparent refusal to short-cut the trial by accepting the proffered concession. He can very properly retort: "Although I have no doubt that my opponent would have to concede the expert qualifications of this witness, I feel certain that the jury would be interested to know his background and why he is fully qualified to render an authoritative opinion."

Consider the type of disaster which can ensue when counsel too readily accepts an opponent's concession of the qualifications of an expert witness. The witness takes the stand and gives his name and address. The opponent then concedes his qualifications. The witness is then asked (either by the utilization of a hypothetical question or, in some jurisdictions, through a simple question asking his opinion) to state his opinion. He voices an opinion in very short form.

Counsel producing this witness eagerly awaits cross-examination, since he is sure that the expert can confound the opponent by his answers. But skillful adversary counsel says that *he does not desire to cross-examine.* It is too late, now, to establish the witness' qualifications (or the reasons for his conclusion). Obviously, the court will not allow redirect examination when there has been no cross-examination. What is the net result? The witness, about whom the fact-finder knows absolutely nothing except his name and address, has testified to an opinion (possibly without even amplifying his answer by a statement of the reasons therefor). All the careful preparation of this witness' proposed testimony goes down the drain. If opposing counsel thereafter calls an expert witness of his own and carefully establishes his qualifications and fully explores the basis for his opinion, the original disaster is emphasized. Here, the fact-finder is practically compelled to choose between the testimony of a faceless, substantially anonymous witness and the testimony of a demonstrably qualified expert.

There are few principles of law subject to more constant change than the requirements for establishing qualifications of expert witnesses, particularly in the fields where an expert is to testify as to his opinion. In some rare instances statutes prescribe qualifications. Of course, where such a statute exists the problem of "qualifying" the expert is greatly simplified. However, in the vast majority of jurisdictions it is decisional law which sets the criteria. Although it would be misleading to a reader if specific qualifications for any type of witness were set forth in a text, certain general principles can be stated as a basis for individual research by counsel in his preparation for direct examination of an expert witness.[45]

It is a general rule that it is a matter of law resting in the sound discretion of the trial court whether a proffered witness is qualified to render an expert opinion. The exercise of discretion by the court in this respect will rarely be disturbed on appeal. The weight to be accorded to the testimony of an expert is within the province of a fact-finder. As has been indicated, above, where qualified experts give different opinions, the fact-finder may be in a situation where the acceptance of one opinion or the other rests on an assessment of credibility.

It is not necessary that a person be qualified as an expert in every situation where he is called upon to state an impression or opinion.[46] For example, a non-expert can state whether it grew

---

[45] Standard works on the law of evidence are helpful starting points for individual research. Among the best are: *Wigmore on Evidence* (3rd Ed., 1940) vol. 2, pp. 633 *et seq.* and Pocket Supplement (1964), pp. 209 *et seq.*; *The Chamberlayne TRIAL EVIDENCE* (Tompkins, 2nd Ed., 1936), pp. 937 *et seq.* It should be emphasized that consulting these and other texts is not sufficient preparation. It is vital that the *latest* cases in the trial jurisdiction be examined.

[46] This subject is learnedly discussed in *Kelley v. Richardson*, 69 Mich. 436.

warmer or colder during the course of a day on which a happening took place. He can also say whether a person's countenance was flushed, but here it would probably have to be shown that the witness was familiar with the ordinary appearance of that person. In some jurisdictions a witness who has had considerable experience in driving an automobile is permitted to give his estimate of the speed of a moving vehicle. In others, a subscribing witness to a will is allowed (and in some instances is required by statute) to state his opinion that the testator, at the time he signed his will, was sane, or at least that the testator knew what he was doing and that the document to which he affixed his signature was, in fact, his last will and testament.

The cases in which a non-expert can give an opinion or state an impression are legion. As a general rule it may be said that a lay witness may give his impression of physical facts which an ordinary person without special training could assay. The key, here, is the ability to observe and to place that observation against a background of ordinary experience. An extension of this principle is the proposition that one who has had a special type of experience over a protracted period may give an opinion if such opinion is clearly within the demonstrable ambit of his experience and is coupled with positive testimony of the witness' personal observation.

There are, in general, two types of experts who are permitted to testify to their opinions: first, those who are trained in a scientific discipline (for example, physicians, physicists and certain types of chemists); second, those who possess extensive practical experience and skill (for example, a skilled and experienced mechanic, builder, real estate broker, or practical metallurgist). In addition, there are the types of experts who, ordinarily, couple their opinions with demonstrations (for example, handwriting and ballistic experts). Finally, there is the quasi-expert, who may be permitted to state an opinion within a very limited field (for example, experienced businessmen who testify as to customs of a trade or business and, sometimes, as to value).

Although, as we shall presently see,[47] special problems involved in the introduction of expert witnesses arise in individual cases, certain generalizations are appropriate as to each of the types of expert "opinion" witnesses referred to in the foregoing paragraph.

---

[47] Sections 9:8 to 9:17, inclusive, *post.*

The following are requirements for the testimony of each of these broad types to establish qualifications as experts:

A witness trained in a scientific discipline should testify to: his formal education (precisely stating the colleges and graduate schools which he has attended, the degrees awarded to him and the dates of such awards); [48] his quasi-educational experience after his formal education was completed (for example: in the case of a physician, his internship, residency and subsequent acceptance by the formal action of an appropriate governing body of his qualification as a specialist; in the case of an engineer, physicist, architect, or metallurgist, his apprenticeship and practical training); his practice of his profession; his experience in the very type of professional activity which equips him to render an authoritative opinion on the matter at bar; the articles or books or technical papers written by him concerning the scientific field in which he is engaged; his teaching activities (professorships and the like); and his officerships and committee activities in and with scientific societies. [49]

A witness whose expertise is founded upon extensive practical experience and the acquisition of skills should testify to: his present job or position, his title, the name of his employer, the nature of the employer's business and the type of duties performed by the witness, if the witness has been licensed by any official body (such as a state board of examiners for a particular trade or occupation), the name of the license, a description of its requirements and the examinations or experience required before licensure; [50] the total period of time in which he has been engaged in the trade or occupation from which his expertise derives; each step in his practical experience, coupled with a statement of the knowledge gained by him from each such step; the various jobs held by him (from the lowest apprenticeship to the highest executive position), the length of time in each such job,

---

[48] If the witness has received honorary degrees, this may impress the fact-finder. However, there is danger that, on cross-examination, the expert may be compelled to admit that the awarding of an honorary degree to him had nothing to do with his talent in the field within which he is testifying.

[49] Where the expert has acquired knowledge through extensive reading of scientific publications and investigation rather than through practical experience, some cases have held that this is sufficient to qualify him as an expert. *Isenhour v. State*, 157 Ind. 517; *Hardeman v. Brown*, 162 Mass. 585. Whether a fact-finder will be impressed by this species of qualification is another matter. *Soquet v. State*, 72 Wis. 659.

[50] If the witness is a member of a union, which has gradations of membership (apprentice, journeymen, etc.) he should describe the same in the same manner as his statement of licensing.

the name of the employer and, where applicable, the promotions gained while in each employ; a description of his studies "outside of the job" (for example, attendance at night schools, vocational schools, mechanics arts institutes, lectures or symposia in the field and industrial conferences); a description of the successive and increased responsibilities of the witness during the course of his career, including, where applicable, a statement of when the witness went into business for himself and the nature and extent of his business.

A demonstrating expert witness should state his training and background in substantially the same manner as one who depends upon extensive experience as a basis for his expertise. Of course, if such a witness has had formal education leading to a college or university degree, this fact should be established. In addition, if the witness has undergone specialized education in his field, he should not only set forth what that education was but also describe its nature and extent (for example, a ballistics expert may have taken special courses in a police academy or in the program for law enforcement officers conducted by the Federal Bureau of Investigation). The demonstrating expert should, very clearly in his testimony, establish the scientific basis for his experiments and conclusions.[51] This testimony will not only act as a guide to the understanding of the demonstration but will also make known to the fact-finder the nature of the witness' expertise.

The quasi-expert (who is called upon to give his opinion with respect to a very limited field) should, in addition to establishing his extensive practical experience in a business or trade, testify in minute detail about the particular facet of his experience which enables him to render an authoritative opinion.[52]

No matter how well qualified an expert witness may be to render an opinion, it should be noted that expert testimony given in a vacuum is practically meaningless. The fact-finder is not interested in the exposition of theories unless there is demonstrated the applicability of those theories to the *facts* of the case at bar.

An exception to this generality may arise in a situation where the statement of an established scientific principle is requisite to an understanding of facts which have been established through the testimony of non-expert observers.

---

[51] As to a handwriting expert, for example, see section 9:4, *supra.*
[52] See section 9:15, *post.*

Where the expert has *personally observed* facts upon which his opinion is based and states that his opinion flows from such observation, great weight should be accorded that opinion. Some cases have so held as a matter of law.[53] However, rendering of an opinion based upon evidence in the case, resulting from observations of facts by persons other than the expert, is admissible.[54]

The present section has been devoted to the *broad and general* proof requisite to the establishment of the qualifications of the various major classes of expert witnesses.[55] The appropriate type of evidence, as hereinabove outlined, should be introduced with respect to *every* expert witness. However, more may be needed than this broad and general proof when an individual expert is called to the stand. The peculiar facts of the case or the refinements of required expertise can create the necessity for such *additional* proof.

In sections 9:8 to 9:17, *post,* inclusive, we discuss the problems presented in the establishment of the qualifications of *individual* expert witnesses and the *additional* proof which may be necessary. Again, it is appropriate to emphasize the word "additional." The broad and general proof is *always* required. The *additional* proof is a supplement thereto.

Sec. 9:8   Physicians.

A duly licensed physician can be called as an "opinion" expert witness. Unless a statute so provides, the physician need not be a specialist.[56] However, where the matter at bar is a highly technical one beyond the ken of a general practitioner, the danger arises that, upon cross-examination, the weight to be accorded the witness' testimony may be greatly impaired. Therefore, it is wise, where a non-specialist physician is called, to establish that he has had extensive practical experience in treating the conditions as to which he renders an opinion.

If a physician has not been licensed to practice in the jurisdiction

---

[53] *Cf., Loveridge v. Brown,* 98 N.J.L. 381; *Cadwell v. Arnheim,* 152 N.Y. 182.

[54] The use of a hypothetical question to establish the connection between record facts and the expert's opinion is discussed in section 9:3, *supra.*

[55] It should be noted that every "opinion" expert falls into one of these classes.

[56] An example of such a statute is found in some jurisdictions where there is a requirement that only a specialist in psychiatry may certify a person for commitment to a mental institution or testify as to his sanity.

in which he is called to testify, even though he has been duly licensed in another jurisdiction, a serious question may arise as to whether he can testify to his opinion.[57] Of course, such a witness can give evidence as to his observations when he was actually attending a patient, provided he was licensed in the jurisdiction where he rendered medical services. This type of witness is commonly referred to as the "treating physician." Such a witness will be regarded as something more than a layman, because his observations will probably extend beyond what would be apparent to a non-physician. For example, the witness can describe, in technical terms, the portion of the body of his patient where a bruise or wound was seen and whether a wound was "deep" or superficial and will, in all probability, be permitted to state that the patient suffered a fracture or compound fracture of a limb. However, beyond these obvious fact-opinions he may not be permitted to go.

In order to lay the foundation for an expert opinion, counsel may be compelled, where the treating physician is not available, to call non-physicians to establish the medical facts upon which the expert opinion will be premised. A nurse who attended the patient may have to be the "observation" witness. A member of the patient's family can also be used for this purpose. But in neither case will such a witness be considered other than as a layman and the only facts as to which such a witness can testify are those which a layman without scientific training could observe. The ability of this type of witness to observe the facts should be clearly established. The time when and the place where the observations were made, the lighting conditions and similar matters are important. If there has been more than one observation or a continuous course of observation, each incident should be separately described.

Although it must be borne in mind that lay testimony of observations amounts to no more than a statement of observable *physical* facts and that the lay witness may not express a technical opinion, some of these facts may necessarily have to be stated with precision in order that the expert can draw scientific conclusions therefrom. For example, a member of the family cannot say that there was a compound fracture of a leg, but he can testify that he observed a wound in the leg and that a jagged piece of bone was protruding

---

[57] This problem arises not only when the physician is a general practitioner but also if he is a specialist; but a specialist of nation-wide repute will generally be allowed to render an opinion in any jurisdiction.

therefrom. A nurse can testify that a patient vomited constantly, became incoherent at times, or lapsed into long or short periods of unconsciousness.

A physician (whether he be a treating physician or a specialist) may testify to the fact of any bodily condition, the symptoms of the patient and the effect of injuries and may give his diagnosis that the patient was suffering from a certain disease and may state his opinion as to the cause of death. *The extent of a physician's testimony is necessarily limited by the proof of his personal competence with respect to the subjects on which he is testifying.*[58] Therefore, as has been heretofore stated, specific proof of particular competence should be offered. If this proof is forthcoming, a duly qualified physician can even render an opinion on subjects not necessarily encompassed within the discipline of medicine. He may, for example, testify to his opinion, based upon personal observation or other established record facts, about what was the probable cause of an injury, the force required to produce it and the direction from which that force was delivered. Very often, a qualified expert testifies about the permanency of injuries, and the effect thereof upon the body and nervous system of the patient.

An opinion as to the cause of death may be testified to by a physician who conducted an autopsy. Here, expertise must be established by a detailed recital of this physician's training and experience in the art of performing autopsies and drawing conclusions therefrom. At times, the physician who performed the autopsy renders only an intermediate opinion (for example, that a certain type and quantity of poison was found in the brain of a deceased). The final opinion as to the cause of death is testified to by another expert, who premises this final opinion on the autopsy findings.[59]

There is, of course, a distinction between what a physician testifies to as a matter of pure observation and the type of testimony he gives requiring the establishment of his qualifications as an expert. Since a layman would be permitted to give evidence about physical facts (for example, that a patient was suffering from a nosebleed, or had a black eye, or a bruise on his forehead), a physician's testimony as to the same facts is receivable and it makes no difference

---

[58] A comprehensive discussion of the scope of medical testimony is found in *The Chamberlayne TRIAL EVIDENCE* (Tompkins, 2nd ed., 1936), pp. 956–964, wherein are cited numerous decisions. Note that the experience of the physician is an important factor when he states a diagnosis or prognosis.

[59] See section 9:10, *post.*

whether that physician is licensed in the jurisdiction of the forum or has any special skill which would enable him to draw and express conclusions from the observed physical facts. The physician when he gives this type of testimony (simple observation) is under no disability because of lack of expertise. In other words, to all practical intents and purposes, such a physician-witness may be regarded as a layman. In these circumstances, the only criteria in the case of either the physician or layman are the opportunity to observe and the ability intelligibly to relate his observations.

Beyond this point, we move on an ascending scale of requirements for establishing expert qualifications, *under the particular circumstances of the case at bar.* The grade of ascent depends upon the extent to which a witness will be permitted to draw conclusions from presented facts. Counsel should, in preparation for the adducing of expert testimony, consult the *latest* decisions about necessity for establishing expertise, with specific reference to the very fact situation with which he is confronted; because the tendency of decisions over the last several decades has been to allow broader conclusions to be drawn from certain fact situations and, consequently, to relax the need for specific qualifications and to permit general practitioners to render opinions in cases where they might have been previously precluded from doing so.[60] An important limitation must here be noted. Although the "modern rule relative to opinion evidence is liberal," there must be "more than possibility of result, if weight and credit are to be given the opinion of a medical expert. . . . While no special form of words is required in framing the question, the answer must disclose that in the mind of the witness there exists a reasonable certainty that a given condition or result has occurred or will probably occur from the original injury or ailment." [61] It follows that, despite the relaxing of requirements for establishing expertise, the medical witness must at least be shown to have sufficient experience and skill to express an informed opinion with "reasonable certainty."

Sec. 9:9   Analytical chemists, metallurgists and physicists.

Where expert witnesses testify to their opinions, using as a factual basis for such testimony tests conducted by them, proof of their

---

[60] *Cf., Peo. v. Caricco*, 310 Ill. 543; *Fournier v. Zinn*, 257 Mass. 575; *State v. Moordiam*, 132 Wash. 37.

[61] *McLaughlin v. Curtis Quillen Co. et al.*, 223 App. Div. 208, 227 N.Y.S. 712, 714–715, and cases therein cited.

personal qualifications must be fortified by additional testimony establishing the controlled conditions under which the experiments were conducted and the scientific basis therefor. Although, at first blush, this might not seem to fall within the category of establishing qualifications of the expert, himself, further analysis indicates that it is part of the qualification process; because the opinion of the expert becomes viable only where its underlying facts add to his general qualifications and he can hardly be deemed an expert *in the case at bar* unless these underlying facts establish his familiarity with the subject-matter of the litigation.

An analytical chemist, metallurgist and experts of a similar genre are called for the *primary* purpose of proving that a given article has certain physical characteristics or properties. The same witness may also be in a position to testify that the presence of such characteristics, in his opinion, did or could have produced certain results material to a solution of the issues at bar. The ability to render this latter type of opinion probably calls for qualifications beyond those required of the analyst. In an appropriate case, these additional qualifications should be proved. But the analytical expert is ordinarily called *solely* for the purpose of establishing the physical characteristics of an article and an opinion as to the material *result* of that condition is very often elicited from another expert.[62]

A common and simple example of the use of analytical chemists as experts is a case where the issue at bar is whether a stain found on a garment is human blood.[63] After he has testified to his general qualifications (education, experience, etc.), the expert states his specialized education, experience and work in the field of blood analysis.

The next steps are to qualify as valid the tests conducted by the expert. These steps encompass separate stages of testimony:

(a) The expert first testifies to general and well-established scientific principles, such as the reaction of human blood stains to the application of certain chemicals. He may say, for example, that when a given chemical compound is applied to a blood stain or when the stain is dipped into such a compound either the stain or the com-

---

[62] See section 9:10, *post.*

[63] Serological blood analyses, commonly used to establish exclusion in cases involving paternity, are more complicated than simple blood-identification cases; because, in a serological examination there must be a differentiation between types of blood and not merely an identification of a specimen as human blood. In section 9:5, *supra,* there is a verbatim report of the testimony of an expert who has made a serological test.

pound will turn a certain color; but that if the stain is not human blood the color reaction will not appear or there will be a different color reaction.

(b) There must now be established that the garment which was tested by the expert is the same garment as bore the stain at issue.[64]

(c) The chemist now describes his tests in great detail. He tells what chemical reagents were used by him, how they were applied to the garment and what the resultant color reaction was.[65]

(d) The witness now states his expert opinion that the stain on the garment was (or was not) human blood.

Up to this point, the witness' direct examination, *solely* as an analytical chemist, has been completed. Whether or not he can render an opinion on other factors depends both on his further qualifications and the nature of the case at bar.

A different type of example of the use of an expert analyst is furnished by the expert metallurgist-witness. Primarily, this witness is called upon to testify as to the composition of a section of metal (for example, a part of a building beam, where the cause of action is for negligence in using that beam as part of the construction of a floor which collapsed). Here, the witness' testimony, in general, follows the outline for the testimony of an analytical chemist (proof of special qualifications of the witness to conduct relevant experiments, the statement of general scientific principles, establishment of the fact that the piece of metal tested was the same as that involved in the issue being tried, the details of the experiment and the expert conclusion of the witness that the piece of metal was composed of certain ingredients in stated proportions). At this point, the testimony of the metallurgist, *as such*, is complete. However, it is obvious that this testimony is not sufficient, standing alone, to establish a cause of action. There must be proof that material composed of the ingredients testified to by the metallurgist has insufficient tensile strength to support the weight which would ordinarily be found on the floor of the premises in question. Thus, unless by sheerest coincidence the metallurgist is qualified to render an

---

[64] It may be necessary, in this connection, to prove by other witnesses the continuous custody and possession of the garment until it reached the hands of the expert.

[65] This portion of the testimony must clearly establish that the chemicals used in the experiment were the same as those described in the expert's earlier testimony about established scientific principles. The purity of the chemicals used can be established on direct examination; but it is wiser to leave this subject for redirect examination only if the cross-examination casts doubt on the purity of the chemicals.

opinion on the subject, other witnesses (for example, a physicist or an experienced master builder) must be produced to establish the ultimate fact that the material in question was too weak to bear the normal load to which it would be subjected (or the actual load at the time of the floor collapse).

The testimony of an expert physicist-witness is ordinarily given (after the witness' general and special qualifications have been established) through response to a hypothetical question. He is asked, for example, to assume (as has been established by record testimony): that, on a certain date, a floor beam was part of the construction of a floor which collapsed; that at the time of such collapse the weight of objects on this floor was a certain amount; [66] and that an analysis of the composition of the floor beam disclosed the components theretofore testified to by the metallurgist. He then testifies to his opinion as to whether the beam had sufficient tensile strength or supporting vigor to sustain the weight-load to which it was subjected and whether, if his testimony has negatived the presence of sufficient tensile strength, the lack of such strength was the probable cause of the collapse.

The foregoing example of the testimony of an expert physicist occurs in cases where the witness, himself, did not conduct tests. However, he may have made observations. Thus, in a case involving the amount of force which would have had to be applied to break a fence, shear down a tree or cause a hole or depression in a sidewalk or highway, the physicist may well have personally looked at the fence, tree, street or highway after the catastrophe at issue had taken place. Here, the testimony should establish that the object in question was in the same condition when examined by the physicist as it was *immediately* after the happening. A similar situation arises where a physicist is called upon to express his opinion of the speed of vehicles in collision. If, as part of his professional engagement, the physicist examined tire tracks, the condition of the two vehicles after the collision and like observable physical facts, he will first detail his observations, then state the scientific principles through which these observations can act as a basis for his conclusion and then give his opinion.[67]

There are cases in which the physicist-witness, himself, has con-

---

[66] If possible, the weight of objects resting directly upon the beam should be proved and that factor may be part of the hypothetical question.

[67] It may be necessary in an instance of this sort, for the physicist to testify to certain specialized experience and training that enabled him to reach his conclusion.

ducted tests from which his opinion derives. Here, he is not basing his opinion on the prior opinion of another expert who conducted tests nor upon partial observation of but a few facts. For example, the physicist-witness in his own laboratory may have applied different degrees of heat to a metallic substance in order to determine its bending or melting point. After testifying to his general qualifications and experience, his special qualifications and experience, and, in full detail, the tests conducted by him and their controlled conditions, the witness gives his opinion.

Sec. 9:10 Derivative and compound opinion experts.

In certain types of cases, the opinion of an expert about an ultimate material fact necessarily depends upon another expert's opinion concerning an intermediate contributing factor. This presents a dual problem for establishing qualifications. Not only must the qualifications of the expert to render his opinion be shown but the earlier expert must also have been demonstrated to be qualified to render his opinion.

More is involved here than a matter of law. The court must first rule, in the case of each expert, that he is qualified to render his opinion and that he may testify to that opinion. However, equally important and probably finally decisive is the question whether the fact-finder believes *both* experts. If the fact-finder disbelieves either, the entire fabric of expert testimony falls as a unit.

The hypothetical question directed to the ultimate expert must assume as a *fact* the conclusion stated by the intermediate expert. For example, in a bastardy proceeding, if the earlier expert made blood tests as the result of which he testified to his opinion that a putative father had one type of blood and the child whose legitimacy is in question had another, the proof is incomplete unless there is further expert testimony that such difference in blood types establishes an exclusion of paternity. The expert whose testimony to this effect is required and who may not have personally done the blood testing is subjected to a hypothetical question which states, in part: "and further assuming that William Smith [the child] had a different type of blood than Henry Smith [the defendant], can you state, in your opinion and with reasonable certainty, whether this difference in blood type excludes the defendant as the possible father of the child?".[68]

---

[68] We have set forth the quoted portion of the hypothetical question in

Because the opinion of the ultimate expert, if believed, will (counsel hopes) be decisive of the litigation and because the intermediate expert's opinion is merely a step in the course of final proof, some lawyers have treated the qualifications, methods and conclusions of the intermediate expert in a cursory or perfunctory manner. This is a great mistake. The axiom that a chain is only as strong as its weakest link here comes into play. Opposing counsel, realizing that the opinion of the ultimate expert is, of itself, unassailable on any scientific basis, may concentrate his fire on the testimony of the intermediate expert.

We have, thus far in this section, discussed derivative expert testimony. This is the type where the opinion of one expert necessarily is premised upon the prior opinion of another. Compound expert testimony is another matter. It arises in situations where a series of expert witnesses testify to their conclusions, but where the ultimate solution of the case at bar depends upon a *composite* of all of these conclusions, *none of which is specifically derived from another*. As in the case of derivative expert testimony, counsel must carefully qualify each expert and have that expert convincingly testify to his methods and the scientific principles underlying his conclusions.

The expert testimony in two sensational murder trials illustrate, respectively, a method of attack on an intermediate expert and the presentation of proof through composite (instead of derivative) expert opinions: [69]

In the first case, a defendant, who was a physician, was charged with murdering his wife by injecting into her buttocks a rare poison, the presence of which was hard to detect. At the request of the prosecutor, the body of the wife was disinterred and an autopsy was performed. A physician who participated in that autopsy and made a chemical analysis of the brain of the deceased described the autopsy and his methods of analysis fully and then testified that he found, in the brain of the victim, a considerable quantity of the poison. A world-renowned medical expert, called as the ultimate expert, testified that, in his opinion, the amount of poison found in the deceased's brain was the cause of death. Defendant's counsel, while questioning the scientific basis for the testimony of the ulti-

---

general terms. Actually, such a question should state the precise blood type of the child and the precise blood type of the putative father.

[69] The actual testimony, in each case, has been slightly modified in our outline so that it will be better illustrative of the points now under consideration.

mate expert, did not make this his important point. Instead, he attacked the qualifications of the doctor who participated in the autopsy and his procedures.[70] Thus, counsel for the defendant was able to raise the question whether the qualifications and procedures of the *intermediate* expert were sufficient to create a reasonable doubt of the validity of the ultimate expert's opinion.

The second case presents a masterpiece in the use of compound expert testimony. There, the defendant was charged with kidnapping and murdering a young child. An important question in the case was whether a ladder, used to gain access to the bedroom of the kidnapped child, belonged to or was under the control of the defendant. An expert forester testified that the grain of wood is so peculiar to each piece that it is virtually impossible precisely to match grain patterns unless they come from the same piece of wood. He then testified that a portion of a certain wooden fixture in the defendant's home had been cut away. He then established that the grain pattern of this wooden fixture precisely matched the grain pattern of the wood in the ladder and voiced his conclusion that the ladder was made, in part, from wood taken from the defendant's home wooden fixture. Another expert, a carpenter, also testified that a piece had been cut from the wooden fixture in the defendant's home. He then asserted, based on long experience, that the rough edges of a piece of wood from which part has been cut, would not exactly fit a piece of wood other than the one originally cut away. He then testified that he had matched the remaining wooden fixture in the defendant's home with a portion of the ladder in question and that one precisely fitted the other. He then testified that, in his opinion, part of the ladder was made of the wood cut from the defendant's home wooden fixture. Thus, the prosecution was able to present the opinions of two experts, *neither of whose opinions was derived from that of the other,* although both reached the same ultimate conclusion.

The use of compound expert opinion is sometimes in the nature of corroborative evidence. In such a case, each opinion can, standing alone, establish the ultimate point sought to be proved. Thus, in the foregoing example about the composition of the kidnap ladder, a finder of the facts might have been justified, solely on the opinion

---

[70] He even went so far as to contend that the ultimate expert could not render an opinion because, in depending on the intermediate opinion, he was relying on hearsay proof. This contention was overruled.

of one of the two experts, in finding that the ladder was partly made from a piece of wood torn from an appliance in the defendant's home.[71]

There are some instances in which the opinions of several experts are utilized to establish *different* ultimate points in the same case. These are neither derivative nor compound expert opinions.

Sec. 9:11   Fingerprinters and other impression takers.

In addition to establishing the general qualifications of one who takes or analyzes fingerprints, special training and experience should be brought out. Examples of such special training and experience are courses given in police academies or by the Federal Bureau of Investigation, practical work in the art of "lifting" fingerprints and preserving the impressions so obtained, and particular experience in analyzing prints, comparing them with others and thus identifying the person, impressions of whose fingerprints have been obtained.

The taking and analysis of fingerprints are akin to other types of tests. As is true of all tests, the expert's evidence should first state the general principle (which is so well known that some courts will take judicial notice thereof) that no two persons have the same fingerprints. He should explain the various individual characteristics of fingerprints which aid in making identification (lines, circles, arcs, etc.).

The evidence of identification established by fingerprints is tripartite:

First, proof should be adduced, in detail, as to where and when the original fingerprints were found and as to how they were "brought out" or "lifted," with an explanation of precisely what the bringing out consists of and how it works. The process of bringing out a fingerprint is sometimes referred to as "dusting." It is done by blowing a thin dust-like substance over the fingerprint and then blowing gently on the dusted print, as a result of which a white impression of the fingerprint remains, due to the fact that the moisture and convex reverse pressure of the print causes the dust to cling to it

Second, there should be evidence that the fingerprint impression from which identity is sought to be established was preserved (usually by photographing) and that the preserved impression was the

---

[71] There was, actually, further expert testimony to the effect that a nail hole in the defendant's wooden fixture matched a nail hole in part of the ladder.

one actually used in making identification. It may be necessary to prove custody of the preserved impression through several witnesses, particularly where one witness (for example, a specially trained police officer) "lifted" the print and another witness (the identification expert) examined, analyzed and compared the same.

Third, the expert should state that he has compared the preserved fingerprint impression with another fingerprint (or the impression thereof) *unquestionably* shown to be the defendant's fingerprint. It is the best practice to produce enlarged photographs of the two prints. The expert can then make a demonstration in the presence of the fact-finder, pointing out the similarities by which identification is established.[72]

If the defendant's "unquestioned" fingerprint is shown by a court record (particularly if the record comes from a jurisdiction other than that of the forum), it may be necessary to establish through a witness, present when the defendant was convicted on an earlier occasion, that the defendant at bar is the same person whose fingerprint was taken after the earlier conviction. This proof can be strengthened if the earlier fingerprint record is on the same sheet or card as a photograph of the defendant. But such a sheet or card does *not*, in and of itself, prove that the fingerprint is actually that of the defendant at bar, because it is obvious that there could be an error whereby the fingerprint of one person, through accident or negligence, could be put on a card bearing the photograph of another.

Where comparison is made between a "lifted" fingerprint and a central identification fingerprint-record (such as those maintained by the Federal Bureau of Investigation and the armed services), some statutes and some decisions are to the effect that there need be no further proof about the accuracy of the central record. However, there may be serious doubt as to the constitutionality of such a provision in the light of the principle guaranteeing the right of confrontation to defendants in criminal cases.

In some hospitals, an impression of the footprints of a newly born baby are taken. These impressions become part of the hospital records and would probably be admissible as an entry made in the regular course of business.[73] Where an issue arises as to the identity

---

[72] The demonstration here made *is*, in its general nature, very similar to demonstrations made by handwriting experts. In this connection, see section 9:4, *supra.*

[73] As an analogy, consider section 11:10, *post.*

of an infant (for example, in a case where there is a claim that one child was substituted for another), an impression of the footprint of the child whose identity is sought to be established may be made under the same conditions as the original impressions were made. A properly qualified expert can testify on the subject of identification. Here, a demonstration can be made in the presence of the fact-finder. The difficulty with this type of case arises from the fact that, unless the second set of prints were made within a relatively short time of the first, controlled condition of the print-taking procedures is almost impossible to establish.

Impression takers other than fingerprinters are employed as expert witnesses in a variety of fields. A common example occurs in situations where fresh footprints are found leading to or from the scene of a crime or other occurrence. Trained police officers may not only take photographs of these footprints but may also make impressions of them. This is ordinarily done by "pouring" the footprint through placing therein plaster of paris or a similar liquid which subsequently solidifies with the result that a converse mould is created. An expert, by comparing the underface of the mould with shoes owned by a defendant, can testify that the footprints were made by these shoes. Indeed, a demonstration to that effect can often be made in the presence of the fact-finder, by means of which demonstration there is established visual evidence of identity. The expert making this demonstration should, as part of his testimony, point out to the fact-finder that the mould is an impression of a convex pattern while the shoe presents a concave appearance. Thus, if a nail protrudes from the surface of the shoe, the mould will display a hole.

In some instances, counsel have deemed it wise to have the expert prepare a model from the original mould, with the result that the model (as far as surfaces are concerned) bears the same convex-concave appearance as the shoe to which it is being compared.

Where a mould or similar sculptured impression has been made, the most important facts to be shown are when, under what conditions and how the processing was done. The skill of the mould-maker is relatively easy to establish. It does not take a particular type of genius to pour a liquid substance into a depression, wait until the liquid substance hardens and then extract the mould. But it is vitally important to show that the mould ultimately used for comparison purposes was in the same condition when it was so used as when it was made and it is of equal vital importance to prove that great *care* accompanied the mould-making process to ensure that the mould would not, in any manner, be distorted. Particularly is this true if the mould was broken or even partially fragmented and then put together so that the whole could be observed.

Where a model is made from a mould, the training and skill of the model maker as well as a description of the exact method used by him should be established. The degree of skill and training required depends on the nature of the mould and model making problem. For example, a dentist who presents as evidence a model of his patient's teeth, which he made, must be shown to have had extensive experience in preparing such models. If, because of breakage, he had to "patch" the mould before making the model, the dentist should testify (possibly on redirect examination) about the exact method employed by him in so patching the mould that there would be no distortion of the shape and position of the teeth. Similarly, a skilled mechanic or physicist who makes a mould of a portion of a piece of machinery has to be a highly qualified person, using scientifically approved methods and exercising not only personal skill but great care.

Sec. 9:12 Photographers.

Ordinarily, a photograph may be received in evidence without the testimony of the photographer if a witness testifies that the photograph is a fair representation of what it purports to show.[74] However, where the precise dimensions or other special characteristics of the photographed object are in issue, the photographer must not only be produced but his special qualifications to take the picture in question must be shown and he must testify to every step in the taking of the picture, the developing of the film or plate and the making of the print.

Different types of pictures require varying degrees of skill, which encompass not only the ability of the photographer, as such, but also special techniques and individual methods. For example: (a) a picture of a depression or hole in a sidewalk must be so taken that there is neither exaggeration nor diminution of the depth, grade or circumference of the hole; (b) a photograph of an exposed internal portion of a human body should be so made that the relationship of

---

[74] See cases cited in footnotes 24 and 25 of Chapter X, *post*.

various organs to one another can be observed; (c) where relative sizes of various objects are at issue, the angle of photography must be such that there is no distortion with respect to size; and (d) where color photographs are used, they must be so taken, developed and printed that the colors will be as nearly natural as possible.

Obviously, in some instances, special lighting techniques must be used to give meaningful content to photographs offered in evidence. But, sometimes, the very use of these techniques may lead to partial and unintentional distortion. For example, where a photograph is taken of the exposed interior of a human body, the light-angles requisite to showing the relationship of one organ to another may result in the casting of shadows which would not appear in non-photographic observation of the cadaver. Here, the testimony of the photographer should carefully explain the unintended distortion. His testimony in this respect may be accompanied by a photograph taken from the same angle but without special lighting effects.

Where, because of the nature of the proof sought to be established by a given photograph, lighting effects or photographic angles create a distortion, the photographer should bring out this fact and explain the nature of the distortion on his *direct* examination. If he so testifies, the opponent is deprived of the opportunity to capitalize on the distortion during cross-examination.[75]

It is not uncommon, where a photograph encompasses a broad field, to offer in evidence an enlarged picture of a portion instead of the whole of the photograph. There is nothing illegitimate in this practice if the enlargement will be of greater help to the fact-finder than would the entire original photograph. However, in *every* case where such a selective enlargement is offered, the entire picture should simultaneously be produced so that there can be no claim of an attempt to mislead the fact-finder. In a celebrated senatorial investigation, an enlargement of a portion of a picture was offered in evidence, presumably to show that two people were together at a given time. Opposing counsel, during cross-examination, produced the entire original photograph, claiming that the enlargement was misleading, because it failed to show that certain other people were present when the picture was taken. The presence of the other

---

[75] For a discussion of the general method of handling unfavorable facts during direct examination, see section 5:7, *supra*.

people did have some significance, but the failure to produce the entire picture had a dramatic effect far out of proportion to the ultimate conclusion that other persons were present.

As has been indicated, above, a lay witness as well as a photographer can testify that a given photograph is a fair representation of that which it purports to show and is also a fair representation of the condition pictured at the time the incident, which is the subject of litigation, took place. Such testimony is sufficient foundation, as a matter of law, for the introduction of the picture in evidence. However, it is not conclusive proof. Either a lay witness or a photographer may testify that the picture received in evidence is *not* a fair representation. Where the photographer so testifies, he may point out the technical considerations that lead to his conclusion; for example that artificial lighting as evidenced by shadows of objects close to one another run in different directions although all of the objects are meant to have been lighted from the same light source.

Testimony that a photograph is not a fair representation may be based on external proof, which the expert photographer can state he took into consideration in reaching his opinion.

An interesting example of such compound proof occurred in a suit involving the holding over of premises by a corporate tenant. There, the last day of the written lease was a Thursday. The tenant corporation claimed that it had surrendered the premises on that Thursday, removing all of its equipment. The landlord claimed that the tenant still had much of the equipment in the premises on Friday. In the circumstances of the case, under the law of the forum wherein it was tried, if the tenant had not removed its equipment by midnight on Thursday, it would be liable, as a holdover, for an additional year's rent, at the option of the landlord.

The landlord introduced in evidence a picture of the premises showing a substantial amount of heavy equipment remaining therein. The photographer who took this picture testified that it was taken in the afternoon of Friday. The picture showed sunlight streaming through two windows, the reflection of that sunlight on the tenant's equipment and shadows thrown on the floor of the premises.[76]

On cross-examination, the tenant's attorney caused the landlord's photographer to state unequivocally that the photograph was taken on Friday, that Friday was a sunny day, that no artificial light was

---

[76] There was no dispute about the identity of either the premises or the equipment or about the fact that the equipment belonged to the tenant.

used when the picture was taken and that sunlight was streaming through the windows.

In rebuttal, the tenant produced a representative of the United States Weather Bureau. Through this witness, the tenant introduced in evidence an official Weather Bureau chart, which showed that Thursday was a clear, sunny day but that Friday was a rainy day, during the course of which no sunlight was visible.[77] The tenant thereupon produced his own photographer, who examined the photograph which had been introduced in evidence by the landlord. He confirmed the testimony of the landlord's photographer that no artificial light was used when the picture was taken and that the sunlight streaming through the windows was the sole source of light. He buttressed this testimony by indicating to the jury the reflections of light on the equipment and the direction of the shadows cast. He then stated his opinion that, in view of the proof of weather conditions on Friday, the photograph could not have been taken on that day. He further testified, also basing his opinion on the Weather Bureau proof, that the photograph could have been taken on Thursday.

Sec. 9:13 Mechanics and skilled craftsmen.

When a mechanic or skilled craftsman is called as an expert, the most important facet of his qualifications is the practical experience he has had in his field. In section 9:7, *supra*, we have set forth the items used to establish qualifications of this type of witness in a general way. This proof, insofar as it is available, should be made with regard to every mechanic or skilled craftsman expert.

In the light of the facts of each individual case and the type of testimony the expert is called upon to give, it is essential that additional qualifications be established. It should, of course, be shown that the witness is generally experienced and skilled in his field. However, this may not be enough. It should be established further that the witness has had sufficient experience with regard to the very type of thing he is testifying about that his opinion is entitled to weight. For example, a mechanic may give his opinion that the manner in which two pieces of metal were joined was improper and unsafe. It is not enough to qualify this witness merely by showing

---

[77] Proof of weather conditions by official Weather Bureau charts is discussed in section 11:15, *post*.

that he has had experience in making joinders of this type. It must also be shown that his experience includes examinations of improperly made joinders and his observation of the bad results flowing from such a method of joining. Likewise, where such a mechanic is called upon to testify as to the reasonable value of doing certain repair work, he must be shown not only to have skill in making these repairs but also experience in charging for them and in being paid his charges.[78] His testimony should also include proof that he is familiar with charges made for such repairs in the neighborhood by other mechanics.

Where a mechanic or skilled craftsman is the expert witness, it is almost invariably necessary that, as one of the bases for his opinion, he must have actually examined the object or contrivance at issue. This will enable him to state *facts* observed by him. From these facts he is enabled not only precisely to state the condition of the object or mechanical contrivance but also what is wrong with it and even what would have to be done to put it in proper condition.

There are some cases where a mechanic or skilled craftsman is asked to express a general opinion not based on personal observation. If it is shown that the witness possesses sufficient skill and experience, this type of testimony is admissible. For example, such a witness may testify that certain materials are or are not proper for manufacturing an article where that article is intended to be used for a particular purpose. In the same general category is the expression of opinion by an expert as to why a certain thing happened; for example, why a metal component in an automobile was unable to stand the strain put upon it and, hence, broke and why such breakage was the proximate cause of an accident.[79] Conversely, such an expert can testify that certain causes would not have produced the deleterious effects in issue.

Of a somewhat greater breadth of expertise than is possessed by a skilled mechanic or craftsman is that resulting from the knowledge and experience of a master builder, industrial designer, or experienced industrial or mechanical engineer. However, the difference is one of degree, based on essentially narrowly qualitative considerations. Once the qualifications of this type of expert are established,

---

[78] The proof in this respect is somewhat analogous to the type of evidence under the ancient "shop-book rule." See section 11:10, *post*.

[79] An analogous situation is discussed in section 9:9, *supra*, in connection with the testimony of a metallurgist about tensile strength of floor beams.

the end result is merely that he may testify to opinions in a broader field and may, in reaching such opinions, indulge in more extended inferences. For example, such a witness can give his opinion as to whether a piece of machinery was properly operative, whether a given piece of equipment (or building) was properly constructed, whether there was an undue disregard of safety precautions in certain operations and whether a manufacturing procedure was economically undertaken, including a conclusion as to the ability of those engaged in the work and the method by which the total operation has been set up. This type of witness is often permitted to express an extremely broad opinion about the cause of accidents and the value of objects damaged or destroyed.

A master builder (or a prime or subordinate contractor), if his underlying knowledge is established through proof of experience, may testify about the availability of materials, their cost and the appropriateness of their use in a given construction.[80]

Although he is not narrowly classifiable as a skilled craftsman, the qualifications of an expert on the authenticity and value of works of art are established by criteria similar to those of the skilled craftsman. The basic formula for qualifying such an expert is to exhibit that he has such *knowledge* as to enable him to render an opinion which will be helpful to the fact-finder because this knowledge is beyond that possessed by an ordinary person.

That a questioned work of art is or is not the authentic product of the artist to whom it is sought to be attributed usually has an important bearing on its value. However, the type of knowledge required to establish expertise as to authenticity is different from that requisite to expressing an opinion of value. True it is that the same expert often possesses expertise in both fields; but this is coincidental and the two subjects should be considered separately in the course of the expert's testimony.

The development of expertise leading to the expression of an opinion as to authenticity is, of necessity, highly practical, though extensive reading in the field may add to the qualifications of the witness. It should be shown: that the expert has examined and studied a substantial number of the works of the artist in question

---

[80] In section 9:14, *post*, is treated the calling of a master builder as a specialized type of "real estate expert" to establish the proper cost of construction in cases involving, among others, assessments for purposes of taxation or involving valuation in eminent domain or other condemnation proceedings.

and that from this study he has noted characteristics and special idiosyncrasies of that artist's technique and style (as simple examples, types of brush-strokes, combinations of colors, arrangements of figures, use of backgrounds and the like); that the expert has studied the history of the artist and of the periods in which that artist worked; that the expert has studied the development of the artist and, where applicable, the different periods of that artist's development leading to changes in style and technique; and, although this may be difficult to explain to a fact-finder, that the expert has noted the infusion of the personality of the artist into his work.

Skilled forgers of works of art have been known to create pictures that apparently have all the characteristics of work produced by famous artists. Indeed, to the lay eye it may be practically impossible to tell which is the original work of art and which is a copy thereof. Where art experts differ in their opinions as to authenticity, the fact-finder is necessarily puzzled, particularly where he has little choice in determining which expert is possessed of greater skill or experience. Therefore, the introduction of the expert to the fact-finder should, among other things, harp on the *reputation* of the expert. He can, for example, testify about his employment by museums and well-known collectors to authenticate proposed purchases, to the fact that he has written books or articles covering the artist whose work is the subject of inquiry in the case at bar, to the fact that he has lectured on this subject and to his teaching positions in the same field.

Objective evidence to buttress the opinion of the expert (or to act as a partial basis for that opinion) should be produced, whenever possible. When the question at bar is the genuineness of a painting attributed to an old master, there are certain types of tests which can be conducted and the results of which should be the subject of testimony.[81] For example, each of the following is an important element of supporting proof: (a) that the canvas upon which a painting is done or the paint used in making the picture was not in existence at the time when the alleged artist was living or working; (b) that the alleged artist never used the quality of paint now

---

[81] Sometimes, the tests are done by persons other than the testifying expert. The testers should be produced in advance of the expert so that, as to the derivative portion of his testimony, a proper foundation will have been laid. See section 9:10, *supra.*

appearing on the canvas; (c) that x-ray studies establish that under the painting is an earlier painting but that this earlier painting was made at a time subsequent to the death of the artist who is alleged to have produced the masterpiece under consideration.

The testimony of an art expert called to give his opinion of the value of a painting must necessarily be predicated upon his familiarity with the art market and of the prices paid for the type of work under consideration. If the expert has acted as agent for collectors or museums in buying or selling similar works of art (preferably by the same artist) this should be established. If there is a history of one or more past sales of the very picture which is the subject of litigation, this past history should be proved.[82]

Past or current sales prices of works by the same artist are admissible, but not necessarily of controlling importance because the same artist may have painted in different "periods" of his development and it may well be brought out that the market for his paintings is higher or lower depending upon the period when he produced them. Furthermore, even a great artist does not necessarily produce only good pictures. Therefore, it may be established through the expert's knowledge that some of the works of this artist bring higher prices than others. Indeed, a certain species of snob appeal attaches to some pictures because, at one time or another, they were in the collection of a famous personage. It must be remembered, in this connection, that the question of market value is not necessarily confined to the intrinsic quality of the work of art.

The fact that a given work of art attributed to a particular artist is established to be a counterfeit, forgery or copy does not, by any means, have to result in a determination that the copy is worthless. The expert may well testify that, even though the picture in litigation is not an original, it nevertheless has substantial value either because the artist who produced it is, himself, a well-known painter, or an apprentice of the famous painter, or because the picture, itself, is a fine work of art.

It seems to be the general public belief that cases involving authenticity or the value of paintings and other works of art are confined to situations where someone is seeking to recover because a false product was foisted upon him or where a prospective buyer

---

[82] If the last sale took place a substantial time before the trial, there should be testimony as to the variance in prices between that last sale and the time of the trial.

refuses to go through with a purchase because the picture is not what it was claimed to be at the time the sales agreement was made. There are, however, two additional subjects of litigation which should be noted. They are suits to recover insurance after the partial or total destruction or mutilation of a work of art and cases involving taxation (such as the value to be set in inheritance tax proceedings and the value to be determined when a work of art is donated to a tax-exempt organization and the value of that work of art is attempted to be set up as a deduction from taxable income).

Sec. 9:14   Real estate experts.

The real estate expert is called, primarily, to testify to the value of land and buildings. Ordinarily, such an expert is either a real estate operator, a real estate broker, a city assessor or a master builder. At times, one type of expert is called to testify to the value of land and another to the value of a building; but it is more usual for a single expert to render his opinion on both factors.

> "The opinions of experts as to the value of lands and rentals, and of the rise and depreciation thereof, when such witnesses have a practical knowledge of the neighborhood and its surroundings, founded on actual experience and observation, are, as a rule, competent evidence as to such matters, and often the only attainable proof of the fact. . . . Though not of a conclusive character, such evidence, if satisfactory, at times furnishes a safe and reliable guide which would be unsafe to dispense with. A defendant can always protect himself against any danger arising from it by furnishing, in answer thereto, evidence of the same general character." [83]

To qualify the real estate expert, it should be shown: (a) that he is active in the real estate market in which the subject premises are located (or, in the case of a master builder, that he is familiar with the method and cost of producing construction similar to that in the case at bar); (b) that he has access to comparative prices for prop-

---

[83] *Butler v. Manhattan Ry. Co.*, 3 Misc. 453, 23 N.Y. Supp. 163, 169, a case involving the opinions of experts as to the depreciation in value of property when an elevated railroad was built along a street on which the property abutted. See, also, *Hunter v. M. R. Co. et al.*, 141 N.Y. 281, 287, involving the same type of situation.

erties similar to the one under consideration; and (c) that, where applicable, he has knowledge of rental values for properties similar to the one involved in the case at bar (or, indeed, in the same building).[84]

It is the rule that the real estate expert must have personally actually seen the premises concerning which he is giving a value opinion. The details of his inspection of the premises should be set forth early in his testimony.

The value of the land and the value of the building are separate matters and should be individually treated. While it is true that, where land is improved, ordinary purchasers or sellers would base their estimates on the entire parcel (land *and* building), statutes or constitutional provisions in some jurisdictions require that land value and building value be separately stated where an award is made in a condemnation proceeding or values are fixed for tax assessment purposes.[85] An important factor may be whether the improvement constitutes the best possible use of the land. Here, an expert should be shown to have so extensive a knowledge of the neighborhood and surrounding area that he can express an opinion on this subject.

In general, there are three methods of valuation: (a) comparative sales, which apply to land, only; (b) the cost of reproducing the building, new, less depreciation, which, obviously, can only apply to fixing the value of the building; and (c) economic valuation.

The comparative sales method requires the production by the expert of sales prices of similar properties. He will be permitted to testify, where the properties are in different locations, or where other variations appear, that the differentiating factors have been considered and applied by him in expressing his opinion of the value of the subject premises. He must be shown to have had experience which would enable him to apply the differentiating factors. For example, he may testify that one parcel of land, although near the subject premises, is in a more desirable neighborhood, or has better transit facilities, or is in such a busy portion of the city that stores

---

[84] In some situations, the expert is called upon to testify about trends in prices or rental values over a period of time. Here, it is one of his qualifications that he has a sound basis for "trending"; but this need not be separately proved if his evidence establishes trends of purchase or rental values.

[85] In some jurisdictions there are constitutional or statutory provisions that the land must be valued as though vacant and unimproved, despite the fact that a structure is erected thereon.

erected thereon will rent at a higher amount because more people would pass the building at various times of the day. The general criterion covering the establishment of comparative prices as a guide to fixing valuation is that these prices, coupled with the explanations given by the expert, will enable the fact-finder to fix a value for the subject land better than he could have done without the production of comparative sales.

Attempts have been made to apply comparative sales to buildings as well as land; but the variations between two buildings are so great that this method has been almost universally rejected. It would seem, at first blush, that a recent sale of the building whose value is at bar is the best proof of its present value. However, this is not always true, because there may have been special matters involved when the sale was made. For example, the sale may have been part of a group of simultaneous transactions and the sales prices put on these particular premises may have had slight relation to their value. Likewise, if there was a sale and a lease-back, the court may very well determine that this was merely a financial transaction (undertaken for tax or other non-real estate considerations).[86] Also, there are situations where, in order to wind up an estate, property is sold at less than its true value.

The determination of the value of a building may be proved by one of two methods: first, the cost of reproducing such a building, new, less the application to that cost of depreciation; second, the so-called "economic method", which requires the capitalization of *net* rental. If the economic value of the structure is less than the reconstruction cost less depreciation, it has been authoritatively stated that economic value governs and must be adopted for purposes of assessment.[87]

A master builder (such as the prime contractor in erecting buildings of the type whose value is at bar) is the best kind of witness for expressing his opinion as to the cost of reconstruction. He should be carefully qualified to show not only his experience in building, but also his knowledge of the cost of materials, labor and other factors. His testimony should set forth every item that would be required to reproduce the building in question. Very often the actual cost of

---

[86] *Peo. ex rel. 100 E. 57th Street Corporation v. Chambers*, N.Y.L.J. May 10, 1951, 281 App. Div. 815, 2 App. Div. 2d 965.
[87] *Peo. ex rel. Parklin Operating Corporation v. Miller*, 287 N.Y. 126, 141; *Peo. ex rel. Luce v. Lewis*, 257 App. Div. 724, 15 N.Y. Supp. 2d 180.

erecting the building in question is important. If the master builder is of the opinion that this cost was excessive due to uneconomical procedures, he may so testify.

An expert witness who testifies to the "economic value" of the building should be qualified by establishing his familiarity with rentals in similar buildings. An active real estate broker, who specializes in renting space, is the prime type of witness in this situation.

In the first instance, the witness as to economic value should produce the actual rent roll of the premises.[88] Then, he should produce the expenses for running the building. It would seem that subtracting the latter figure from the former would conclusively prove net rentals. However, either or both of two variations may appear: (a) the actual rentals charged may be considerably more or less than true rental value; and (b) the cost of running the building may be excessive. In the former case, the witness can testify, basing his testimony on data produced by him, what the true rental value should be. In the latter, the witness should be prepared to state in detail the amounts by which the maintenance figures exceed normal requirements.[89]

Data used by a witness to show a variance between actual rent roll figures and true rental value generally consists of proof of rentals charged for similar premises in the immediate neighborhood of the building whose value is in question or in a neighborhood so closely comparable that the figures are acceptable.

After net rentals have been established, the next question to be considered is what figure should be used to capitalize these net rentals in arriving at the value of a building. Basically, this question is best answered by testimony from an expert as to the figure which individuals purchasing properties of this sort would use as a multiplier applied to net rentals in determining their willingness to pay a given price. But this is not the only method. Recent decisions of courts, wherein, on similar edifices, a capitalization rate has been determined are helpful. The expert witness should be prepared to refer to such decisions in the course of his testimony.

The question has arisen whether offers to purchase property are

---

[88] A rather special situation arises where the owner of the building occupies space therein. Here, the question whether the owner is charging himself a proper rental is important.

[89] It may be necessary to produce a special witness to testify, in detail, about what would be proper maintenance charges.

admissible as some proof of the value of that property. The great weight of authority is against the admissibility of this evidence and the few cases which seem to permit it are easily differentiatable on the basis of their particular facts.[90]

There are some cases other than condemnation and tax proceedings in which real estate expert witnesses are used. However, in the last analysis their employment generally touches questions of value. Examples are computations involving damages by reason of injury to real property, where opinion evidence may be introduced as to the respective values before and after the injury to the property, and a holdover proceeding wherein the proper rental value of the property held over is an appropriate subject for opinion evidence. A master builder may, of course, render his opinion about whether an edifice was properly constructed.

Sec. 9:15   Businessmen and other witnesses as to trade customs.

Where, without the help of a person engaged in a particular business or trade, it would be difficult for a fact-finder to determine certain matters, evidence from such persons may be received. The criteria for receiving this testimony are two-fold: (a) could an ordinary fact-finder be expected to know the subject-matter of the testimony without aid; and (b) does the witness have a peculiar knowledge that can assist the fact-finder. Whether or not this type of witness is technically an "expert" is unimportant.

In order for a witness to be permitted to testify about customs or usages, it must be shown that he has been engaged in the applicable trade or profession for a considerable time, that he is familiar with its customs and usages and that he has had actual *experience* in the application of those customs and usages. Beyond this general statement, it is almost impossible to indicate the qualifications required of such a witness.

When properly qualified, one connected with a particular business may testify as to methods of conducting that business, general usages with regard to the same and usages peculiar to a given business community, standards of doing business and inferences from facts observed by him as to technical matters which would not be familiar to those outside his special calling.

---

[90] *Sharp v. United States*, 191 U.S. 341, 348–350.

There is a narrow line between that to which an expert of this type can testify and that of which the court will take judicial notice. For example, a court may presume that a signature upon a letter sent in answer to another letter was authorized by the responder or that the seal of a corporation was, itself, a duly authorized seal. These are presumptions of law. The court may assume that a businessman will give credit to a solvent principal rather than to an irresponsible agent. This is a presumption of fact. However, although the court may assume that customary methods of business were followed in a given transaction, it may be necessary to have testimony as to what those customary methods were.

A very usual type of proof as to custom and usage is found in cases where a written contract or memorandum contains words or terms that are ambiguous. Here, a person familiar with the use of that term in a given business may state what it would ordinarily mean to other persons engaged in that business.

With the increasing complexity of business over the past half century and the concomitant wide spread ownership through publicly-held corporations, the value of corporate shares and of the assets of corporations has become a matter of increasing interest. Many litigations turn on the conclusions of experts in this regard. Auditors and accountants are now used for more than a mere recital of accounting practices. Their judgment as to methods of accounting is often important. By the same token, the opinion of businessmen about the value of inventories may well be sought. In either case, the witness should be qualified to establish not only his general knowledge of a business but his particular knowledge respecting the operations of the corporation whose value is at stake in the litigation.

It should be noted that, in some jurisdictions, the testimony of a certified public accountant is given greater weight than that of an ordinary accountant. It may also be borne in mind that, under certain circumstances, the testimony of a mere bookkeeper is superior to that of an outside accountant, since the bookkeeper is in a position to state the precise methods used in the individual business for the maintenance of its records.

Sec. 9:16 Experts on foreign law.

Some statutes require a court to take judicial notice of foreign law, but it is unreasonable to assume that a court will know the law of all jurisdictions without help from counsel.[91] This help is furnished in various ways, one of which is the calling of an expert in foreign law. Where no such statute exists, foreign law must be proved.

Strange as it may seem, what the foreign law *is* is a matter of *fact*. Assuming that a principle of law has been settled in a foreign jurisdiction, there should be no dispute about what that principle is.[92] If the principle has not been settled that also is a fact, which can be simply stated and possibly embellished by further testimony about what the divergencies of foreign courts are.

An expert on foreign law is, preferably, a lawyer who has practiced in the foreign jurisdiction. But, through reading and research, one can make himself an expert on foreign law without having practiced and, in some instances, courts have accepted the testimony of such a self-created expert.

If the question at bar involves a foreign statute, the best method of proving the contents of that statute is to present an authenticated copy thereof.[93] Where the statute is in a foreign language, a witness must be produced who can testify to his familiarity with that language and can translate the statute. In some cases, the courts have accepted a certified translation. It is essential that the foreign law expert be prepared to testify that the copy of the statute produced for the court is the latest statute on the subject (or the statute that was in effect when the matters involved in the litigation took place).

A more difficult matter is presented where decisional law of a foreign jurisdiction is in question. Many courts refuse to accept a statement of foreign law based on decisions unless those decisions are of the highest court of the foreign jurisdiction. In any event, the expert must be prepared not only to cite (and, if necessary, translate) the foreign decision, but to differentiate other decisions and to fully acquaint the trial court with all applicable decisional law on the subject.

Sec. 9:17   Method of examination of experts.

In the course of the examination of an ordinary witness, counsel should try to establish an easy type of conversation between him

---

[91] See section 2:7, *supra*, which discusses the preparation for producing proof of foreign law where the court is required to take judicial notice thereof.

[92] Reference to "foreign law," as used herein, means the law of any jurisdiction outside the trial forum.

[93] For the method of authentication, see section 11:9, *post*.

and the witness, through which the witness is enabled to tell his story in a natural way and the questions act solely as a guide to the order in which the story is related.

An entirely different situation is presented in the case of an expert witness. Here, the witness, if he is indeed an expert, has the type of knowledge which, in its particular field, surpasses that of both the fact-finder and the questioning attorney. The expert is not merely (and sometimes not at all) stating his observations. He is giving a professional opinion. It is this opinion upon which counsel is asking the fact-finder to rely. In questioning an expert witness, counsel must attempt to impress the jury with the fact that the superior knowledge of this witness is so important that the approach to his testimony requires a special type of consideration. There is nothing light about this process. The keynote is the utmost seriousness and the approach of counsel to his own witness should be almost diffident.

The questioning of an ordinary witness, when appropriate, can sometimes be lightened by a semi-humorous approach to some matters. This is *never* true when examining an expert. At no time should the fact-finder be permitted to forget that the expert witness is in a special class and is entitled to a unique type of respect.

In section 9:6, *supra*, we have discussed special preparation for direct examination of expert witnesses and in section 9:3, *supra*, has been covered the form of expert testimony. Each of the propositions therein referred to finds reflection in the method of examining such witnesses and need not be repeated here.

It cannot be too strongly emphasized that the whole ultimate effect of the testimony of an expert may depend on the impression created by his introduction to the fact-finder.[94] The impression must be created that the expert witness is one of such skill and experience that his opinions can be depended upon and that his knowledge of the facts of the case at bar are sufficiently precise so that he is not testifying in a vacuum.

Counsel should let the witness do the testifying and, no matter how great the temptation, should avoid leading questions. Although it is true that in the direct examination of an expert it is a safeguard for counsel to have written out his questions in advance,[95] it will probably be helpful, from time to time, to interject side material in order to prevent boring the fact-finder. Great care should be taken,

---

[94] As to the method of establishing qualifications of expert witnesses, see section 9:7, *supra*.

[95] For a discussion of the reasons for this safeguard, see section 9:6, *supra*.

however, that the introduction of this additional material does not in any manner weaken, modify or change the expert's basic testimony.

Experts sometimes have a tendency to speak in technical terms beyond the comprehension of laymen not skilled in their disciplines. It is an important function of counsel to be sure that the fact-finder understands precisely what the witness is talking about. Therefore, counsel may interrupt the expert's testimony by asking him what a certain term used by him means in lay language. This should *never* be done in a sarcastic or humorous vein and, even if the process has to be repeated, counsel should avoid any sign of irritation. The worst mistake counsel can make is to cause antagonism on the part of the witness or in the mind of the fact-finder. An expert witness may be difficult to handle but the difficulty should be overcome in a friendly way.

The order of calling experts is sometimes of great importance. Obviously, if one expert is to render an opinion derived from an earlier opinion by another expert[96] the earlier opinion must be introduced, first, in order to lay a basis for the latter. Where several experts are to be called on the same subject, opinions differ as to whether the more interesting expert should be called first or last. There can be no fixed rule, here. However, it is better to call only one interesting expert than to dilute the impression made by him through the interrogation of a pedantic and dull other expert.

As a general rule, an expert should never be the last witness. If it becomes necessary to call an expert at the end of one's case, it is wise to use a hypothetical question in interrogating this witness, since it gives counsel an opportunity to sum up his case.

Sec. 9:18   The unwilling expert.

It is not always possible for counsel to get an expert witness who is willing to testify. Particularly is this true in cases involving professional malpractice or negligence. Obviously, no professional man takes pleasure in asserting that one of his fellow professionals has caused injury by being careless. Furthermore, there seems to be an unholy conspiracy, particularly among physicians, to refuse to testify against their brethren.

In some jurisdictions an attempt has been made to ameliorate this difficulty by the voluntary action of courts, lawyers, bar associations

---

[96] See section 9:10, *supra.*

and medical societies; but, to put it mildly, none of these efforts has been crowned with outstanding success.

The unfortunate result is that, in order to establish a prima facie case under some circumstances, counsel is compelled to bring an unwilling expert witness to the stand and to try to force a situation where that witness will act as an expert for his side. There is no uniform formula for success in this endeavor. At best, it is a hit and miss attempt, born of the direst necessity.

The only general rule that can be stated is that counsel should try to get enough expert testimony into the record so that he can reduce the case to the determination of a question of *fact*.

In a typical case involving an unwilling expert, we have a situation where it is necessary to establish that a given course of conduct would, reasonably probably, result in an actionable injury. An expert can be called as a hostile witness and, by questioning him with the aid of the latest and most authoritative texts on the subject, it can be shown that certain professional actions are improper, careless or unskillful. This showing is made in the absence of any direct reference to the facts in the case at bar and the court is asked to accept it subject to connection. Then, having proved the scientific principle, the evidence in the case can show that the defendant was guilty of the very conduct condemned by the expert.

One must not be deceived into believing that the foregoing procedure is easy of accomplishment. It requires great skill, based upon counsel's completely mastering the technical matters presented so that he can prevent the expert from escaping conclusions by some such convenient statement as that the matter in question is not established with scientific certainty.

Another method used where a willing expert is not available is to place the defendant, himself, on the witness stand and get him to commit himself about the proper scientific procedures. This is somewhat easier if the defendant has done any writing on the subject. He can be confronted with his own writings and forced to admit either that he falsely stated correct procedures in his published work or that the things done by him in the case at bar were careless or negligent.

The utility of examinations before trial is often debated by experienced trial lawyers. However, there can be little doubt that, in a malpractice case, the defendant physician or other professional should be carefully examined in advance of trial so that he cannot escape the results of his misdeeds through a change of mind in the light of expert testimony. When a defendant is so examined, he has no way of knowing that an expert witness is not available to the examiner. Therefore, he is liable to admit that certain types of procedures would be careless or negligent, since his failure so to admit might establish him as an unfit professional.

When counsel calls an unwilling expert witness, the best he can hope for is that this witness will state scientific principles, even though he couples his statements with hedging commentary. If counsel can succeed in reducing the sum total of the expert's testimony to the proposition that *if* certain facts were established these facts would prove carelessness or negligence, he has narrowed the entire matter at bar to a question of *fact*. If he can then establish as a *fact* the underlying premise of the expert's conclusions, he has proved a prima facie case in this respect. The fact-finder will then be free to disregard the hedging statements of the expert and apply the principles enunciated by him to the facts established.

It has been recognized by all trial attorneys in the field that, if severe injury to a plaintiff is shown, the fact-finder will be anxious to reach a determination in the plaintiff's favor. If the one thing that would block such a determination is the failure of expert testimony, it is obvious that such testimony must be produced. In the light of the fact that many situations arise in which a willing expert cannot be put on the stand, courts have, to a great degree, accepted as sufficient a relatively slight amount of favorable expert proof. Indeed, the tendency of modern decisions is to minimize the necessity for expert testimony. For example, where it is shown that a plaintiff has sustained a severe injury and that, between the time of the alleged negligence and the time the case is reached for trial the plaintiff is still unable fully to use one of his limbs, the court will permit counsel to argue that the injury is permanent, even though expert testimony to that effect is unavailable.

If there is one rule which can be stated without qualification in regard to the calling of unwilling experts, it is that only *one* such expert should be produced. Otherwise, there is the danger that multiple unwilling experts may minimize or destroy the compelled conclusions of others.

In some cases, where a motion to dismiss is made at the close of the plaintiff's case, the judge reserves decision on that motion. This may necessitate the defendant's calling of an expert witness in his own behalf. Such a witness can, through cross-examination, be turned into an expert on behalf of the plaintiff. The circumstance is so fortuitous that reliance can hardly be placed upon it.

Chapter X

MISCELLANEOUS TECHNICAL PROOF

Sec. 10:1 Establishing competency of evidence by technical proof.

The evidence used, substantively, to prove a cause of action or defense is often inadmissible in its available form without *preliminary* proof to establish its *competency*. A copy of a letter, for example, is inadmissible without proof that the original was actually mailed, or received, or answered. Similarly, a telephone conversation is inadmissible without proof of the actual *knowledge* of the person testifying to it that he was speaking to the very person alleged to have been a party to the conversation.

The present chapter is devoted to the types of proof, in common situations, necessary to establish competency of substantive evidence.

We are not here referring to the elements of proof necessary to establish prima facie cases or defenses. These are matters of sub-

stantive law peculiar to individual situations.[1] What is here covered
is the purely technical proof, common to the trial of most cases, and
necessary to establish competency of *other* proof.

Sec. 10:2   Requesting court to take judicial notice.

In section 2:7, *supra,* discussing preparation for inviting judicial
notice, we have set forth the principles of law governing whether or
not foreign law must be pleaded and proved. As therein appears,
some statutes *require* courts to take judicial notice of the law of other
jurisdictions and some of the cases make a distinction between the
law of another state and the law of a foreign country.

Of course, where foreign law is required to be pleaded, it should
be proved during the course of the trial either through the production of an expert witness or by means of one of the appropriate
statutory aids to proof.[2] In situations where the pleading and proof
of foreign law is not required, the attention of the court is ordinarily
drawn to the applicable foreign law by a trial or post-trial memorandum.

It should be remembered, however, that trial memoranda are not
part of the record. Therefore, it is appropriate that a statement of
counsel should be made *on the record* of the principles of foreign
law of which he desires the court to take judicial notice. This need
not be a lengthy dissertation on the foreign law, but it should be
sufficiently detailed so that there can be no doubt that the matter
was called to the attention of the trial judge.

It has been suggested by some trial counsel that the reference on
the record to foreign law should be very brief, because the setting
forth of details may inadvertently eliminate some matters and act
as a quasi admission that the material not set forth is deemed by
counsel unnecessary to the decision of the case. How to present the
subject must be dictated by the circumstances of the case being
tried. For example, in some instances, it will serve the necessary
purpose by simply referring to section numbers of a foreign statute.
In others, where decisional law is depended upon, it is wiser not
to cite the cases on the record, but to refer to the principle involved

---

[1] For full coverage of these substantive questions, see Spellman, *How to
Prove a Prima Facie Case* (Third Edition, 1954), pp. 11–605, and Spellman,
How to Prove a Prima Facie Defense (Second printing, 1947), pp. 13–507.
[2] See, for example, as to means of making such proof, sections 11:8, 11:9
and general discussion in Chapter XI, *post.*

and to state on the record that the matter has been or will be covered in a brief.

Where a question of foreign law arises in a case tried to a jury, the requests to charge should encompass the matters of foreign law, but *not as such*. It is the *court* which takes judicial notice. The court's determination as to foreign law, the same as its determination as to local law, is given to the jury as a principle which the jurymen are obliged to follow. Reading the text of foreign statutes or decisions to a jury is confusing and has often been held to be error. Counsel should not, by his request to charge, lead the court into such error.

Situations may arise in a particular case where a court is asked to take judicial notice of something other than foreign law. The general rule about judicial notice is that the court is required to judicially note matters of common knowledge, shared in by the community as a whole; for example, the fact that in a certain city the numbered streets run from south to north.

There are other matters which are not of common knowledge and, both technically and as a matter of common sense, no court should be required to judicially know. Here, proof is required. It is wrong, for example, to ask a court to judicially note that on a certain remote date it was raining in the morning and clear in the afternoon. On the other hand, weather conditions on the day of trial or on one or two days prior thereto are the subject of a reasonable request that the court take judicial notice thereof.

An interesting facet of the "common knowledge" rule is that a court will take judicial notice of its *own* record of the case before it and *also of all cases in its own files* involving the same or other parties, but will *not* take judicial notice of proceedings in *other* courts. "Formal proof is required and, as such, the records in the other court must be introduced as evidence." [3]

To summarize the method of requesting a court to take judicial notice, the following four principles state the proposition: (a) counsel should specifically request the court to take judicial notice either of a principle of foreign law or a fact of common knowledge; (b) the court should be asked to state for the record whether or not he is taking such judicial notice; (c) if the court grants the request only in part or refuses it altogether, an exception should be taken on the record even in those jurisdictions which do not require exceptions to preserve a point of law; and (d) if the court grants the request in

---

[3] *Berger v. Dynamic Imports*, 51 Misc. 2d 988, 989 [New York].

part and either denies the balance or fails to cover the balance, the exception should specifically indicate what part of the court's ruling is objected to.

Sec. 10:3   Circumstantial evidence.

There is a difference between the nature of the ordinary proof employed to establish the competency of some other evidence and the nature of circumstantial evidence.

Circumstantial evidence has as its purpose the setting up of a factual situation from which the trier of the facts is enabled to draw an inference of fact. There may be a question of law as to whether the circumstantial evidence is sufficient to create a prima facie case. In other words, whether, as a matter of law, the circumstances established are sufficiently clear so that the trier of the facts is enabled to draw a fair and reasonable conclusion.

A classic example of this type of situation is found in wrongful death actions, where no direct witnesses are available to establish the manner in which an accident occurred, but where circumstantial evidence is relied on. A leading decision in the New York Court of Appeals discusses the factors involved in such a case as follows: [4]

> "The accident being unwitnessed, the proof, of necessity, must rely upon circumstantial evidence. In a case such as this the law recognizes that plaintiff will have to establish fault by a showing of various circumstances from which a jury can draw fair and reasonable conclusions. Moreover, in a death case plaintiff is not held to as high a degree of proof of the cause of action as where an injured plaintiff can himself describe the occurrence. (*Cole* v. *Swagler*, 308 N.Y. 325; *Noseworthy* v. *City of New York*, 298 N.Y. 76.) Plaintiffs' evidence is deemed sufficient to make out a prima facie case if it shows facts and conditions from which the negligence of the defendant and the causation of the accident by that negligence may be reasonably inferred. (*Dillon* v. *Rockaway Beach Hosp.*, 284 N.Y. 176; *Ingersoll* v. *Liberty Bank of Buffalo*, 278 N.Y. 1.) . . .
> "The circumstantial evidence offered by plaintiffs need not exclude all other possible causes of the accident. (*Dillon* and *Ingersoll*, both *supra*.) On the evidence produced, viewing it in

---

[4] *Wragge v. Lizza Asphalt Constr. Co.*, 17 N.Y. 2d 313, 320, 321.

a light favorable to plaintiffs, it was more reasonable that the accident was caused by the ice—that the decedents suffered an experience similar to that of the garage employee earlier in the evening but with greater consequence—than that the accident was caused by an oncoming or passing car or some other happening which may have caused the driver to lose control of the automobile. The task of weighing and evaluating the evidence belonged to the jury and the court below erred in overruling the verdict of the jury. Plaintiffs made out a sufficient prima facie case and were entitled to a submission of the case to the jury."

The presentation of circumstantial evidence entails an infinitely more difficult *practical* problem than merely producing a prima facie case. Here, we are asking the trier of the fact to reach a verdict without any *direct* proof of a happening. We do not have a case which can be simply resolved by a determination as to credibility of conflicting witnesses. With *no* witness to the actual happening, we are asking the fact-finder to reach a conclusion as to *probability*.

Where a case is based on circumstantial evidence *every* circumstance which may lead to a favorable conclusion should be presented. It may be necessary to throw caution to the winds and to call weak witnesses. The important thing to remember is that the fact-finder must be convinced without the use of *any* eye-witness testimony.

Evidence of surrounding circumstances may be used to buttress direct evidence. Technically, such proof is not circumstantial evidence, since there are direct eye-witnesses. However, where such proof of surrounding circumstances is available, it should be brought out with the same fulsomeness as technically circumstantial evidence, particularly when the evidence of surrounding circumstances is used to support or buttress the testimony of a weak witness.

Sec. 10:4 Proof of agency.

The acts done, the words spoken, the letters written, or admissions made in whatever form by an authorized agent within the scope of his agency and within the issues of a litigation are clearly admissible in evidence as a matter of substantive law. However, agency must be established as a prerequisite to the ultimate admissibility of this proof.

The three most common methods of establishing such agency are:

(a) By an admission of the principal (either through advance authorization or subsequent approval or ratification);[5]

(b) By establishing a course of dealing from which the inference may be drawn that a given person was the authorized agent of another;[6] and

(c) By proof that the person sought to be charged was the undisclosed principal of the actor, whose agency is sought to be established.[7]

One general principle must be borne in mind: declarations made by the alleged agent outside of court cannot, in and of themselves, establish agency; but the *testimony* of the agent during the course of the trial can prove such agency.[8] This does not mean that acts of the agent cannot be used as a basis for establishing a course of dealing which could reasonably lead to an inference of agency.

---

[5] *Dothan Grocery Co. v. Pilcher*, 200 Ala. 151; *Strumpf v. State*, 31 Ala. App. 409; *Bazemore v. A. B. Small Co.*, 9 Ga. App. 29; *Davis v. Metropolitan Life Ins. Co.*, 196 Ga. 304; *Ballard v. Ballard*, 226 Iowa 699; *D'Armour v. Beeson Hardware Co.*, 217 N.C. 568; *Ellenberg v. Fremont Land Co.*, 165 Or. 375; *Hearn v. Hanlon-Buchannan Inc.*, (Tex., 1944) 179 S.W. (2d.) 364; *Stouffer-Bowman, Inc. v. Webber*, 18 Wash. (2d.) 416.

[6] *Kent v. Addicks*, (C.C.A., Pa., 1903) 126 Fed. 112; *Shama v. U.S.*, (C.C.A., Iowa, 1938) 94 Fed. (2d.) 1; *Colley v. Atlanta Brewing & Ice Co.*, 196 Ala. 374; *Syar v. U.S. Fidelity & Guaranty Co.*, 51 Cal. App. (2d.) 527; *Rhodes v. Industrial Commission*, 99 Colo. 271; *Coe v. Kutinsky, Adler & Co.*, 82 Conn. 685; *Lawhon v. Henshaw*, 63 Ga. App. 683; *Fredrich v. Wolf*, 383 Ill. 638; *Morehead v. Murray*, 31 Ind. 418; *Cumnock-Reed Co. v. Lewis*, 278 Ky. 496; *Culver v. Nichols*, 140 Md. 448; *Eisenberg v. Matthew*, 84 Minn. 76; *Barr v. Howe*, (Mo., 1943) 166 S.W. (2d.) 244; *Standley v. Clay, Robinson & Co.*, 68 Neb. 332; *Young v. Anthony*, (N.Y., 1907) 119 App. Div. 612; *Del Piccolo v. Newburger*, (N.Y., 1939) 9 N.Y. Supp. (2d.) 512; *D'Armour v. Beeson Hardware Co.*, 217 N.C. 568; *Georgia State Sav. Ass'n of Savannah, Ga. v. Elias*, 192 Okl. 227; *City of Greenville v. Washington American League Baseball Club*, 205 S.C. 495; *Pullman-Palace-Car Co. v. Nelson*, 22 Tex. Civ. App. 223; *Holbrook v. J. J. Quinlan & Co.*, 84 Vt. 411; *Cooper v. Farmers' & Merchants' Bank of Wenatchee*, 68 Wash. 310; *Domasek v. Kluck*, 113 Wis. 336.

[7] *Ferguson v. Huddleston*, 208 Ark. 353; *Marr v. Postal Union Life Ins. Co.*, 40 Cal. App. (2d.) 673; *McCabe v. Williams*, (Del., 1946) 45 A. (2d.) 503; *Byers v. Harper*, 64 Ga. App. 404; *Klassie v. Holt*, 233 Iowa 826; *Unruh v. Roemer*, 135 Minn. 127; *Yates v. Repetto*, 65 N.J. Law 294; *Raymond Commerce Corp. v. Warner*, 16 N.J. Misc. 548; *Foote v. De Bogory*, (Tex., 1944) 179 S.W. (2d.) 983.

[8] *Steuerwald v. Jackson*, 123 App. Div. 569 [New York]. See, also, 2 *Greenleaf on Evidence* (15th ed.), sec. 63.

For example, in a leading case involving automobile negligence, it was held error for the court to refuse proof that the person who was driving the truck which ran down the plaintiff had, on that very day, used the truck to make multiple deliveries on behalf of the defendant.[9]

Another salutary rule is that one who takes the proceeds of a transaction is estopped from denying the agency of the person through whose intermediacy he obtained such proceeds.[10]

The method by which agency is established varies with the facts of each case.[11] However, unless direct appointment of the agent can be shown either by a written document (such as the authority of the agent to collect rents in a lease) or by a specific admission by the principal (for example, by his having introduced the person in question as his agent), care should be taken to introduce *all* available evidence to establish agency. Although not technically so denominated, the introduction of extraneous evidence to establish agency is very similar to the uses of circumstantial evidence as more fully discussed in section 10:3, *supra.*

Where it is sought to prove that one person was the undisclosed principal of another, it is often fairly simple to get the alleged agent to testify that he was, in fact, merely an agent; because, unless such testimony is available, the agent might find himself in a position where he, personally, could be charged as the principal and thus become liable to plaintiff's claims.

The fact of agency is rarely pleaded, as such. A complaint ordinarily states the ultimate fact that a principal has done certain acts. Sometimes, this allegation is enlarged by a phrase to the effect that the defendant acted "through his agents, servants and employees." The same observations apply, of course, to allegations in a counter-claim or separate defense.

A denial in an answer that a principal acted as complained of

---

[9] *Thiry v. Taylor Brewing & Malting Co.*, 37 App. Div. 391 [New York], also holding that although single circumstances might not, if separately considered, be sufficient to establish agency, a series of such circumstances, taken together, might prove a course of conduct demonstrating agency and that plaintiff was entitled to prove each of the elements making up the course of conduct.

[10] *Adams v. Irving National Bank*, 116 N.Y. 606. See, also, *Krumm v. Beach*, 96 N.Y. 398.

[11] For the types of questions that are asked in each situation, see Spellman, *How to Prove a Prima Facie Case* (3rd ed.), pp. 609 (admission of principal), 611 (course of dealing) and 614–615 (undisclosed principal).

may mean that the charged principal is, in fact, denying that a person acted as his agent. Therefore, whenever it is claimed that a principal is liable for the acts of an agent, it is essential that agency be proved. Counsel should be alert to the possibility that a mere denial is not intended solely to put in issue the ultimate allegation of fact, but may have the hidden danger of denying agency.

Sec. 10:5   Mailing of letter or notice.

If a letter or notice has been mailed, its substantive effect is determined by the law of the particular case in which it is sought to be introduced in evidence. This effect may vary from jurisdiction to jurisdiction. For example, some courts hold that the mailing of a letter accepting an offer operates as an acceptance whether or not the letter is received by the offerer. Others hold that the acceptance letter must be received before the offer and acceptance merge to form a binding contract.

Statutes providing for a type of service by mail operate on the presumption that the letter or notice (or even summons) was, in fact, mailed as prescribed by the statute. However, in order for such a statute or principle of law to take effect, there must be actual proof that the mailing, itself, was accomplished.

The three items which complete proof of mailing are:

    (a) That the letter or notice was actually mailed;

    (b) That the address to which the letter was sent was correct; and

    (c) That the copy of the letter or notice offered in evidence is a true copy of the original, as mailed.[12]

---

[12] *Swinehart Tire & Rubber Co. v. William Whitman Co.*, (C.C.A., Ohio, 1920) 266 Fed. 45; *Franklin Life Ins. Co. v. Brantley*, 231 Ala. 554; *Cady v. Guess*, 197 Ark. 611; *Schneider v. Oakman Consol. Mining Co.*, 38 Cal. App. 338; *First Nat. Bank of Denver v. Henning*, 112 Colo. 523; *Womack v. U.S. Fidelity & Guaranty Co.*, 85 Ga. App. 564; *Alger v. Community Amusements Corp.*, 320 Ill. App. 184; *Glaser v. Williamsburg City Fire Ins. Co.*, 72 Ind. App. 319; *DeBolt v. German-American Ins. Co.*, 181 Iowa 671; *Shriver v. Union Stockyards Nat. Bank*, 117 Kan. 638; *Home Ins. Co. of New York v. Roll*, 187 Ky. 31; *Gulf Refining Co. v. Bagby*, 200 La. 258; *McFerren v. Goldsmith-Stern Co.*, 137 Md. 573; *Anderson v. Inhabitants of Town of Billerica*, 309 Mass. 516; *Long Bell Lumber Co. v. Nyman*, 145 Mich. 477; *Outcault Advertising Co. v. Farmers' & Merchants' State Bank of Greenbush*, 151 Minn. 500; *Senaca Co. v. Ellison*, 203 Mo. App. 179; *W. J. Lake Co. v.*

The mailing of a letter or notice properly directed to the party to be charged raises a common-law presumption that the letter or notice was received; but this is a presumption of fact and not of law and may be repelled by proof.[13] Although it has been stated that, even if the letter is misdirected, the fact that it was received may act as adequate statutory notice,[14] this begs the question now under discussion. We are now considering *how* proof of mailing is established irrespective of whether there is proof of receipt. Isolated dicta should not be considered sufficient to overcome the general rule, which is as stated above.

Obviously, the best method of proving that a letter was properly mailed is to produce the person who mailed it and to have him testify when and where he mailed it, that there was sufficient postage on the envelope, that it was addressed to the correct address and that the copy which he produces was compared by him with the original at the time of mailing and is a correct copy.[15]

But the simple proof just outlined is often not available. Several alternative methods of proof are acceptable. These are either directly involved in or are analogous to the rules with respect to entries kept in the regular course of business.[16] The exigencies of an individual case may suggest numerous types of presentation. The following are common examples:

(a) A log-book for outgoing mail is kept in the regular course of business, which indicates the date on which letters are mailed, the addressees, the amount of postage and the

---

Montana Horse Products Co., 109 Mont. 434; *City of Omaha v. Yancey,* 91 Neb. 261; *Whelton v. Daly,* 93 N.H. 150; *New York Cent. R. Co. v. Petrozzo,* 92 N.J. Law 425; *Curry v. MacKenzie,* 239 N.Y. 267; *Dulberg v. Equitable Life Assur. Soc. of U.S.,* 277 N.Y. 17; *Carden v. Sons and Daughters of Liberty,* 179 N.C. 399; *Kuale v. Keane,* 39 N.D. 560; *Miller v. Penwell,* 112 Okl. 163; *Coffey v. Northwestern Hospital Ass'n,* 96 Or. 100; *Weathers v. Sovereign Camp, W.O.W.,* 119 S.C. 402; *Fountain City Drill Co. v. Linquist,* 22 S.D. 7; *Boorum & Peas Co. v. Armstrong,* (Tenn., 1896) 37 S.W. 1095; *Southland Life Ins. Co. v. Greenwade,* 138 Tex. 450; *Town of Barnet v. Town of Norton,* 90 Vt. 544; *Kubey v. Travelers' Protective Ass'n of America,* 109 Wash. 453; *Frank v. Metropolitan Life Ins. Co.,* 227 Wis. 613; *First Nat. Bank v. Ford,* 30 Wyo. 110.

[13] *Austin v. Holland,* 69 N.Y. 571, 576. See, also, *Best on Presumption,* sec. 403.

[14] *Wilson v. Peck,* 66 Misc. 179, 121 N.Y. Supp. 344, 345. See, also, *Carter v. Bradley,* 18 Me. 62 and *Marshall v. Sonneman,* 216 Pa. 65.

[15] For the questions properly asked in this circumstance, see Spellman, *How to Prove a Prima Facie Case* (3rd ed.), p. 673.

[16] Compare section 11:10, *post.*

initials of the person mailing letters. An individual is called to the stand, testifies as to the method of keeping the log-book and further testifies that, although he does not remember mailing the letter, itself, it was his practice not to make the entry in the log-book until he had mailed the letter after comparing its contents with the copy retained. A carbon or Xerox copy is customarily produced, in which case there is no need for proof of actual comparison. All that is required is that the employee testify that this is a true copy placed in the files after mailing.

(b) Where the employee who made the entry in the log-book is no longer available, his absence should be explained and another person familiar with the method of maintaining the log-book can testify in his place.

(c) An employee produces a copy of the letter from the files. He testifies that copies of letters are not placed in the files by him until they have been mailed. He identifies the sub-dictation initials on the letter as his and states that it is his practice, where the letter has been dictated to him, to transcribe the letter, mail it with proper postage and then place it in the files.

(d) Where the employee whose sub-dictation initials appear on the letter is no longer available, his absence should be explained and another person, familiar with the office practice, should testify with respect thereto.

(e) Where an affidavit of service has been made (as, for example, where a document has been served by mail or a notary has served a notice of protest by mail) and where such an affidavit is authorized by law, the affidavit, itself, is prima facie proof of mailing, provided it complies with the applicable statute.[17]

(f) As a last resort, when none of the above types of proof is available, a person familiar with the filing methods in an office may testify (though it is by no means certain that this testimony is sufficient) that the copy of the letter was found in the files in its normal place and that it is the custom never to file such a letter until it has been properly mailed to the addressee.

---

[17] See section 11:5, *post*.

In each of the above situations, it should be remembered that there must be some type of independent proof that the address to which the letter was sent was the correct address of the person sought to be charged with its receipt. If the letter is in answer to an earlier communication from that person, it is sufficient to prove that it was mailed to the address on the letterhead of the original letter or communication. Proof of a correct address rarely presents a real problem; but counsel offering a letter should be prepared to make proof of a correct address in the event the question of address should arise.

Sometimes the copy of a letter offered in evidence varies in some slight detail from the original letter as mailed. For example, in accordance with office practice, the copy may be signed with initials, or not signed at all, or the signature may not appear but the name of the signer may have been typed. This variation should be explained by the person testifying to the mailing, who should also state that the variation is in accordance with the standard office practice of his firm. Similarly, the copy of the letter sometimes contains either a filing notation or some handwritten marginal notes (referring, for example, to later conferences had or work done in connection with the subject-matter of the letter). This variation should also be explained.

If an answer is received to the letter claimed to have been mailed, proof of mailing is adequate upon production of the answer, properly authenticated. Proof of mailing can similarly be made by testimony that a conversation between the addressee and the person mailing the letter took place at a later date in which conversation the subject-matter of the letter and a reference to its receipt appears.

It is unfortunately too readily assumed by some counsel that, upon adequate proof of mailing, they may introduce a copy of the letter without further ado. Under the law of most jurisdictions this is not the fact. A copy of the letter is secondary evidence. The best evidence is the original letter, itself. In order for the copy to be technically admissible, a notice to produce should be served in advance of trial requiring the opponent to produce the original letter under penalty of having a copy offered in evidence if such production does not take place. This subject is more fully discussed in section 10:9, *post*.

Sec. 10:6 Telephone conversations

Communications, when material to the issues, through the medium of the telephone, may be shown in the same manner and with like effect as conversations had between individuals face to face.[18]

However, in order for testimony as to such a conversation to be admissible, there must be proof of identity of the person or persons holding the conversation in order to fix a liability upon them or their principals.[19]

The ordinary method of proving the identity of the person speaking on the telephone is for a witness to state that he knew that person and recognized his voice. But such proof is not absolutely essential. A witness who did not know the voice of the person to whom he was talking at the time of the original conversation may nevertheless testify to the conversation if he further testifies that he met the person in question later and then recognized the voice as that of his original telephone communicant.[20]

The identification of a person engaging in a telephone conversation is established when that person, on a later occasion when

---

[18] *Young v. Seattle* (Wash., 1903) 63 L.R.A. 988 and cases therein cited. See, also, *Knickerbocker v. Gardner*, 107 Md. 556; *Theisen v. Detroit*, 200 Mich. 136; *De Lore v Smith*, 67 Or. 306. We are, of course, assuming that the telephone conversations are not subject to exclusion because they resulted from an illegal wiretap or illegal interception.

[19] *Sawyer v. Eaton*, 293 Fed. 898; *Western Union v. Rowell*, 153 Ala. 295; *Schubkegel v. Gardino*, 56 Cal. App. (2d.) 667; *Kent v. Cobb*, 24 Colo. App. 264; *Reardon v. Mutual Life Ins. Co. of N.Y.*, 138 Conn. 510; *Stewart v. Fisher*, 18 Ga. App. 519; *Garden City Foundry Co. v. Industrial Comm.*, 307 Ill. 76; *Greenberg v. Greenberg*, 79 Ind. App. 218; *Smith v. Farm Property Mut. Ins. Ass'n of Iowa*, 199 Iowa 693; *Bradley v. Illinois Cent. R. Co.*, 291 Ky. 25; *Miller v. Leib*, 109 Md. 414; *Irving Tanning Co. v. Shir*, 295 Mass. 380; *Miller v. Kelly*, 215 Mich. 254; *Katzmarek v. Weber Brokerage Co.*, 214 Minn. 580; *St. Paul Fire & Marine Ins. Co. v. McQuaid*, 114 Miss. 430; *Meeker v. Union Elec. Light & Power Co.*, 279 Mo. 574; *Jendresen v. Hansen*, 50 Mont. 216; *Nat. Bank of Ashland v. Cooper*, 86 Neb. 792; *Smarak v. Segusse*, 91 N.J. Law 57; *Bonner Mfg. Co. v. Tannenbaum*, 169 N.Y. Supp. 43; *Pitt Lumber Co. v. Askew*, 185 N.C. 87; *B. Dannemiller & Sons v. Leonard*, 15 Ohio Cir. Ct. R. 686; *Heckman v. Davis*, 56 Okl. 483; *Johnston v. Fitzhugh*, 91 Or. 247; *Ehrenstrom v. Hess*, 262 Pa. 104; *G. W. McNear Inc. v. Am. & British Mfg. Co.*, 44 R.I. 190; *Cohen v. Standard Accident Ins. Co.*, 194 S.C. 533; *Colbert v. Dallas Joint Stock Land Bank*, 136 Tex. 268; *Atlantic Coast Realty Co. v. Robertson's Ex'r*, 135 Va. 247; *Beeler v. Pacific Fruit & Produce Co.*, 133 Wash. 116; *Stein v. Jaseulea*, 165 Wis. 317.

[20] *People v. Dunbar Contracting Co.*, 215 N.Y. 416. The types of question that are addressed to a witness in both situations are set forth in Spellman, *How to Prove a Prima Facie Case* (3rd ed.), p. 386.

he met the witness, referred to the prior telephone conversation or to facts then discussed, which were not discussed on any other occasion.[21]

Records of telephone companies establishing a "person-to-person" call cannot be said necessarily to prove that the individual responding to such a call was, in fact, the person sought to be charged with the contents of the telephone conversation.

Sec. 10:7 Photographs and mechanical recordings.

One of the most common incidents (particularly in personal injury, injunction, land title, condemnation or real estate tax cases or in criminal prosecutions) is the offer in evidence of photographs. Such photographs may, for example, depict the locus of an accident or the condition of a plaintiff after an injury or assault, a dead body prior to or after autopsy, an allegedly excessive picket line, land which has been condemned, or a building whose value is a matter of dispute in a tax certiorari proceeding. It is a uniform rule that such photographs, properly authenticated, are admissible in evidence.[22]

Photographic evidence is one of the best tools that counsel can employ. It not only has the advantage of making a vivid impres-

---

[21] *Woodruff v. Benesch,* 112 Misc. 489 [New York].

[22] *Bradley v. Lewis,* 211 Ala. 264; *Sloan v. Newman,* 166 Ark. 259; *Berkovitz v. American River Gravel Co.,* 191 Cal. 195; *Parris v. Jaquith,* 70 Colo. 63; *Cagianello v. City of Hartford,* 135 Conn. 473; *Phillips v. Wilmington & Philadelphia Traction Co.,* (Del.), 1 W. W. Harr. 593; *City of Thomasville v. Growell,* 22 Ga. App. 383; *Department of Public Works and Bldgs. v. Chicago Title & Trust Co.,* 408 Ill. 41; *Walker Hospital v. Pulley,* 74 Ind. App. 659; *Coonley v. Lowden,* 234 Iowa 731; *Griffin v. Fredonia Brick Co.,* 90 Kan. 375; *Lee Lewis, Inc. v. Dosch,* 193 Ky. 163; *Rosenberg v. Robbert,* 155 La. 557; *McPhee v. Lawrence,* 123 Me. 264; *Buch v. Hulcher,* 180 Md. 309; *Howe v. City of Boston,* 311 Mass. 278; *Potvin v. West Bay City Shipbuilding Co.,* 156 Mich. 201; *Wallstedt v. Swedish Hospital,* 220 Minn. 274; *Young v. Dunlap,* 195 Mo. App. 119; *Stokes v. Long,* 52 Mont. 470; *Harrell v. People's City Mission Home,* 131 Neb. 138; *Braelow v. Klein,* 100 N.J. Law 156; *Marion v. B. G. Coon Const. Co.,* 157 App. Div. 95, aff'd. 216 N.Y. 178; *White v. Hines,* 182 N.C. 275; *Wyldes v Patterson,* 31 N.D. 282; *Luebbering v. Whitaker,* 101 Ohio St. 292; *Colonial Refining Co. v. Lathrop,* 64 Okl. 47; *Northwest Door Co. v. Lewis Inv. Co.,* 92 Or. 186; *Taylor v. Bland,* 77 Pa. Super. Ct. 551; *Curtis v. New York, N.H. & H.R. Co.,* 32 R.I. 542; *Brown v. Southern Ry. Co.,* 111 S.C. 140; *Figland v. Jones,* 42 S.D. 92; *Southern Pac. Co. v. Eckenfels,* (Tex.), 197 S.W. 1003; *Blake v. Harding,* 54 Utah 158; *Silveira v. Croft,* 116 Vt. 420; *Staples v. Spence,* 179 Va. 359; *Brewer v. Berner,* 15 Wash. (2d.) 644; *Merrill v. Marietta Torpedo Co.,* 79 W.Va. 669; *Prideaux v. Milwaukee Auto Ins. Co.,* 246 Wis. 390

sion on the finder of the facts,[23] but in a jury trial where the jurors are permitted to take exhibits for examination during the course of their deliberations (not permitted in a criminal case except with the consent of the defendant), the visual impression persists.

The "authentication" of a proffered photograph does *not* require testimony of the photographer.[24] If a witness testifies that the photograph is a fair representation of what it purports to show, sufficient foundation has been laid.[25] Of course, the authenticating witness so testifying may be cross-examined concerning the accuracy of the picture and evidence may be introduced to rebut his testimony. But the privilege of cross-examination and rebuttal has no connection with the original admissibility of the photograph, unless it is shown, as a matter of law, that the photograph is so inaccurate that its value as evidence is nil. In an appropriate case, the witness who authenticates the photograph must be able to testify, of his own knowledge, that a later-taken picture is a fair representation of the scene at the time of an earlier occurrence, which is in issue.

A motion picture of an event is admissible to prove the facts therein depicted. In a leading case, where plaintiff had claimed that he was totally disabled and unable to work or earn a living at any useful employment, the court held that a motion picture showing great physical activity on the part of plaintiff presented a case which was "a striking illustration of an instance where moving pictures are not only admissible but very important." [26]

---

[23] The concept that "a camera does not lie" is almost universally held. In the absence of proof of trickery in the taking of photographs, a finder of the facts will, ordinarily, grant a photograph his complete attention, sometimes to the exclusion of much oral testimony.

[24] *Roosevelt Hospital v. New York El. R. Co.*, 21 N.Y. Supp. 205. This may not be true in the case of exhibits offered to support the testimony of an expert (for example, handwriting and ballistic experts). In such a case the photographer should be called to testify that he, personally, took the picture and that it is an exact photograph of the object in question.

[25] *Archer v. N.Y., N.H. & H.R.R. Co.*, 106 N.Y. 589.

[26] *Boyarsky v. G. A. Zimmerman Corporation*, 240 App. Div. 361, 270 N.Y. Supp. 134, 137–138, wherein the court also pointed out that in most cases the question should be left largely to the discretion of the trial judge and that if a trial is to be unduly delayed by exhibiting motion pictures or if such pictures "are sensational only and unnecessary, the court should refuse to permit such evidence, particularly where the facts may be described or the evidence submitted in another form and thus avoid the delay and difficulty which will result from their introduction. If their use is solely for the purpose of advertisement or in an effort to obtain publicity, they should not be allowed in evidence."

The use of mechanical sound recordings is now a common device. Subject to prohibitions contained in local statutes requiring exclusion of such recordings as evidence, "[n]o persuasive reason exists why the reproduction of the sounds of an original event if material and when a proper foundation is laid should not be admissible." [27] The authentication here required would probably necessitate the calling of a witness who actually made the recording and the testimony of that witness, after the recording has been played back in the courtroom, that it *precisely* (not merely reasonably) sets forth the words in the recorded conversation.[28]

Sec. 10:8   Proof of contents of lost instruments.

Where a document has been lost, destroyed, or, for sufficient reason, is shown not to be in the possession of the party whose duty it was to keep it, secondary evidence of its contents may be given.[29] In such a case, the party desiring to proffer the contents of the document has the same right to give secondary evidence of those contents, even if it is an official document, as in the case of any other instrument in writing incapable of production.[30] Indeed, where it is shown that an original official document cannot be found in the particular place provided by statute for its deposit the presumption is that it has been lost or destroyed.[31]

A party alleging the loss of a material paper, where such proof is necessary for the purpose of giving secondary evidence of its contents, must show that he has in good faith exhausted, to a reasonable degree, all the sources of information and means of discovery which the nature of the case would naturally suggest and which were accessible to him.[32] It has been said that the person last known to have been in possession of a missing paper must be examined as a witness to prove its loss and that, even if he is

---

[27] *Frank v. Cossitt Cement Products,* 197 Misc. 670, 97 N.Y. Supp. 2d 337, 340.

[28] The proper questions to be asked to lay a foundation for the admission of a recording are found in Spellman, *How to Prove a Prima Facie Case* (3rd ed.), p. 689.

[29] *Mendeville v. Reynolds,* 68 N.Y. 528. For the requirement that a notice to produce must be served before secondary evidence is admissible in certain circumstances, see section 10:9, *post.*

[30] *Leland v. Cameron,* 31 N.Y. 115.

[31] *Rex v. Stouerbridge,* 8 B. & C. 96.

[32] *Kearney v. Mayor, et al.,* 92 N.Y. 617. See, also, *Simpson v. Dall,* 3 Wall. 460, 475.

out of the State, his deposition must be procured if practicable, or some good excuse given for not doing so.[33]

The ordinary, usual and accepted method of proving the contents of a lost paper or instrument, after a foundation has been laid for secondary evidence, is to produce a copy, properly authenticated.[34] However, it is also a general rule, in common with other rules concerning secondary evidence, that the contents of written instruments, when lost or destroyed, may always be proved by parol.[35]

---

[33] *Dickinson v. Breeden*, 25 Ill. 186. In *Kearney v. Mayor, et al.*, 92 N.Y. 617, the New York Court of Appeals stated of this proposition, citing cases from other jurisdictions, that "it has been repeatedly held."

[34] *Penix v. Sloan*, (C.C.A., Tex., 1924) 3 Fed. (2d.) 258; *Stockburger v. Aderholt*, 204 Ala. 557; *Robert v. Brown*, 157 Ark. 230; *Edmunds v. Atchinson, T. & S.F. Ry. Co.*, 174 Cal. 246; *Bay State Milling Co. v. Sussman Feuer Co.*, 91 Conn. 482; *Bible v. Sommers Const. Co.*, 197 Ga. 761; *City of Berwyn v. Man*, 345 Ill. App. 86; *Pittsburgh, C.C. & St. L. Ry. Co. v. Brown*, 178 Ind. 11; *Geddes v. McElroy*, 171 Iowa 633; *McAuley v. Siscoe*, 110 Kan. 804; *Little v. National Colortype Co.*, 197 Ky. 524; *White v. White*, 156 La. 324; *Isaacs v. Williams*, 149 Md. 19; *Eveland v. Lawson*, 240 Mass. 98; *Fremont Canning Co. v. Pere Marquette R. Co.*, 180 Mich. 283; *Stevens v. Minneapolis Fire Dept. Relief Ass'n*, 219 Minn. 276; *Panola County Bank v. J. O. Nessen Lumber Co.*, 117 Miss. 593; *Kline v. Groeschner*, 280 Mo. 599; *Rogness v. Northern Pac. Ry. Co.*, 59 Mont. 373; *In re Baker's Estate*, 144 Neb. 797; *Richardson v. Boston & M. R.R.*, 80 N.H. 370; *Smith v. National Union Fire Ins. Co.*, (N.J., 1925) 130 A. 371; *March v. Wycoff, Church & Partridge*, 111 N.Y. Supp. 669; *Universal Oil & Fertilizer Co. v. Burney*, 174 N.C. 382; *Serking v. Laidlaw*, 59 Or. 116; *Brenner v. Lesher*, 332 Pa. 522; *Dawley v. Congdon*, 42 R.I. 64; *Inman v. Tucker*, 138 Tenn. 512; *Pate v. Gallup*, (Tex., 1917) 195 S.W. 1151; *Chadwick v. Wiggin*, 95 Vt. 515; *Swingley v. Daniels*, 123 Wash. 409; *Larson v. A. W. Larson Const. Co.*, (Wash., 1950) 217 Pac. (2d.) 789; *State v. McComas*, 97 W.Va. 664; *Hoeffler v. Carew*, 135 Wis. 605. For the proper types of questions to be asked in this situation, see Spellman, *How to Prove a Prima Facie Case* (3rd ed.), p. 668.

[35] *State of Louisiana v. Clark*, 142 La. 305. See, also, *Jefferson Lumber Co. v. Berry*, 247 Ala. 164; *Cotton v. Hudson*, 42 Cal. App. (2d.) 812; *Woicicky v. Anderson*, 95 Conn. 534; *People's Nat. Bank of Middletown v. Rhoades*, (Del., 1913) 5 Boyce 65, 90 A. 409; *Williams v. Richardson*, 66 Fla. 234; *Carrie v. Carnes*, 145 Ga. 184; *Mould v. Rohm*, 274 Ill. 547; *Olson v. New York Life Ins. Co.*, 229 Iowa 1073; *Marcotte's Estate v. Clay*, 170 Kan. 189; *Hehr's Adm'r v. Hehr*, 288 Ky. 580; *Perley v. McGray*, 115 Me. 398; *American Fidelity Co. of Montpelier, Vt. v. State*, 135 Md. 326; *Cumberland Glass Mfg. Co. v. Atteaux*, 199 Mass. 426; *Munroe, Boyce & Co. v. Ward*, 207 Mich. 369; *Berryhill v. Clar*, 137 Minn. 135; *Bullock v. E. B. Gee Land Co.*, 347 Mo. 721; *Nelson v. Geough*, 61 Mont. 301; *Powers v. Murray*, 185 N.C. 336; *Winters Nat. Bank & Trust Co. v. Grether*, 69 Ohio App. 461; *Smith v. Dunn*, 165 Or. 418; *Del Vitto v. Schiavo*, 370 Pa. 299; *Arnold v. Barrington*, 44 R.I. 298; *Bank v. North Carolina Mut. Life Ins. Co.*, 186 S.C. 394; *Miller Management Co. v. State*, 140 Tex. 370; *Town of Barnet v. Town of Norton*, 90 Vt. 544; *Murray v. Chamberlain*, 126 Wash. 642; *Boardman v. Lorentzen*, 155 Wis. 566. For the appropriate questions to be asked when proof of a lost or destroyed instrument is made by parol evidence, see Spellman, *How to Prove a Prima Facie Case* (3rd ed.), p. 671.

In some of the cases hereinabove cited in this section, courts have permitted parol evidence as to the contents of a lost or destroyed document or instrument to be made by the testimony of a witness summarizing the contents of a lost document, when the witness cannot, from memory, give its exact text. Obviously, if the document in question is a very long one, such evidence may have slight persuasive effect. When the instrument is a simple promissory note or a simple receipt, for example, the summary of its contents is almost as good as a verbatim account thereof. In some situations, even a long document can be summarized, where the document is a printed form in which the salient facts were set forth. An example, of such a document would be a form lease in which the period of the lease and the rental were filled in. If the printed form is available, the witness may testify that this identical form was used. The blank form may be introduced in evidence with the testimony of the witness as to how the blanks were filled in.

Sec. 10:9   Notice to produce.

It has been shown, in section 10:8, *supra*, how the contents of a lost document or instrument may be proved if a proper foundation is laid establishing that the document in question is, in fact, or must be presumed to be lost or destroyed. There is no need in such a situation to call anyone else to produce the document and there is, obviously, no possibility of subpoenaing it.

However, it is a familiar principle of the law of evidence (sometimes buttressed by specific statute) that secondary evidence of the contents of a document, other than one which has been proven to be lost or destroyed, may not be introduced if the original is in the possession or under the control of an adverse party, unless that adverse party is first notified to produce the original.[36] This notification is generally described as a "Notice to Produce." As an incident to the use of a notice to produce, it must be shown by the party offering a copy of a document or parol evidence of its contents as secondary evidence that the opponent actually has, or should have, possession of control of the original.[37] The test is

[36] *Abat v. Riou*, 9 Mart. 465, 467 (La.). See, also, *Kerr v. McGuire*, 28 N.Y. 446, 453.

[37] *Lally v. Cash*, 18 Ariz. 574; *Sun Ins. Co. v. Earle*, 29 Mich. 406; *Desnoyer v. McDonald*, 4 Minn. 515, 518; *Elmslie v. Thurman*, 87 Miss. 537; *Peo. v. Dolan*, 186 N.Y. 4.

"whether it is sufficiently proved that the letter or document has come to the hands and is in the possession and power of the opposite party." [38] A common method of proving that the original document is in the possession of or under the control of the opponent is to show that it was mailed to him at his correct address.[39]

A notice to produce is a paper served on the opposing counsel to the effect that he is required to produce a *specific* document or documents upon the trial of the action and that, in the event of his failure to produce it or them, secondary evidence of its or their contents will be offered.

The document or documents demanded for production should be described in detail. It is not sufficient, for example, to require one's opponent to produce "all correspondence between the parties." The requirement should be that the opponent produce "a certain letter from plaintiff to defendant, dated June 3, 1966; and a certain letter from plaintiff to defendant, dated June 9, 1966; and a certain receipt dated June 16, 1966 from John Jones, Inc., to defendant" etc. The description of the documents to be produced must be such "as will apprize a man of ordinary intelligence of the documents desired." [40] Although it has been said that a notice is sufficiently particular where, from its contents, it is "impossible for the defendant to have doubted" what documents were required,[41] it is wise, if possible, to describe the documents precisely.

It should be observed that a notice to produce merely lays the foundation for the introduction of secondary evidence. Unless a statute otherwise provides, the notice to produce does *not* have the force of a subpoena.[42] If the party served with the notice fails to produce the document, the burden of proving its contents by secondary evidence rests with the party demanding its production. Counsel is ill-advised to assume that the document will be

---

[38] *Dana v. Kemble,* 12 Pick. 112, 114 (Mass.).
[39] *Rosenthal v. Walker,* 111 U.S. 185, 193.
[40] *Burke v. T. M. W. Co.,* 12 Cal. 403, 408.
[41] *Bemis v. Charles,* 1 Metc. 440, 443 (Mass.).
[42] A somewhat different rule sometimes applies where the notice to produce is served in connection with pre-trial proceedings (such as the taking of a deposition or proceedings upon a discovery). There, a statute or rule of court may make the failure to produce a document ground for an order of preclusion. See, for example, rule 36 F.R.C.P., which permits a notice to produce to take the place of an order. As to the procedure where there is a captious refusal to make discovery, see *Burgin v. Ryan,* 238 App. Div. 122 [New York].

produced. He must be prepared to offer secondary proof. If he desires to have greater assurance that the document will be in court, he should serve a subpoena for its production; but even when such a subpoena is served, it is wise to have secondary evidence at hand and not to depend on the hope that the court will strike the opponent's pleading for contempt of court.

The length of time in advance of trial required for service of a notice to produce is often set forth in statutes or court rules. In some jurisdictions, such statutes or rules require "reasonable notice." Cases construing these provisions, as well as decisions in other jurisdictions, ordinarily hold that the term "reasonable notice" must be construed in the light of the facts of each case, or that it is within the discretion of the court to determine whether reasonable notice was given, based on the situation presented by the particular litigation at bar.[43] It has been stated that a notice must be sufficiently long to enable the notified party to procure and produce the document without undue inconvenience.[44]

When the notice to produce has been served, the serving party's counsel may ask for the production of the notice by stating in open court:

> "I call upon my opponent to produce a certain letter written by plaintiff to defendant dated on or about June 16, 1966, pursuant to notice to produce served upon him on February 15, 1967."

If the opponent fails or refuses to produce the document, the notice to produce with proof of due service should be offered in evidence and, upon its receipt, the serving party may proceed to adduce secondary evidence.

Although a written notice to produce is the customarily required practice and although sometimes such requirement is set forth in a statute or court rule, a demand for production prior to the introduction of secondary evidence may be made in open court if the document is already there and in the possession of the opponent. Such an oral demand is, in and of itself, sufficient notice.[45]

---

[43] *Burke v. T. M. W. Co.*, 12 Cal. 403, 407; *Cummings v. McKinney*, 5 Ill. 57; *Greenough v. Shelden*, 9 Iowa 503, 507; *Glenn v. Rogers*, 3 Md. 312, 320; *Worth v. Norton*, 60 S.C. 293.
[44] *Littleton v. Clayton*, 77 Ala. 571, 574.
[45] *Dana v. Boyd*, 2 J. J. Marsh. 587, 592 (Ky.).

Similarly, where the very nature of the action, as disclosed by the pleadings makes it clear that a certain document will be required in court, no notice to produce is necessary, since the pleading, itself, is deemed an implied notice.[46]

When a party is called upon, after proper notice either express or implied, to produce a document and the party declines or refuses to do so, that party is thereafter prevented from introducing the document in evidence.[47] Although this rule is of ancient origin, modern decisions are more generally to the effect that one who refuses to produce a document upon proper demand is thereafter forbidden to introduce it in evidence for the purpose of contradicting the other party's copy or evidence of its contents.[48]

---

[46] *Nicholson v. Tarpey*, 70 Cal. 608, 610; *Commonwealth's Ins. Co. v. Monninger*, 18 Ind. 352; *Howell v. Huyck*, 2 Abb. App. 423 [New York]; *Nichols & S. Co. v. Charlebois*, 10 N.D. 446; *Niagara Ins. Co. v. Whittaker*, 21 Wis. 335.

[47] This principle is sometimes the subject of a statute or court rule. However, even in the absence of such rule, the earliest decisions recognized the principle. *Roe v. Harvey*, 4 Burr 2484, 2489 (England, 1769); *Doe v. Cockell*, 6 C. & P. 525, 528 (England, 1834); *Doe v. Hodgson*, 12 A. & E. 135 (England, 1840).

[48] *Bank v. M'Williams*, 2 J. J. Marsh (Ky.) 256, 259; *Gage v. Campbell*, 131 Mass. 566; *McGinness v. School District*, 39 Minn. 499.

Chapter XI

STATUTORY AIDS TO PROOF

Sec. 11:1 Nature of statutory aids.

Under common law rules of evidence, great hardship sometimes occurs in the purely mechanical proof of relatively simple facts, miniscule in nature and ultimate effect but necessary for the establishment of a cause of action or defense.

Over the years, the realization that inordinate amounts of time are wasted by meeting technical requirements of proof has forcibly come to the attention of courts and (often through the medium of the courts) of legislatures. As a result, either by court rule or legislative action short-cuts have been evolved, enabling proof to be made through such means as certified copies of papers, certificates of public officials and the like.

Trial lawyers should be familiar with these statutory short-cuts, since their utilization will not only save trial time but also cut down the time consumed in preparation and obviate the necessity for calling unnecessary witnesses.

In this connection, it should be noted that each jurisdiction has its own statutory aids. They are not interstate in nature unless they are passed by interstate compact (uniform laws). Furthermore, it is not sufficient for the lawyer preparing his case for trial to consider only the text of statutory aids. Their construction is often decisive of their meaning and application in a given jurisdiction.

In some instances, even where statutory aids are couched in *identical* language, they are differently construed by courts in different jurisdictions. Indeed, occasions sometimes arise where the same statute is construed differently by courts of the *same* state, sitting in varying judicial departments or sections of that state. And, under the Federal system, different United States Courts of Appeals have construed some of the same Federal Rules of Civil Procedure in a contradictory manner, with the result that, unless these diversities are settled by the Supreme Court of the United States, we have, in effect, different rules in different circuits.

The foregoing considerations may sometimes lead to the determination where venue should be set for a specific trial so as to take full advantage of the court rule or statute involved in important technical proof *and its construction.*

Basically, a statutory aid to proof is formulated as a *convenience* for counsel. Due to the language of some statutes, these aids are sometimes categorized as "presumptions." Except in a very limited sense, they are no such thing as far as ultimate proof is concerned unless a statute directly or inferentially so provides. All they accomplish is permission to prove a given fact in a shorthand manner. This proof establishes the fact, *prima facie,* thus shifting the burden of going forward with the proof to the opponent. If uncontradicted, the shorthand method establishes the fact for all purposes of the case;[1] but there is nothing to stop an opponent

---

[1] Compare section 1:2, footnotes 7, 8 and 9, *supra.*

from proving, for example, that a certificate of a foreign court official is contradicted by actual facts, or that a certified copy of a document is not a true copy thereof.

No matter how strongly worded (for example, by a statement that a certain certificate is "conclusive evidence" of a fact), no legislative aid to proof can foreclose the establishment of the truth. In a landmark decision on this subject, the New York Supreme Court was confronted by a novel but vitally important illustration of this principle.[2] There, a provision of the New York State Constitution set out the exact method by which legislation could be enacted. It required that, in order for a bill to be legally passed and "become a law" it must have been printed and upon the desks of the legislators in its final form at least three calendar legislative days prior to its final passage; but that, if the Governor sent a message of necessity to the legislature, the bill could be passed without printing, "in which case it must nevertheless be upon the desks of the members in final form, not necessarily printed, before its final passage."

Section 40 of the New York Legislative Law, presumably implementing the constitutional provision, reads, in part:

> "No bills shall be deemed to have so passed unless certified in the manner provided by this section, *which certificate to such effect shall be conclusive evidence thereof.*" (Emphasis supplied)

During the trial of the cause, the plaintiff (claiming that the bill was not on the desks of the legislators in its final form at the time it was finally voted upon and that, despite the fact that the Governor had sent a message of necessity, the bill did not become a law) sought to introduce evidence that the bill was not on the desks of the legislators in its final form at the time of the final vote. Objection was made to the introduction of this evidence upon the ground that the statute had been certified in the manner provided by section 40 of the Legislative Law (quoted above) and that this certification was "conclusive evidence" of proper passage. The trial court admitted the evidence and, after making a finding of fact that the bill was not on the desks of the legislators in its final form when it was finally voted upon, held that the statute was never passed and never "became a law."

---

[2] *Franklin National Bank of Long Island v. Clark*, 26 Misc. 2d 724, 212 N.Y.S. 2d 942, 947 *et seq.*

This case and the arguments and reasoning contained in a number of authorities quoted in the opinion, clearly establish that, although a type of certification provided by statute may act as an aid or convenience, the certification, no matter how strongly the statute may be worded, cannot foreclose proof of the truth. The case is of particular importance since it was decided against the background of a strong argument that the courts could not interfere in the legislative processes where the appropriate legislative officers had certified that their legislative proceedings were regular.

Although most of the States have separate enactments of statutory aids to proof, some of them have a general statute to the effect that the Federal Rules of Civil Procedure are adopted as operative within such States. Other States have adopted some but not all of the Federal Rules of Civil Procedure. However, even where there has been an adoption *in toto* or an adoption of specific rules, the problem heretofore adverted to still often arises—to wit, that some of the State courts construe certain of the Federal Rules of Civil Procedure differently from the construction in Federal courts. Thus, it must be emphasized that, before depending upon a statutory aid to proof which is stated to be an adoption of one of the Federal Rules of Civil Procedure, counsel should investigate the construction given to such rule by the State court in which he intends to utilize it.

In later sections of the present chapter, we set forth the most common aids to statutory proof, indicating in appropriate footnotes the States wherein each statutory aid exists. Minute variations in the text of the statutes are not set forth, because the citation of the legislative enactment should only be taken by the reader as a starting point for his own investigation. Individual practice statutes are so often amended that it would be dangerous to take a statutory citation, in this respect, as a final word on the subject.

Sec. 11:2 Classes of statutory aids.

There are nine major classes of statutory aids to proof. As has been noted, these aids have been adopted as a *convenience* to facilitate technical proof. In and of themselves, they are not intended to add anything to the substantive proof, although they sometimes have that effect, depending upon which class of statutory aid is being used. The major classes of statutory aids to proof are:

1. Certification by a public officer of a copy of a document in his official files or official custody. This is the familiar "certified copy" of a paper.[3]

2. A certificate by a public official or some other person authorized by statute to furnish the same, which relates to the *existence of facts*, as such. Typical of the use of this class of statutory aid is a certification by a governor, secretary of state, or legislative officer to the effect that a statute was passed in a certain manner. Somewhat less typical, but permitted under certain statutes (and required under others to complete corporate acts), is a certificate by a corporate officer, under the seal of the corporation, that a corporate meeting was held on a certain date and that certain things transpired thereat. This latter type of certificate is sometimes in the form of a certified copy of corporate minutes by an authorized corporate officer under the seal of the corporation.

The most often employed of this class of statutory aids to proof is a certificate of conviction of crime.[4]

3. A certificate by a public official or some other person authorized by statute to furnish the same, which relates to the *absence of facts*. This class of statutory aids to proof typically consists of a certificate by a public official that he has searched his official files and, as a result of that search, certifies that a certain document or class of documents is *not* in his official files. A familiar example is a certification by the clerk of a probate court that there is no document on file in his court indicating that a prior application to admit a will to probate has been made, or that prior letters testamentary or letters of administration have been issued.

4. A certificate of an authorized public official appended to a printed official compilation. For example, a certificate of a secretary of state to the effect that the printed compilation has been compared with the original text of statutes and is a true copy thereof.

5. A certificate attached to an original document produced in

---

[3] In this class also fall certified copies of judgments, findings of fact and conclusions of law, often utilized in proving the defense of *res adjudicata*.

[4] In this connection, the certificate, standing alone, is not sufficient. There must be some independent proof by a living witness that the person who is accused of having been previously convicted and who is in court is the same person as the one referred to in the certificate. In some instances, special statutes permit this proof to be made by a comparison of the finger prints of the person in court with the finger prints annexed to the record of conviction and officially certified.

court, thus permitting the use or introduction in evidence of the document without the necessity of calling as a witness the person who prepared it. An example of the use of this type of statutory aid is a certification by an official court stenographer that a transcript of testimony to which it is attached was made by him and is correct.

6. Original certificates or certified copies thereof produced in court as proof of facts. Typical of this class are birth certificates, death certificates and marriage certificates.

7. Miscellaneous documents accepted as *prima facie* proof of facts. Within this class are ancient filed maps, surveys, title searches and the like affecting real property, affidavits of service and of the posting and publication of notices.

8. Official or standard unofficial compilations accepted as *prima facie* proof of facts. Within this class are such things as reports of past weather and tide conditions, certificates of population, census reports and stock market reports (sometimes including newspaper reports of stock market operations).

9. Permission granted by statute to use official or unofficial documents or entries in books as *prima facie* proof. An example of an official document used in this respect is a report by a policeman of his investigation of happenings concerning the commission of a crime or the circumstances of an accident.[5] An example of unofficial documents or entries is found in statutes permitting the introduction into evidence of books of account and other company records, regularly made and maintained in the course of business. The most salient effect of this latter aid is the elimination of the ancient shop-book rule, which required not only proof of the entry in a book of account but also proof that such entries were used in the regular course of business as a method of settlement with persons other than the parties to the action.

The foregoing general classification of statutory aids to proof may be used by trial counsel as a convenient *aide memoire* in determining whether there will be available to him a short-cut method of proof in the circumstances of his particular case. Details of individual statutes and their scope are hereinafter set forth.

---

[5] Some statutes provide that an official entry of this type is not necessarily excludable because the person making the entry was repeating hearsay, but decisions very often exclude such hearsay as proof of a fact. In a criminal trial, the construction of this type of statute is often conditioned upon the right of a defendant to confront witnesses against him.

Sec. 11:3 Tactical disregard of statutory aids.

As has been stated hereinabove, statutory aids to proof have been enacted as a *convenience* for counsel, having as their main purpose the elimination of time-wasting and expensive procedures. As has also been indicated, the existence of a statutory aid merely establishes certain facts, *prima facie*, and, no matter how worded, a statutory aid does not foreclose proof of the truth, even though such proof may contradict or modify the contents of an official certificate. There is an important corollary of this latter principle. In the course of a trial, counsel is not *obliged* to make his proof via the convenience afforded by a statutory aid. He may establish facts by direct evidence, disregarding such convenience. Some statutes specifically so provide.[6]

The ultimate purpose of direct examination is to convince the trier of the facts (court or jury) not only that certain happenings took place in the manner suggested by examining counsel, but also—and of the utmost importance—that it would be right and proper, morally as well as legally, for the cause to be decided in favor of that counsel's contention. Courts and juries, however technically their functions may be delineated in reported decisions, are human beings, whose emotions often play as large a part as their logical processes in reaching a decision. This is particularly true where the measure of damages is entrusted to the fact-finders. Although appeals to passion or prejudice are properly condemned, trial counsel is fully justified in presenting his case in such manner as to appeal to the non-prejudiced emotions of the finder of the facts. In this connection, it is a legitimate tactic for trial counsel to disregard the convenience offered by a statutory aid to proof and to offer, instead, direct proof by the old-fashioned method of calling witnesses without short-cuts. Consider the following example:

---

[6] LOUISIANA: LSA-C.C.P. art. 1397. NEW JERSEY: N.J.S.A. 2A:84A, Rules of Evidence, Rule 5. NEW YORK: C.P.L.R. 4543. Some of these statutes cover only proof of official records or entries or lack of the same. FEDERAL: F.R.C.P., Rule 44(c). ALABAMA: Code, Title 7, §431. ARIZONA: R.C.P. Rule 44(i). COLORADO: R.C.P., Rule 44(c). DELAWARE: 13 Code Ann.; Super. Civ. Rule 44(c), Chan. Rule 44(c). KENTUCKY: R.C.P., Rule 44.03. NEW MEXICO: §21-1-1(44)(c), N.M.S.A. 1953. TEXAS: Vernon's Tex. Civ. Stat., Art. 3731a, Sec. 6. UTAH: 9 Code Ann. 1953, R.C.P., Rule 44(c). VIRGINIA: §8-272(c), Code 1950, 1957 Repl. Vol. WEST VIRGINIA: R.C.P., Rule 44(c). WYOMING: R.C.P., Rule 44(c).

In a suit for wrongful death as the result of an unjustified assault, wherein damages are claimed not only for the death, itself, but also for conscious pain and suffering before death, trial counsel can establish the death and the cause thereof by a coroner's or medical examiner's certificate. The certificate states that the cause of death was brain damage resulting from a series of blows about the head and face. If counsel desires to take advantage of a statutory aid to proof, all he needs is the death certificate (accompanied, of course, by establishment of the fact that the certificate applies to the person whose death is the subject of the trial). However, counsel is not obliged to rely on the death certificate. Instead, we may assume that he would prefer to use the following questions and answers:

Q. Are you the widow of the deceased? **A.** Yes.

Q. On June 1, 1967, did you go to the morgue in this City? **A.** Yes.

Q. What did you there see? **A.** There was a table on which there was a large sheet.

Q. What then happened? **A.** The sheet was drawn aside and I saw my husband's body.

Q. What did you observe on the body? **A.** There were big bruises on the left cheek, there was a deep cut on the lower part of that cheek extending to the chin. There was another deep cut on the upper part of my husband's forehead which went from just below the hairline and continued on through the hair. My husband's nose was flattened and his whole face was covered with blood.

Certainly, this testimony is better and more persuasive than a mere death certificate. The certificate may, thereafter, be introduced to corroborate the testimony of the wife.

The use of evidence other than that made possible by the utilization of the statutory aid to proof does not prevent using that statutory aid in addition to the other evidence. Indeed, this is sometimes a wise procedure, since it guarantees that there will be no deficiency in *technical* proof.

In the foregoing hypothetical case, the wife's testimony is justified not only as direct proof of facts at issue, but also as proof of identification of the body. The medical examiner or coroner can be called to establish the fact that, before the wife viewed her husband's body, there had been no autopsy which might have caused the wounds she observed. Where, as in the hypothetical case presently under discussion, the claim is made that the deceased suffered conscious pain and suffering prior to his death, the widow might be in a position further to testify that, after the assault and before her husband died, he was conscious and was obviously suffering great pain. In such a situation, her testimony is even more dramatic if the deceased was brought to his home after the assault and she actually saw him die.

The evidence employed in tactical disregard of the statutory aid to proof should not be "dragged in by the heels." Each of its elements must have a legitimate, legal reason for its introduction. It would result in reversible error to introduce extraneous evidence, such as additional gory details not legitimately necessary for proof of the issues at bar. Thus, in a criminal prosecution for murder,[7] a conviction was reversed when the prosecution offered in evidence "[p]hotographs showing the bodies of the decedents in the barn depicting grisly scenes." The court held that the photographs "had no probative value and were highly inflammatory. . . . We can conceive of no other purpose than to excite the sympathy and passion of the jury."

There are certain instances in which statutory aids to proof may not be disregarded, because a statute requires that a certain type of certificate be used in order to complete some legal proceeding. In this context, the certificate or similar document is not solely a statutory aid to proof, but is, in and of itself, a jurisdictional requirement, the meeting of which requirement is simplified by a short-cut method of presenting the facts. Typical of this class is the requirement, under certain corporate statutes, that a change in the corporate structure (for example, an increase in the amount of authorized stock or some other amendment to a certificate of incorporation) can only be accomplished by the filing with an appropriate state officer of a document effecting such change, *plus* a certificate by a designated corporate officer under seal of the corporation to the effect that, under the applicable statute, a meeting of stockholders was held and, at such meeting, the required percentage of the affected stockholders voted in favor of the proposed corporate change. Another example is the requirement, in some jurisdictions, that a petition for the probate of a

---

[7] *People v. Rial,* 25 A.D. 2d 28, 30 [New York].

will must be accompanied by a certificate of the clerk of a probate court that no other will of the decedent has been admitted to probate and that no other petition has been filed.

Sec. 11:4   Authentication of out-of-state oaths.

The statutes of all states provide for the persons or officials before whom oaths may be taken. From the point of view of statutory aids to proof, these statutes are important insofar as they set forth the official before whom an affidavit may be sworn to.

There is no problem when the affidavit is taken by a notary public, court clerk or similar official within the jurisdiction where the affidavit is to be offered in evidence or upon the hearing of a motion. However, where such an affidavit is sworn to in a state other than that in which the cause is being tried or the motion argued, it is essential that the official character of the person before whom the oath was taken be authenticated.[8]

The exact method by which such authentication must be evidenced is provided for by statutes in individual jurisdictions. Some of these statutes set out in more or less precise terms the requirements for foreign authentication, usually providing the character of officer in the foreign jurisdiction who must (either under the seal of a court or by means of some similar formality) attest to the official character of the oath-administrator.[9] Other statutes provide that such authentication should take the same form as would be required to entitle the acknowledgement of a deed or other document concerning realty to be recorded.[10]

---

[8] In some jurisdictions, the processes of authenticating the official character of the person administering the oath is known as "exemplification." In common parlance, since the authenticating certificate is very often oblong in shape and is physically attached to the document below the signature of the oath-administering officer, the process of attaching this authentication is known as "putting on the flag."

[9] ALABAMA: Code, Title 7, §§416–418. FLORIDA: F.S.A. §§695.03–695.04. INDIANA: Burns' Stat. §§56-125, 56-126 and 56-130b. IOWA: 36 Code Ann., §§558.20–23; 43 Code Ann., §622.26. MISSISSIPPI: 2 Code 1942 Ann., §§1746–1747. MISSOURI: V.A.M.S. §§490.410 and 490.530. NEW HAMPSHIRE: RSA 456:10–456:11.

[10] ARKANSAS: Stat. Ann., §28-919. CALIFORNIA: Code Civ. Proc., §1951 (Deering's); Evidence Code §1451 (Deering's). CONNECTICUT: C.G.S.A. §47-5. HAWAII: Rev. L. Hawaii 1955, §343-29. IDAHO: Code, §9-409. ILLINOIS: Smith-Hurd Ill. St. Ch. 30, §19. KENTUCKY: KRS 423.020. LOUISIANA: LSA-R.S. 35:513. MAINE: 3 M.R.S.A. §203. MICHIGAN: Stat. Ann., §27A. 2131. MINNESOTA: M.S.A. §§600.09 and 600.14. MONTANA: Sec. 93-1101-19, Repl. Vol. 7, Revised Codes of Montana 1947. NEVADA: NRS 111.295. NEW JERSEY: N.J.S.A. 2A:82-17. NEW YORK: C.P.L.R. 4538. NORTH DAKOTA: NDCC 31-08-06. OHIO: Page's Rev. Stat. Ann., §§5301.05–5301.06. UTAH:

From the point of view of litigation, the important factor which *must* be borne in mind is that, if an affidavit is taken in a foreign jurisdiction, it may not be used in a litigation unless the official character of the oath-administrator has been authenticated in the manner provided by local statute.[11] A motion based upon an affidavit sworn to before a foreign notary, whose official character has not been authenticated as provided by statute, must be denied, since, when the moving affidavit is not properly authenticated "the motion is not properly before the court."[12] However, the failure of authentication may be regarded as a mere defect, which may be cured by appropriate motion.[13]

The authenticating certificate should comply *exactly* with the statute of the forum wherein the trial is held or the motion made embodying its use. Thus, where a statute provided that the authentication of a foreign oath-administrator's official character must be to the effect that he is "an officer authorized by the law of the state to take and certify the acknowledgement and proof of deeds, to be recorded in the state" but the authenticating certificate was to the effect that the officer "was duly commissioned, sworn, and acting as such, and authorized to administer oaths," the authentication was held defective.[14]

There are various requirements for authenticating certificates. In some jurisdictions, all that is required is that an appropriate official of the foreign jurisdiction certify that the person administering the oath had the official capacity so to do (the precise nature of the official capacity varying under different statutes). In others, there are further requirements: for example, that the signature of the oath-administrator has been compared with his official signature, or that the seal affixed to the authenticating certificate or to the original jurat is a correct official seal.[15]

9 Code Ann. 1953, §78-25-7. VIRGINIA: §8-277, Code 1950, 1957 Repl. Vol. WEST VIRGINIA: Michies W.Va. Code 1961, §§5721 and 3952. WISCONSIN: W.S.A. 327.23.

[11] *Schon v. Ortner* [New York] 21 Misc. 2d 612, 613.

[12] *Majestic Co. Inc. v. Wender* [New York] 24 Misc. 2d 1018, 1019.

[13] *Gordon v. Gordon* [New York] 17 Misc. 2d 734, 735.

[14] *Miller v. Jones*, 67 Hun 281, 22 N.Y. Supp. 86, 90–91, holding, however, that since the invalidity of the authenticating certificate had not been raised during the hearing of the motion in which it was employed, the point would be deemed waived and the defect cured. The court added that the defect in the certificate, if one existed, "was such that it could be cured by producing on the appeal a proper certificate."

[15] Under some old statutes, there are actually required to be *two* authenticating certificates. One had to be made by an appropriate official, who authenticated the signature, seal and official capacity of the oath-administrator.

It is important for counsel, who intends to depend upon a foreign jurat, either to ascertain that the authenticating certificate furnished in the foreign jurisdiction complies with local law, or else to send a form of authentication to the foreign jurisdiction so that the form may be executed (and, if necessary, sealed) by an appropriate officer in that foreign jurisdiction.

Some examples of authenticating certificates are enlightening. In each instance, it will be noted that the certificate conforms with the law of the state wherein it was issued. This does not necessarily mean that it meets the requirements of the statute in the state where it is intended to be used. (See Form 7.)

Form 7.

Authenticating Certificates.

MASSACHUSETTS

"STATE OF MASSACHUSETTS
COUNTY OF BARNSTABLE } SS.

I, [   ], Clerk of the County of Barnstable, and also Clerk of the Superior Court in and for said county, which court is a court of record having a seal, do hereby certify that [   ] by and before whom the foregoing acknowledgment or proof was taken, was, at the time of taking the same, a NOTARY PUBLIC residing in said county, [SEAL] and was duly authorized by the laws of said state to take and certify acknowledgments or proofs of deeds of land in said state, and further that I am well acquainted with the handwriting of said notary public, and that I verily believe that the signature to said certificate of acknowledgment or proof is genuine.

In testimony whereof, I have hereunto set my hand and affixed the seal of said court at Barnstable in said County of Barnstable this 21st day of June 1965.

[   ] Clerk."

The other, by a superior official, who was required to authenticate the signature, capacity and seal of the first authenticating official. This process is technically known as "exemplification."

NEW JERSEY

"In the Atlantic County Court

STATE OF NEW JERSEY } SS.
COUNTY OF ATLANTIC

I, [   ], Clerk of the County of Atlantic and Clerk of the Court of said County, said Court being a Court of Record, having a common seal, being the officer authorized by the laws of the State of New Jersey to make the following certificate. **DO HEREBY CERTIFY,** that [   ] whose name is subscribed to the certificate of the acknowledgment, proof or affidavit, was at the time [SEAL] of taking such acknowledgment, proof or affidavit, a **NOTARY PUBLIC** of the State of New Jersey, residing in the County aforesaid, duly commissioned and qualified to administer oaths and affirmations and to take acknowledgments and proofs of deeds or conveyances for lands, tenements and hereditaments and other instruments in writing to be recorded in said State of New Jersey, and to all whose acts, as such, full faith and credit are and ought to be given, as well in Courts of Judicature as elsewhere; and that I am well acquainted with the handwriting of the said **NOTARY PUBLIC** and verily believe the signature to the attached certificate is genuine. Impression of Notary Public Seal not required by law to be filed in this office.

IN TESTIMONY WHEREOF, I have hereunto set my hand and affixed the seal of the said County and Court this *8th* day of *October* in the year of our Lord, one thousand nine hundred and *Sixty-five* (1965).

[   ]
Clerk"

FLORIDA

"STATE OF FLORIDA } SS.
COUNTY OF PINELLAS

I, [   ], Clerk of the County of Pinellas, and also Clerk of the Circuit Court of the said County, the same being a Court of Record, **DO HEREBY CERTIFY THAT.** [   ]

whose name is subscribed to the certificate of the proof or acknowledgment of the annexed instrument and thereon written, was at the time of taking such proof and acknowledgment, a Notary Public, in and for said County, residing therein, duly commissioned and sworn, and authorized by the laws of said State to take the acknowledgments and proofs of deeds or conveyances, for land, tenements or hereditaments in said State, to be recorded therein.

[SEAL]   And further, that I am well acquainted with the handwriting of such Notary Public, and verily believe the signature to said certificate of proof or acknowledgment is genuine; that I have compared the impression of the seal affixed thereto with a specimen impression thereof filed or deposited in my office, and that I believe the impression of the seal upon the original certificate is genuine.

IN WITNESS WHEREOF, I have hereunto set my hand and affixed the seal of the said Court and County, this 9 day of *November, 1965.*

[   ], Clerk Circuit Court

By [   ]

Deputy Clerk."

In the present section, we have considered the authentication of the official capacity of an oath-administrator. This required authentication is for the *sole* purpose of establishing the power of the oath-administrator to take the oath of an affiant. The function of this type of authenticating certificate is to lay the groundwork for the introduction in evidence (or the use upon a motion) of a document or affidavit. Whether or not such document or affidavit, in turn, is a statutory aid to proof depends upon a different statute of the forum of litigation. The difference between the two types of enactments may be summed up as follows: the document or affidavit may not be utilized *at all* unless the capacity to administer an oath is authenticated by a proper official in the state wherein the oath was administered; however, even though this authentication is complete and proper, the *effect* of the document or affidavit depends entirely on the substantive law of the trial forum. It may, *or may not,* be an ultimate statutory aid to proof.

In succeeding sections, we discuss and illustrate enactments which are true statutory aids to proof. The operative effect of those statutes is a subject entirely apart from the sufficiency of authentication of the foreign official. However, some of those statutes combine a statement of the effectiveness of a given document (as, for example, that it is *prima facie* proof) with special provisions as to the type of authentication required. For example, the authentication of the official character of a person administering an oath may be different from the authentication required for the receipt of an official foreign document under the seal of a foreign official. The *local* statute should be carefully examined to determine, in each instance, whether the foreign authentication meets the requirements for the use of a foreign document or affidavit in the circumstances of the case at bar.

Sec. 11:5   Affidavit of service or posting notice.

The most common form of statutory aids to proof is the affidavit of service, customarily used to support the taking of a default judgment where no appearance has been made by the defendant or no answer filed by him.[16]

The affidavit of service is required to bear the title of the action and to state the date (and sometimes the time of day) and place of service, plus a general averment to the effect that at the time of service the process server personally knew the person so served to be the defendant in the action.[17]

---

[16] In matrimonial actions, some statutes, court rules or decisions are to the effect that an affidavit of service may not be used in support of a default judgment. The process server must be produced and must be prepared to testify not only that he served the process but that he personally knew the person so served to be the defendant and the spouse of the plaintiff. If he did not personally know the person so served to be the defendant and the spouse of the plaintiff, his testimony may be supported by that of an identifying witness (other than the plaintiff). Proof of identification of the person served may also be made by producing a picture of the defendant, the process server testifying that the person he served was the person whose picture was produced, and, by the testimony of another witness (other than the plaintiff) to the effect that the picture is that of the defendant, who is the spouse of the plaintiff.

[17] CONNECTICUT: C.G.S.A. §52-52. FLORIDA: R.C.P., Rule 1.4. KANSAS: K.S.A. 60-312. KENTUCKY: R.C.P., Rule 5.03. MONTANA: Sec. 93-1701-1, Repl. Vol. 7, Revised Codes of Montana 1947. NORTH DAKOTA: N.D.C.C. 31-04-05. OHIO: Page's Rev. Stat. Ann., §2319.03. OKLAHOMA: 12 Okl. St. Ann. §431. WASHINGTON: RCWA 4.28.310. WISCONSIN: W.S.A. 328.18. WYOMING: R.C.P., Rule 4(m). In some jurisdictions there is a requirement that, at the time of service, the process server ascertain that the defendant was not in military service. Or the affidavit may be required to be made by a particular type of agent. Rev. L. Hawaii 1955, §224-29.

Some statutes provide that an affidavit by a person who served, posted or affixed a notice, showing such service, posting or affixing, is *prima facie* evidence of the service, posting or affixing, if the affiant is dead, insane or cannot be compelled with due diligence to attend the trial.[18]

The Federal rule as to proof of service reads as follows:

> **"Return.** The person serving the process shall make proof of service thereof to the court promptly and in any event within the time during which the person served must respond to the process. If service is made by a person other than a United States marshal or his deputy, he shall make affidavit thereof. Failure to make proof of service does not affect the validity of the service." [19]

In footnote 16 of this section, *supra,* we have referred to the fact that in matrimonial actions in some jurisdictions proof of service by an affidavit may not be made, whereas in footnote 18 we have cited statutes indicating that where an affiant is dead, insane or cannot be compelled with due diligence to attend the trial, proof of service may be made by the affidavit of the absent witness. In the presence of this latter type of statute, it is clearly arguable that, even in a matrimonial case, where the process server is dead, insane, or cannot be compelled with due diligence to attend the trial, proof of service may be made by his affidavit, coupled of course with the necessary proof of identification of the person served unless the process server's affidavit states that he, personally, knew the defendant so served to be the defendant in the action and the spouse of the plaintiff.

Sec. 11:6   Affidavit of publication in newspaper.

Where publication of a notice or other advertisement authorized or required by law or court order is a necessary step in a case, various statutes permit proof of such publication by affidavit.

---

[18] ALABAMA: Code, Title 7, §404. CALIFORNIA: Code Civ. Proc. §2009 (Deering's). INDIANA: Burns' Stat. §2-1637. IOWA: 43 Code Ann., §§622.94–622.96. MISSISSIPPI: 2 Code 1942 Ann., §1759. NEBRASKA: R.R.S. 1943, §25-1275. NEW YORK: C.P.L.R. 4531. TEXAS: R.C.P., Rule 21a.
[19] F.R.C.P., rule 4(g).

The most common requirements for such an affidavit are the following: [20]

    1. That the affidavit be made by the printer or publisher of a newspaper published within the state, or his foreman or principal clerk.

    2. That the affidavit show the publication of the notice or other advertisement.

    3. That there be annexed to the affidavit a printed copy of the notice or other advertisement.

Under these statutes, the affidavit is *prima facie* evidence of publication and of statements showing that the deponent is authorized to make the affidavit.

In some jurisdictions, the affidavit may be made by any person.[21]

In Hawaii proof of publication may be made by physical production of the newspaper containing the advertisement or notice. In Oklahoma the statute says that such an affidavit may be used, but there is no specific mention of whose affidavit is required.[22]

Different court orders and statutes may provide for more than one publication. In such a case, the proffered proof of publication should clearly indicate that the publication was made on each of the dates (or within the period) required.

As a practical matter, most newspapers have a regularly printed form of publication, prepared by their own lawyers. Although this affidavit should be examined by trial counsel to make sure it conforms with the local statute, there do not appear to have been any decisions holding that such an affidavit so prepared was insufficient.

---

[20] ALABAMA: Code, Title 7, §403. ALASKA: Alaska Statutes, §09.25.070. ARIZONA: A.R.S., §39-205. CALIFORNIA: Code Civ. Proc., §2011 (Deering's). COLORADO: CRS, §52-1-15. FLORIDA: F.S.A. §48.10. IDAHO: Code, §5-511 and R.C.P., Rule 4(g). ILLINOIS: Smith-Hurd Ill. St. Ch. 100, §1. INDIANA: Burns' Stat. §2-1638. KENTUCKY: KRS 424.170. MICHIGAN: Stat. Ann., §27A.2128. MINNESOTA: M.S.A. §§600.10–600.12. MISSISSIPPI: 2 Code 1942 Ann., §1758. MISSOURI: V.A.M.S. §494.060. MONTANA: Sec. 93-1701-2, Repl. Vol. 7, Revised Codes of Montana 1947. NEVADA: NRCP 4(g). NEW YORK: C.P.L.R. 4532. NORTH CAROLINA: Gen. Stat. §1-600. NORTH DAKOTA: NDCC §31-04-06. OHIO: Page's Rev. Code Ann., §2319.03. TENNESSEE: T.C.A. §21-217. UTAH: 9 Code Ann. 1953, §§78-25-14, 78-25-15. VIRGINIA: §8-329, Code 1950, 1957 Repl. Vol. WASHINGTON: RCWA 4.28.310. WISCONSIN: W.S.A. 328.19.

[21] CONNECTICUT: C.G.S.A. §52-52. IOWA: 43 Code Ann., §622.92. KANSAS: K.S.A. 60-312. NEBRASKA: R.R.S. 1943, §25-520. WYOMING: R.C.P., Rule 4(m).

[22] HAWAII: Rev. L. Hawaii 1955, §224-12. OKLAHOMA: 12 Okl. St. Ann. §431.

Sec. 11:7 Certificate or affidavit of public officer.

Many statutes provide that where a public officer is required or authorized by some specific provision of law to make a certificate or an affidavit to a fact ascertained, or an act performed by him in the course of his official duty *and* to file or deposit it in a public office of the state, the certificate or affidavit so filed or deposited is *prima facie* evidence of the facts therein stated.[23]

Other statutes, of similar import, provide that all public records may be offered as proof of the facts therein contained, but such statutes do not generally contain a specific provision that their contents are *prima facie* evidence of the facts therein stated.[24]

It should be noted that three requirements must exist if such official certificates, affidavits or public records are to be admissible. They are:

1. Ascertainment of fact or performance of the act must be required by law as part of the official duty of the person making the affidavit or certificate or an entry in the public record.

2. The public officer must be required or authorized by specific statute to make such certificate or affidavit or public record.

3. The public officer must be required or authorized to file or deposit the certificate or affidavit in a public office of the state.

The use of such certificates, affidavits or entries in records in the actual trial of a case may, under another type of statute, be simplified by submitting a certified copy of the affidavit, certificate or entry, thus obviating the necessity for producing the original.

---

[23] FLORIDA: F.S.A. §92.18. KENTUCKY: KRS 422.020. MINNESOTA: M.S.A. §§599.18 and 600.13. MONTANA: Sec. 93-1001-32, Repl. Vol. 7, Revised Codes of Montana 1947. NEW JERSEY: N.J.S.A. 2A:84A, Rules of Evidence, Rule 63(15). NEW YORK: C.P.L.R. 4520. NORTH DAKOTA: NDCC 31-09-08, 31-09-11. OREGON: ORS 43.370. UTAH: 9 Code Ann. 1953, §78-25-3. WISCONSIN: W.S.A. 327.10.

[24] CALIFORNIA: Code Civ. Proc., §1920 (Deering's); Evidence Code §§1270–1272, 1280 (Deering's). COLORADO: CRS, §52-1-16. IDAHO: Code, §§9-316 and 9-322. ILLINOIS: Smith-Hurd Ill. St. Ch. 51, §56. INDIANA: Burns' Stat. §2-1607. LOUISIANA: LSA-C.C.P. art. 1393. MICHIGAN: Stat. Ann., §27A.2107. NEW HAMPSHIRE: RSA 516:32. OHIO: Page's Rev. Stat. Ann., §2317.42. TEXAS: Vernon's Tex. Civ. Stat., Art. 3731a. WYOMING: Stat. 1957, §1-169.

Sec. 11:8 Authentication of official record of court or government office in the United States.

The first three subdivisions of Rule 4540 of the Civil Practice Law and Rules of New York are typical of many statutes permitting convenient authentication of domestic official records.[25]
These three subdivisions read as follows:

"(a) **Copies permitted.** An official publication, or a copy attested as correct by an officer or a deputy of an officer having legal custody of an official record of the United States or of any state, territory or jurisdiction of the United States, or of any of its courts, legislature, offices, public bodies or boards is prima facie evidence of such record.

"(b) **Certificate of officer of the state.** Where the copy is attested by an officer of the state, it shall be accompanied by a certificate signed by, or with a facsimile of the signature of, the clerk of a court having legal custody of the record, and, except where the copy is used in the same court or before one of its officers, with the seal of the court affixed; or signed by, or with a facsimile of the signature of, the officer having legal custody of the original, or his deputy or clerk, with his official seal affixed; or signed by, or with a facsimile of the signature of, the presiding officer, secretary or clerk of the public body or board and, except where it is certified by the clerk or secretary of either house of the legislature, with the seal of the body or board affixed. If the certificate is made by a county clerk, the county seal shall be affixed.

---

[25] FEDERAL: F.R.C.P., rule 44(a)(1); 28 U.S.C. §§1738–1740. COLORADO: R.C.P., Rule 44(a). GEORGIA: Code Ann., §38-630. INDIANA: Burns' Stat. §§2-1606 and 2-1607. IOWA: 43 Code Ann., §§622.37, 622.43 and 622.52–54. KANSAS: K.S.A. 60-465. KENTUCKY: KRS 422.050. LOUISIANA: LSA-C.C.P. art. 1395. MAINE: R.C.P., Rule 44; 16 M.R.S.A. §§451, 457–460. MONTANA: Sec. 93-1001-17, Repl. Vol. 7, Revised Codes of Montana 1947. NEVADA: NRCP, Rule 44(a); NRS 49.040–49.060. NEW JERSEY: N.J.S.A. 2A:84A, Rules of Evidence, Rule 68. NORTH DAKOTA: NDCC 31-09-02; R.C.P., Rule 44(a). OHIO: Page's Rev. Stat. Ann., §2317.10. OREGON: ORS 43.110 and 43.330. PENNSYLVANIA: 28 P.S. §§121–128. TEXAS: Vernon's Tex. Civ. Stat., Art. 3731a. UTAH: 9 Code Ann. 1953, R.C.P., Rule 44. VERMONT: 12 V.S.A. §§1696–1699. VIRGINIA: §§8-271 and 8-272, Code 1950, 1957 Repl. Vol. WASHINGTON: RCWA 5.44.010 and 5.44.040. WEST VIRGINIA: R.C.P., Rule 44(a). WYOMING: R.C.P., Rule 44(a).

"(c) **Certificate of officer of another jurisdiction.** Where the copy is attested by an officer of another jurisdiction, it shall be accompanied by a certificate that such officer has legal custody of the record, and that his signature is believed to be genuine, which certificate shall be made by a judge of a court of record of the district or political subdivision in which the record is kept, with the seal of the court affixed; or by any public officer having a seal of office and having official duties in that district or political subdivision with respect to the subject matter of the record, with the seal of his office affixed."

In other jurisdictions, similar statutes exist somewhat more narrowly couched than the New York statute.[26]

In some states, the applicable statute does not contain a provision that the official record is *prima facie* evidence, but does state that the record is "competent" evidence.[27] This is a distinction without a difference. If the record is originally admissible as "competent" evidence, the duty to go forward with the proof is obviously thrust upon one who contests the validity of the record. An example of such a contest might arise where it is claimed, under subdivision (c) of the New York statute that the public officer of another jurisdiction did not have "official duties in that district or political subdivision with respect to the subject matter of the record, with the seal of his office affixed." Although the person offering the certificate might, as a matter of excessive caution, arm himself with the statute of another jurisdiction showing the duties of the certifying officer, it is inconceivable that the time taken to obtain and produce such information would be of practical value. It is better to leave the proof of the negative of official capacity to the technical individual who asserts it.

---

[26] ALABAMA: Code, Title 7, §§422–424, 426–429. ARIZONA: R.C.P. Rules 44(g) and 44(j). ARKANSAS: Stat. Ann., §§28-902, 28-903, 28-931 and 28-932. CALIFORNIA: Code Civ. Proc., §§1901, 1905 and 1918 (Deering's); Evidence Code §§1452–1454, 1506 and 1530 (Deering's). CONNECTICUT: C.G.S.A. §§52-162 to 52-165. FLORIDA: F.S.A. §§92.10, 92.29 and 92.32. HAWAII: Rev. L. Hawaii 1955, §224-5. IDAHO: Code, §9-314. ILLINOIS: Smith-Hurd Ill. St. Ch. 51, §§12a and 56. MARYLAND: Code, art. 35, §76. MASSACHUSETTS: Ann. L. Mass., c. 233, §§69, 70 and 76A-B. MICHIGAN: Stat. Ann., §27A.2103. MINNESOTA: M.S.A. §599.11. MISSOURI: V.A.M.S. §§490.130–490.240. NEBRASKA: R.R.S. 1943, §§25-1279, 25-1285 to 25-1286, 25-1289 to 25-1290. OKLAHOMA: 12 Okl. St. Ann. §486.

[27] DELAWARE: 5 Code Ann.; Title 10, §4308. NEW HAMPSHIRE: RSA 516:30.

In some jurisdictions, there are highly specialized statutes, making unique types of certificates *prima facie* evidence of the facts therein contained. For example, inspection certificates issued by such agencies as the United States Department of Agriculture are within this class.[28]

More general statutes in other jurisdictions apply the rule of admissibility in evidence to all public *reports*.[29] Although this general type of statute does not state that the contents of the public records are *prima facie* evidence of the facts therein contained, their admissibility can hardly have any other effect.

There are various types of certificates filed in county, municipal and other local offices within political subdivisions of a state. The statutes or ordinances authorizing the making of such certificates sometimes provide that they should be made by given officers or classes of persons *and* that they shall be filed in some designated office of the political subdivision. Such certificates are encompassed within the state-wide provisions for authentication of official records, covered by the present section.

In later sections of the present chapter, reference is made to state-wide statutes covering specific certificates (such as marriage and particularized death certificates). However, there are other equally important certificates, such as birth certificates, which are sometimes not specifically mentioned in a state-wide statute. Either by clear inference or specific mention, however, certain general statutes obviously permit the use as evidence of a birth certificate.[30]

---

[28] FLORIDA: F.S.A. §92.20. GEORGIA: Code Ann., §38-631. NEW JERSEY: N.J.S.A. 2A:84A, Rules of Evidence, Rule 63(15). NEW YORK: C.P.L.R. 4529. In Indiana, a commercial feed analysis may be so received but it is not stated to be *prima facie* evidence. Burns' Stat. §16-1024.

[29] FEDERAL: 5 U.S.C. §575; F.R.C.P., rule 44(a). ALABAMA: Code, Title 7, §432. ARKANSAS: Stat. Ann., §28-930. CONNECTICUT: C.G.S.A. §52-165. DELAWARE: 5 Code Ann.; Title 10, §4308. KENTUCKY: KRS 422.050. MINNESOTA: M.S.A. §600.13. OREGON: ORS 43.360–43.370. WISCONSIN: W.S.A. 327.18.

[30] An example of this type of general statute is one which permits "public records" to be proved in a certain manner and to have a certain effect (either, for example, as *prima facie* proof or as admissible evidence). We are here confronted by two concepts. The first is proof of the *existence* of the record. This may be accomplished through the provisions of a statutory aid to proof or by common-law proof (for example, the testimony of an individual that he examined the public record and that the copy which is offered in evidence is an exact copy thereof). The effect that the proved public record will have in a given case depends on other statutory provisions. Whether the public record can act as evidence of the matter set forth in its text may depend on a statute, but could also have this effect as a matter of decisional

Again, even when the statute does not mention that the certificate shall be *prima facie* evidence of a fact, common sense requires us to give it that intendment.

Sec. 11:9 Proof of foreign records or documents.

The use of a foreign document or record in an American jurisdiction is established by provisions of law or court rules. The applicable statutes or rules vary in detail as to the method of authentication, but most of them envisage the use of some original or exemplifying certificate made by an American officer in the foreign jurisdication. Some statutes have different provisions for the authentication of foreign documents in general and for the authentication of foreign court records. Care must be taken to differentiate between these two types.

Some statutes go into the greatest detail in prescribing methods of authentication. Others allow a broader sweep.

There is a difference between the certificate of the custodian of the document and the additional certificate of another person or official stating that such custodian was, in fact, the official he purported to be. The former certificate is known as an "attestation." The latter is denominated an "authenticating certificate." [31]

The use to which a properly attested and authenticated foreign document or record may be put in an American court depends on the substantive law of the jurisdiction in which the cause is tried. It is the general rule that, whether or not explicitly set forth in a local statute, such a document is admissible in evidence as *prima facie* proof of the facts therein set forth.

Typical of a general statute covering foreign documents is the Federal Law, which reads as follows: [32]

> "A copy of any foreign document of record or on file in a public office of a foreign country or political subdivision thereof,

---

law. In California, birth certificates are specifically mentioned in the statutory aid to proof. Evidence Code §1316 (Deering's). The primary purpose of using birth certificates is to establish age. Some special statutes permit the age of a child to be established by the production and exhibition of the child in open court "to determine his age by a personal inspection." KANSAS: K.S.A. 38-836. NEW YORK: C.P.L.R. 4516.

[31] The need for the two certificates is a classic example of "exemplification" as distinguished from mere "certification."

[32] 28 U.S.C. §1741.

certified by the lawful custodian thereof, shall be admissible in evidence when authenticated by a certificate of a consular officer of the United States resident in such foreign country, under the seal of his office, that the copy has been certified by the lawful custodian."

The Federal statute is augmented by Rule 44(a)(2) of the Federal Rules of Civil Procedure, which, in applicable part, reads:

"A foreign official record, or an entry therein, when admissible for any purpose, may be evidenced by an official publication thereof; or a copy thereof, attested by a person authorized to make the attestation, and accompanied by a final certification as to the genuineness of the signature and official position (i) of the attesting person, or (ii) of any foreign official whose certificate of genuineness of signature and official position relates to the attestation or is in a chain of certificates of genuineness of signature and official position relating to the attestation. A final certification may be made by a secretary of embassy or legation, consul general, consul, vice consul, or consular agent of the United States, or a diplomatic or consular official of the foreign country assigned or accredited to the United States. If reasonable opportunity has been given to all parties to investigate the authenticity and accuracy of the documents, the court may, for good cause shown, (i) admit an attested copy without final certification or (ii) permit the foreign official record to be evidenced by an attested summary with or without a final certification."

Certain other American jurisdictions have similarly general statutes, varying in degree of explicitness.[33] Still others are confined in their applicability to foreign court records as distinguished from general foreign records and documents.[34]

---

[33] MAINE: 16 M.R.S.A. §460; R.C.P., Rule 44. NEVADA: NRS 49.070–49.080; NRCP, Rule 44(a). NEW JERSEY: N.J.S.A. 2A:84A, Rules of Evidence, Rule 68. NORTH DAKOTA: NDCC 31-09-04; R.C.P., Rule 44(a). WEST VIRGINIA: R.C.P., Rule 44(a). WYOMING: R.C.P., Rule 44(a).

[34] ARIZONA: R.C.P. Rule 44(g)3. CALIFORNIA: Code Civ. Proc., §§1901, 1906 and 1907 (Deering's); Evidence Code §§1401, 1452–1454, 1530 (Deering's). COLORADO: R.C.P., Rule 44(a). DELAWARE: 13 Code Ann.; Super. Civ. Rule 44(a) and Chan. Rule 44. FLORIDA: F.S.A. §92.032. HAWAII: Rev. L. Hawaii 1955, §224-5. IDAHO: Code, §§9-313, 9-314 and 9-322. IOWA: 43

In some jurisdictions the statutes spell out in great detail not only the precise terms required for attestation and authentication but variations of those terms applicable to individual circumstances.[35]

It is worthy of note that in some instances where minutiae of form are specifically stated, the net result of the statute is to broaden its field of coverage. The mere existence of a statute does not, of course, preclude common-law methods of proof of foreign documents and records, depending upon the general rules of evidence. Nevertheless, assuming that correct technical proof of the contents of a foreign document or record is made, the effect of that proof as a substantive addition to the establishment of a case or defense is often narrowed by the terms of the enabling statutory aid to proof. Some statutes, in effect, restate common-law rules of evidence but add either short-cuts of technical proof or limitations on ultimate effectiveness. Trial counsel should examine and analyze the local statute with great care to determine the extent to which it may be helpful to him or dangerous for him.

A complicated statutory aid to proof, which illustrates all of the problems just adverted to is Rule 4542 of the New York Civil Practice Law and Rules. An examination of the text of that Rule and an analysis of its contents vividly points up the various problems which are faced by trial counsel in considering local statutes in his own jurisdiction. The complete text of the Rule is as follows:

"**Rule 4542.   Proof of foreign records and documents.**

(a) **Attestation in conformity with law of foreign country.**
   1. A copy of a record of a court of a foreign country, or a copy of a patent, record or other document remaining of record or on file in a public office of a foreign country, is admissible in evidence when it is attested, authenticated and accompanied by proof of attestation as provided in this subdivision.
   2. The copy shall be attested as correct, in the manner pre-

---

Code Ann., §§622.55 and 622.57. LOUISIANA: LSA-C.C.P. art. 1395. MICHI-GAN: Stat. Ann., §27A.2104. MINNESOTA: M.S.A. §599.11. MISSISSIPPI: 2 Code 1942 Ann., §1747. NEW MEXICO: §21-1-1(44)(a), N.M.S.A. 1953. OKLA-HOMA: 12 Okl. St. Ann. §485. TENNESSEE: T.C.A. §24-603. WISCONSIN: W.S.A. 327.15. Nebraska confines the application of its statute to foreign court and legislative records. R.R.S. 1943, §§25-1288 to 25-1290, inclusive.
   [35] KANSAS: K.S.A. 60-465. KENTUCKY: KRS 422.080. MONTANA: Sec. 93-1001-18 to 93-1001-19, Repl. Vol. 7, Revised Codes of Montana 1947. ORE-GON: ORS 43.110–43.120, 43.330. TEXAS: Vernon's Tex. Civ. Stat., Art. 3731a. VERMONT: 12 V.S.A. §§1696–1699.

scribed by the law of the foreign country, by the officer, or a deputy of the officer, having legal custody of the record or document, or the officer authorized by the law of the foreign country to make such attestation.

3. The attestation shall be authenticated by a certificate that the person who attested the copy was the officer he purported to be. The authenticating certificate shall be made:

(i) under the seal of the court of which he is an officer, by the clerk or other certifying officer of a court of the foreign country, or of a court of a geographical or political subdivision thereof, other than the clerk or certifying officer who attested the copy; or

(ii) by the officer having charge of the official record of the appointment of the attesting officer or having a record of his signature; or

(iii) under the seal of his office, by any foreign service officer authorized by United States Department of State regulations to authenticate documents who is stationed in the foreign country where the record is kept.

4. The copy shall be accompanied by a certificate to the effect that it was attested in the manner prescribed by the law of the foreign country, and unless it was attested by the officer or a deputy of the officer having legal custody of the record or document, to the effect, in addition, that a person, occupying the office described in the attestation as being the office of the attesting officer, was authorized by the law of the foreign country to make such attestation. The certificate of conformity with the law of the foreign country required by this subdivision shall be made:

(i) by an attorney and counsellor-at-law admitted to practice in the state, resident in the foreign country; or

(ii) under the seal of his office, by any foreign service officer authorized by United States department of state regulations to authenticate documents who is stationed in the foreign country where the record is kept; or

(iii) under the seal of his office, by a consular officer of the foreign country, resident in the state; or

(iv) by any other person deemed qualified by the court.

5. A certificate of conformity as prescribed by this subdivision is prima facie evidence that the attestation is in the form in use in such foreign country and that a person occupying the office

described in the attestation as being the office of the attesting officer was authorized to make such attestation.

(b) Attestation by clerk and certificate of judge and under great seal of country. A copy of a record of a foreign country is admissible in evidence when authenticated:

1. by the attestation of the clerk of the court, with the seal of the court affixed, or of the officer having legal custody of the record, with the seal of his office affixed;

2. by a certificate of the chief judge or presiding magistrate of the court, to the effect that the signature of the person so attesting the record is genuine and that he is the clerk of the court or the officer having legal custody of the record; and

3. by the certificate, under the great or principal seal of the government under whose authority the court is held, of the secretary of state, or other officer having the custody of that seal, to the effect that the court is duly constituted, specifying generally the nature of its jurisdiction, and that the signature of the chief judge or presiding magistrate to the certificate specified in paragraph two is genuine.

(c) Commissioner appointed by secretary of state. A copy of a record of a court of a foreign country, or a copy of a patent, record or other document remaining of record or on file in a public office of a foreign country, certified in the form in use in that country, is admissible in evidence and is prima facie evidence that the copy is certified in the form in use in that foreign country, when authenticated:

1. by a certificate made by a commissioner appointed by the secretary of state to take the proof or acknowledgment of deeds in that country, with his official seal affixed, to the effect that the patent, record or other document is of record or on file in the court or other public office and that the copy is correct and certified in due form; and

2. by a certificate made by the secretary of state, with his official seal affixed, annexed to that of the commissioner, to the same effect as prescribed by law for the authentication of the certificate of such a commissioner upon a conveyance to be recorded within the state.

(d) Witness who examined record. A copy of a record of a court of a foreign country, authenticated by the attestation of the clerk of the court in which it remains, with the seal of the court affixed, is admissible in evidence when a witness testifies that

1. the copy offered has been compared by the witness with the original and is an exact transcript of the whole of the original;

2. the original was, when the copy was compared, in the custody of the clerk of the court or other officer having legal custody of it; and

3. the attestation is genuine."

In addition to the details set forth in subdivisions (a), (b) and (c) of the foregoing Rule, we invite the attention of the reader to the interesting provision of subdivision (d) thereof, relating solely to an attested copy of a record of a court of a foreign country, which is permitted to be authenticated by the testimony of a living witness in open court. An extremely hazardous condition confronting trial counsel may arise if there is no provision by statute or court rule permitting authentication of foreign records by a short-cut method and if there is no provision authorizing a living witness to testify to the contents of such a record. In such a case, it may be necessary to have the actual custodian of the record appear as a witness or to take his deposition in a foreign country and cause the original record to be annexed to the deposition as an exhibit thereof. Foreign officials are understandably loath to permit original records to be taken out of their country. Indeed, it is hard to imagine a situation in which they would allow such extra-territorial extraction. This might lead to the necessity for having a referee or hearing master sent from the United States to take evidence in a foreign country.

As a practical matter, if the foreign record is actually available for examination, a copy of it is often brought into the American court and accepted as genuine by stipulation of the parties. An appropriate arrangement can be worked out by opposing counsel, sometimes with the assistance of the court during pre-trial conferences. If a party unreasonably refuses so to stipulate and thus causes inordinate expense to his opponent, it is probable that the American court would tax the cost of the foreign expedition to the obstructing party, if the latter is unsuccessful on the trial.[36]

---

[36] The cost-taxing (including the charging of disbursements) statutes are becoming increasingly broad in American jurisdictions. Where there is willful obstruction, a judge will probably be eager to discover a way of taxing costs.

As a last resort, counsel may care to consider utilizing the testimony of a witness in open court as to the contents of a document or court record even though a statute does not authorize such procedure. His proffer of evidence would rest upon the general principle that secondary proof is permitted under the "best evidence" rule when satisfactory explanation is made of the unavailability of the described document. The weakness of this type of attempt is that a court might reason that, since the statute permits oral testimony as to the contents of a certain type of document, the same statute inferentially excludes oral testimony as to the contents of other types of documents under the doctrine of *inclusio unius est exclusio alterius*.

Since the use of a consular certificate of authentication is common to so many statutes, we here reproduce a form of such certificate as Form 8.

Form 8.

Sample Form of United States Consular Certificate Of Authentication

"UNITED MEXICAN STATES
STATE OF CHIHUAHUA
CONSULATE OF THE UNITED } ss:
STATES OF AMERICA
AT CIUDAD JUAREZ

I, [   ], Vice Consul of the United States of America at Ciudad Juarez, Chihuahua, Mexico, duly commissioned and qualified do hereby certify that [   ] and [   ], whose true signatures and official seals are respectively, subscribed and affixed to the annexed document, were on the 28 day of DECEMBER 1965, the date thereof respectively, Judge and Secretary of the Second Civil Court (Juez y Secretario del Juzgado Segundo de lo Civil), Bravos District, Ciudad Juarez, Chihuahua, Mexico, duly commissioned and qualified to whose official acts, faith and credit are due.

The Consulate assumes no responsibility for the contents of the annexed document, nor for the validity of this document, or for its acceptability in any state in the United States.

IN WITNESS THEREOF I have hereunto set my hand and affixed the seal of this Consulate at Ciudad Juarez, Chihuahua, Mexico, this 29 day of DECEMBER 1965.

[SEAL]   [   ]
                               Vice Consul of the United States
                                        of America"

Sec. 11:10   Business records (entries made in regular course of business).

For several centuries, courts and legislators have been plagued by the question whether business records made by a party to a litigation should be admissible *in his favor*.[37] Obviously, under both the hearsay and self-serving declaration exclusionary rules, such records would be inadmissible; but business and commercial necessity conspired to create an exception to these rules. This exception was to the effect that a party would be permitted to use his own *account* books as evidence for himself, both in his lifetime and after his death and Professor Thayer has assured us that "[t]here is no sufficient reason to doubt that this had always been allowed." [38] The exception, however, was rigidly circumscribed in order to minimize the danger of false entries or of entries made so long after an event took place that their accuracy might be in grave doubt.[39]

In the early days of English jurisprudence, a party was not competent to testify in his own behalf. Thus, unless his business entries could be received, he might find himself unable to prove the justice of his cause. It was this circumstance that originally prompted permission to introduce in evidence regularly kept and maintained business records. When the inhibitions against a party's testimony were removed by statute, the business records rule nevertheless persisted; but, when the English Parliament found that the rule had been abused, its application was substantially limited by a corrective statute in the year 1609.[40]

The combination of early English statutes and their traditional usage found its way into American common law. This resulted in a series of American decisions that, in collective impact, became known as "the shop-book rule " An example of an application of that rule, which states both its scope and limitations, is found in a leading

---

[37] That such records would be admissible *against* such a party never seems to have been in doubt, since they could be taken as admissions.

[38] *Cases on Evidence* (2d Ed.), p. 509, quoted in Chamberlayne *Trial Evidence* (Second Edition, 1936), p. 834.

[39] For extended discussions of the historical development of these exceptions to the hearsay rule see *Wigmore on Evidence* (3rd Ed., 1940) sections 1517 *et seq.* and Chamberlayne *Trial Evidence* (Tompkins, Second Edition, 1936) sections 866 *et seq.*

[40] St. 7 Jac. I, ch. 12, subsequently continued and amended in 1627 by 3 Car. I ch. 4, §22 and in 1640 by 16 Car. I, ch. 4.

opinion of the New York Court of Appeals, reading, in applicable part, as follows: [41]

"The plaintiff sought to recover a balance due for coal sold and delivered by him to the defendant. He recovered judgment, upon a trial before a referee, and that judgment has been unanimously affirmed by the Appellate Division. Upon his appeal to this court, the defendant assigns as error a ruling of the referee, under which the plaintiff's books of account were admitted in evidence.

"Upon the trial, the plaintiff testified to having had business transactions with the defendant, in the sale of coal to him, for some time past; that his books of account contained a correct statement of the coal sold and delivered within the dates in question and that he, personally, delivered nearly all the coal covered by the account. He testified that his wife kept his books and made the entries therein from memoranda furnished by him, as made after the delivery of the coal. She, also, testified to making the entries in that manner and that they were correctly made. There was evidence on his part, also, to the effect that a copy of the account in the books had been acknowledged by the defendant, with an offer to settle upon some rectification being made. A witness for the plaintiff testified that he had settled with him by his books for eight or ten years and had always found the books correct. Being cross-examined as to that, he said: 'I knew the accounts were correct simply because I had confidence in him and paid what he asked. That is all the reason I had for saying they were correct, because I had confidence in him. . . . I relied on his honesty and not on my recollection as to the amount of coal I ordered.' Another witness testified for the plaintiff that he was a bookkeeper for a firm that purchased coal from the plaintiff on credit and that he had 'settled with him according to his books and according to our own four or five times,' and 'always found them to be correct.'

"Upon this evidence the books of account were offered by the plaintiff and the objection to their admission was placed 'on the ground that they are incompetent; a proper foundation not having been laid for their being admitted as evidence.' The

---

[41] *Smith v. Smith,* 163 N.Y. 168, 169–172.

objection was overruled and the defendant excepted. The question is thus presented whether, in the evidence which preceded, a foundation had been laid for the admission of the books according to the requirements of a rule of evidence, which should be regarded as established since its formulation in the case of *Vosburgh* v. *Thayer* (12 Johns. 461). It was held in that case that books of account ought not to be admitted in evidence, 'unless a foundation is first laid for their admission, by proving that the party had no clerk, that some of the articles charged have been delivered, that the books produced are the account books of the party, and that he keeps fair and honest accounts, and this by those who have dealt and settled with him.' The rule, as thus laid down, has been since accepted as correct. (*Matter of McGoldrick* v. *Traphagen,* 88 N.Y. 334; *Tomlinson* v. *Borst,* 30 Barb. 42; *Dooley* v. *Moan,* 57 Hun, 535.) Under these restrictions account books become evidence for the consideration of the tribunal, with which the determination of the issues rests. As evidence, which is manufactured by the party, they should be received with caution; but that is an objection which goes to the weight of the evidence and not to its admissibility, which is to be determined solely with reference to the foundation which has been laid for it. Their admission in evidence is, of course, not authoritative as to their contents; for the conclusion as to their credit will depend upon their appearance, the manner of their keeping and the character of him who offers them. Although the rule under discussion was established at a time when parties to an action were not allowed to be witnesses, the subsequent legislation, which removed that disqualification and authorized parties to testify in their own behalf, has not deprived them of the right to introduce their books of account in evidence. (*Tomlinson* v. *Borst, supra; Stroud* v. *Tilton,* 3 Keyes, 139) The rule may, still, be an important one in the administration of justice in cases where the party kept no clerk able to testify to the truth of the entries in his books and where, unless they are admitted, great inconvenience and a denial of justice may follow.

"The conditions precedent to the admissibility of the plaintiff's books of account were sufficiently complied with, within the requirements of the rule in *Vosburgh's* case. The plaintiff had sworn that he had personally delivered nearly all the coal charged and that the books which were produced contained his accounts. That he had no clerk was manifest from his testimony. In fact, the appellant does not claim that the plaintiff did have a clerk and, of course, the plaintiff's wife cannot be claimed to be a clerk, within the meaning of the rule. The clerk so intended means one who had something to do with, and had knowledge generally of, the business of his employer and who would be enabled to testify upon the subject of the goods sold. (*Matter of McGoldrick* v. *Traphagen, supra.*)

"The plaintiff had affirmatively shown, not only that his wife kept his books for him, but that it was he who either delivered the coal, or superintended its delivery. The evidence was sufficient to negative the idea that he kept a clerk who could testify, by reason of his employment, to the correctness of the account of goods sold and delivered. The remaining requirement, that proof should be made that the plaintiff kept fair and honest books, by those who had dealt with him and who had settled with him on the books, was sufficiently met in the evidence of the two witnesses, which has been mentioned. The evidence went to establish, not only the character of the plaintiff for honesty, but that in a course of business extending over several years the witnesses had always found his books to be correct. In the one case, the witness paid his bills relying upon the plaintiff's honesty and not upon his recollection as to the amount of coal ordered; in the other case, the witness had settled the plaintiff's bill against his employers according to his books and according to their own books, and had always found the plaintiff's books to be correct. Such evidence should be, and is, quite sufficient to discharge the burden resting upon the plaintiff with respect to that item of proof required by the rule."

Analyzing the foregoing quotation, we note that the court permitted the admission of shop-book entries into evidence because, by the standards of long accepted decisional criteria, it was deemed that their accuracy had been sufficiently established to overcome fear that the entries were manufactured by the plaintiff for the purposes of the trial. The evidence had established that entries of this type were made in the regular course of business, that entries of precisely this type had been used over a period of time to record dealings between plaintiff and defendant *and* that entries so made had been depended upon by both plaintiff and his customers *other than the defendant* as a basis for settling accounts between them. The element of settling accounts with third parties upon the basis of similar entries was an important and decisive factor in encouraging the court to assume the accuracy of the account-book. The course of business was established by the testimony of plaintiff and his wife, the latter having testified that she kept the books and made the entries from memoranda furnished by plaintiff, which memoranda were made after the delivery of coal as part of a regular system employed in keeping the books. Plaintiff, himself, testified that he, personally, delivered nearly all of the coal covered by the account; but this testimony was regarded as proof of the method used in the regular course of business, which resulted in the ultimate making of the book-entries.

The American common-law "shop book rule" was confined to entries in *books of account*, maintained in small businesses, vouched for by persons other than the parties to the action who had occasion to settle on the basis of shop-book entries, and necessarily used because no clerk was employed who could personally testify to the items covered by the entries. The significance of the requirement that no clerk was employed relates to the "best evidence" rule. If there had been a clerk available to testify to the transaction, itself, the use of a shop-book entry would be unnecessary.

Despite the fact that the shop-book rule has now been replaced by evidentiary statutes in most jurisdictions, a consideration of its substance is helpful in the construction of statutes. The rule, itself, is sometimes employed to fill the gaps in statutory provisions.

As business enterprises have increased in size and scope of operations and commercial transactions have become more complicated, the shop-book rule has emerged as an interesting antique with very little modern usefulness. Accordingly, legislatures have enacted broad statutes, permitting the introduction in evidence of records and entries kept in the regular course of business. Primarily these enactments serve to remove the impediments of the hearsay rule; but they constitute a substantial body of statutory aids to proof.

The statutory business record and entry rule has been adopted in a substantial majority of American jurisdictions.[42]

---

[42] FEDERAL: 28 U.S.C. §1732(a). ALABAMA: Code, Title 7, §§414–415. ARIZONA: R.C.P. Rule 44(q); A.R.S. §12-2262. ARKANSAS: Stat. Ann., §§28-928 and 28-929. CALIFORNIA: Code Civ. Proc., §§1953e–1953f(5) (Deering's); Evidence Code §§1270–1271 (Deering's). CONNECTICUT: C.G.S.A. §52-180. DELAWARE: 5 Code Ann.; Title 10, §4310. FLORIDA: F.S.A. §§92.36 and 92.37. GEORGIA: Code Ann., §38-711. HAWAII: Rev. L. Hawaii 1955,

The elements of the rule are as follows:

1. There must be a writing or record "whether in the form of an entry in a book or otherwise";

2. The writing or record must have been made as a memorandum or record of any act, transaction, occurrence or event;

3. There must be a finding that the entry or record was made in the course of "any business" (the term "business" including a business, profession, occupation and calling "of every kind"); and

4. There must be a further finding that "it was the regular course of such business to make it [the record or entry], at the time of the act, transaction, occurrence or event, or within a reasonable time thereafter."

In the presence of the foregoing four elements, the record or entry is "admissible in evidence in proof of the act, transaction, occurrence or event" to which it relates; but all other circumstances of the making of the memorandum or record, including lack of personal knowledge by the maker, may be proved to affect its weight.[43]

The foregoing is the general statutory rule, which is applicable in most American jurisdictions to *all* business records and memoranda and individual entries therein; but in some jurisdictions, the rule is limited to entries in "books of account." [44] In Louisiana, probably as a vestige of the ancient application of the Napoleonic Code,

---

§224-26. IDAHO: Code, §§9-413 to 9-414. IOWA: 43 Code Ann., §622.28. KANSAS: K.S.A. 60-460(m). MARYLAND: Code, art. 35, §59. MICHIGAN: Stat. Ann., §2146. MINNESOTA: M.S.A. §§600.01–600.04. MISSOURI: V.A.M.S. §§490.660–490.690. MONTANA: Sec. 93-801-1 to 93-801-4, Repl. Vol. 7, Revised Codes of Montana 1947. NEBRASKA: R.R.S. 1943, §§25-12,108 to 25-12,111. NEVADA: NRS 51.030. NEW HAMPSHIRE: RSA 521:1 to 521:5. NEW JERSEY: N.J.S.A. 2A:84A, Rules of Evidence, Rules 62 and 63(13). NEW MEXICO: §20-2-12, N.M.S.A. 1953. NEW YORK: C.P.L.R. 4518(a). NORTH DAKOTA: NDCC 31-08-01. OHIO: Page's Rev. Code Ann., §§2317.40–2317.41. OREGON: ORS 41.680–41.710. PENNSYLVANIA: 28 P.S. §§91a–91d. RHODE ISLAND: Gen. Laws 1956, §9-19-13. SOUTH DAKOTA: SDC 36.1001. TENNESSEE: T.C.A. §§24-712 to 24-715. TEXAS: Vernon's Tex. Civ. Stat., Art. 3737e. VERMONT: 12 V.S.A. §1700. WASHINGTON: RCWA 5.45.010–5.45.920. WISCONSIN: W.S.A. 327.25. WYOMING: Stat. 1957, §§1-170 to 1-173.

[43] The precautionary proposition concerning the weight to be given to a book entry is a direct reflection of the similar precaution encompassed in the early shop-book rule. *Cf., Smith v. Smith,* 163 N.Y. 168, 171, quoted *supra.*

[44] COLORADO: CRS, §154-1-3. ILLINOIS: Smith-Hurd Ill. St. Ch. 51, §3. MAINE: 16 M.R.S.A. §356. MASSACHUSETTS: Ann. L. Mass., c. 233, §78. OKLAHOMA: 12 Okl. St. Ann. §501.

the use of records made in the regular course of business is limited to suits against merchants.[45] Under the new California Evidence Code [46] the absence of an entry in a regularly kept business record is admissible for the purpose of showing the non-occurrence of an act or the non-existence of a transaction.

28 U.S.C. §1733(a) provides that books or records of account or minutes of proceedings of any department or agency of the United States "shall be admissible to prove the act, transaction or occurrence as a memorandum of which the same were made or kept." This special statutory provision may be regarded as an extension of the Federal regular course of business entry rule; [47] but, from certain decisions in Federal courts, it would appear that, even without such statute, the types of records referred to would have been admissible under the Federal version of the admissibility of records made in the regular course of business. Numerous Federal decisions have so held.[48]

As we have noted earlier in this section, there are four major elements, including two specific court findings, necessary to establish a foundation for the admissibility of records, memoranda or entries made in the regular course of business. The necessity for the findings is significant. The records, memoranda or entries are only admissible in evidence as proof of acts, transactions, occurrences or events if it is found by the trial court not only that they were made in the regular course of business, but also that it was such regular course to make the entry.

In many cases, a witness, through whose testimony it is sought to introduce business records, is asked the simple question whether those records were made in the regular course of business. In the

---

[45] LSA-C.C. art. 2248.

[46] Section 1272.

[47] 28 U.S.C. §1732(a).

[48] 28 U.S.C. §1733 extends the business records rule to U.S. departments and agencies. But, query whether this statute is necessary. See *La Porte v. U.S.*, 300 F. 2d 878, 880 [Selective Service Records]; *Beaty Shopping Center, Inc. v. Monarch Ins. Co. of Ohio*, 315 F. 2d 467, 470 [Weather Maps]; *U.S v. Rosenberg*, 195 F. 2d 583, 602, cert. den. 344 U.S. 838, rehearing den. 344 U.S. 889, rehearing den. 347 U.S. 1021, motion den. 355 U.S. 860 [Immigration Inspection Report]; *Gimbel Bros., Inc. v. Markette Corp.*, 200 F. Supp. 95, 101, affd. 307 F. 2d 91 [Official Survey]; *Sociedad De Transportes Maritimos, S.A. v. Panama Canal Co.*, 163 F. Supp. 151, 156, affd. 272 F. 2d 726 [Board of Local Inspectors records, findings and opinion]; *Moran v. Pittsburgh-Des Moines Steel Co.*, 183 F. 2d 467, 473 [Bureau of Mines Explosion report]; and, *Lew Moon Cheung v. Rogers*, 272 F. 2d 354, 357–360 [Public Health Service Blood Tests].

absence of objection, an affirmative answer by the witness is sufficient foundation for the introduction of the records. However, if the issue of sufficiency of proof is raised, a generalization by the witness is utterly insufficient. It must be proved that the witness, himself, is familiar with the method of record-making (whether or not he personally made the entry) *and* that he personally knows that, at the time the entry was made, it was the regular course of business to make such an entry "at the time of the act, transaction, occurrence or event, or within a reasonable time thereafter." It should be borne in mind that the witness must have *personal* knowledge of the regular course of business. What was the regular course of business existing at a given time is a fact. Unless the witness is able to testify to this fact, based on his personal observation, his testimony is worthless.

A striking example of failure to establish sufficient basis for introduction of entries made in the regular course of business occurred in a matrimonial action.[49] There, a plaintiff-wife claimed that her husband had told her he was infected with a disease and that she had gone to a physician to be examined for the purpose of determing whether she had contracted this disease. The husband denied that he had ever made such a statement to his wife or that he had ever contracted the disease. The physician, whom the wife claimed she had visited, was dead at the time of the trial. A doctor who had been associated with this physician and took over his practice at the time of his death, produced certain records in court and was asked whether these were the dead doctor's records, kept in the regular course of business. The husband's attorney objected to the question and asked permission to examine the successor doctor on the *voir dire*. Permission was granted.

The *voir dire* examination disclosed that, although the successor doctor had been associated with the deceased physician for a year before his death and knew the method of record-keeping *during that year*, he had *not* been so associated several years earlier, when the wife claimed she had visited the deceased physician. He admitted that he did not know how records were kept in that earlier period. He further admitted that he did not know whether, at that time, it was the custom of the deceased physician to make records at the time he rendered professional services or shortly thereafter. The

---

[49] *Rose v. Rose*, New York Supreme Court, Bronx County, Bronx County Clerk's Index No. 4574/1960 (record sealed).

purported record of the deceased physician concerning a visit made several years earlier by the plaintiff-wife was excluded from evidence upon the ground that no sufficient foundation had been laid for its admission.

Sec. 11:11 Reproductions of original records.

With the increasing complexity of business and commercial ventures, it is often impractical or impossible to bring into court original business records. Many businesses have changed their method of preserving records in the interest of space conservation. For example, microfilm copies are often preserved and the originals destroyed. For the foregoing among other reasons, the legislatures of most states and of the Federal government have enacted statutes permitting the use of reproductions made in the regular course of business in lieu of originals.[50]

Typical (but somewhat more detailed) of such statutes is 28 U.S.C. §1732(b) which reads as follows:

"If any business, institution, member of a profession or calling, or any department or agency of government, in the regular course of business or activity has kept or recorded any memorandum, writing, entry, print, representation or combination

---

[50] FEDERAL: 28 U.S.C. §1732(b). ALABAMA: Code, Title 7, §§415(1)–415(2). ALASKA: Alaska Statutes, §§58-1-21 to 58-1-23. ARIZONA: R.C.P. Rule 44(s). ARKANSAS: Stat. Ann., §28-932. CALIFORNIA: Code Civ. Proc., §1953i; Evidence Code §1550 (Deering's). CONNECTICUT: C.G.S.A. §52-180. COLORADO: CRS, §52-2-1. FLORIDA: F.S.A. §92.35. GEORGIA: Code Ann., §38-710. HAWAII: Rev. L. Hawaii 1955, §224-4. IDAHO: Code, §9-417. ILLINOIS: Smith-Hurd Ill. St. Ch. 51, §3. INDIANA: Burns' Stat. §§2-1649 to 2-1651. IOWA: 43 Code Ann., §622.30. KANSAS: K.S.A. 60-469. KENTUCKY: KRS 422.105. MAINE: 16 M.R.S.A. §456. MARYLAND: Code, art. 35, §60. MASSACHUSETTS: Ann. L. Mass., c. 233, §79E. MICHIGAN: Stat. Ann., §27A.-2147. MINNESOTA: M.S.A. §600.135. MISSISSIPPI: 2 Code 1942 Ann., §1761.5. MONTANA: Sec. 93-801-1 to 93-801-5, Repl. Vol. 7, Revised Codes of Montana 1947. NEBRASKA: R.R.S. 1943, §§25-12, 112 to 25-12, 114. NEVADA: NRS 51.050–51.070. NEW HAMPSHIRE: RSA 520:1–520:3. NEW JERSEY: N.J.S.A. 2A:82-38 to 2A:82-40. NEW MEXICO: §§20-2-20 to 20-2-22, N.M.S.A. 1953. NEW YORK: C.P.L.R. 4539. NORTH CAROLINA: Gen. Stat. §§8-45.1 to 8-45.4. NORTH DAKOTA: NDCC 31-08-01.1. OHIO: Page's Rev. Code Ann., §2317.41. OKLAHOMA: 12 Okl. St. Ann. §§521–523. PENNSYLVANIA: 28 P.S. §§141–143. RHODE ISLAND: Gen. Laws 1956, §9-19-14. SOUTH DAKOTA: SDC 36.1003. TEXAS: Vernon's Tex. Civ. Stat., Art. 3731b and 3731c. UTAH: 9 Code Ann. 1953, 78-25-16. VERMONT: 12 V.S.A. §1701. VIRGINIA: §§8-279.1 to 8-279.2, Code 1950. WASHINGTON: RCWA 5.46.010–5.46.020. WEST VIRGINIA: Michies W.Va. Code 1961, §5714(2). WISCONSIN: W.S.A. 327.29. WYOMING: Stat. 1957, §§1-174 to 1-177.

thereof, of any act, transaction, occurrence, or event, and in the regular course of business has caused any or all of the same to be recorded, copied, or reproduced by any photographic, photostatic, microfilm, micro-card, miniature photographic, or other process which accurately reproduces or forms a durable medium for so reproducing the original, the original may be destroyed in the regular course of business unless its preservation is required by law. Such reproduction, when satisfactorily identified, is as admissible in evidence as the original itself in any judicial or administrative proceeding whether the original is in existence or not and an enlargement or facsimile of such reproduction is likewise admissible in evidence if the original reproduction is in existence and available for inspection under direction of court. The introduction of a reproduced record, enlargement, or facsimile does not preclude admission of the original. This subsection shall not be construed to exclude from evidence any document or copy thereof which is otherwise admissible under the rules of evidence." [51]

In Delaware and Oregon reproductions of original documents are only admissible in evidence if the original is not available.[52]

As a practical matter, quite aside from statutory assistance, counsel will often stipulate that photostats of original records may be used in lieu of originals if it would be inconvenient to produce the originals, even though they are in existence. The usual practice is for a party to deliver these photostats in advance of trial to the other party for inspection and, if desired, for comparison with the originals. Very often this type of mutual convenience is worked out by counsel during the taking of depositions in advance of trial.

Sec. 11:12 Documents or instruments establishing status of property.

Under specific statutes, documents or instruments affecting the status of property are admissible in evidence. These statutes are completely apart from the standard recording statutes, as such.

---

[51] 28 U.S.C. §1733(b) provides that properly authenticated copies or transcripts of records "of any department or agency of the United States shall be admitted in evidence equally with the originals thereof." Rule 44(a) of the Federal Rules of Civil Procedure states the method of authentication.

[52] DELAWARE: 5 Code Ann., Title 10, §4310(b). OREGON: ORS 41.720.

Although they vary in detail, their general purpose is to permit the production of proof, which might otherwise be unavailable or inconvenient to bring into court, but which is of sufficient age and dignity to be entitled to credence, particularly, but not necessarily, where it has been on deposit in a public office.

Ancient maps, surveys and records affecting real property, subject to specific statutory limitations (such as age, length of filing, or the fact that they were made by a person not connected with a party to the litigation) are competent evidence to prove the facts recited in them.[53]

A search affecting real property may be used with the same effect as an official search if it is made and certified by a title insurance, abstract or searching company or some other type of company or individual named in an enabling statute.[54]

A copy of a statement, which is noted or certified by a filing officer pursuant to various statutes involving commercial transactions (such as statements of status and amounts due under chattel mortgages or similar secured transactions) is *prima facie* evidence of the facts stated in the notation or certification and that the copy is a true copy of the statement filed in the office of the filing officer.[55]

Sec. 11:13 Proof of marriage.

It is a general statutory rule that an original certificate of a marriage made by the person by whom it was solemnized, or the origi-

---

[53] ALABAMA: Code, Title 7, §413. CALIFORNIA: Code Civ. Proc., §1936 (Deering's); Evidence Code §1341 (Deering's). COLORADO: CRS, §35-4-13. FLORIDA: F.S.A. §92.08. IDAHO: Code, §9-402. IOWA: 43 Code Ann., §622.23. KANSAS: K.S.A. 60-464. LOUISIANA: LSA-R.S. 13:3728–3729. MISSISSIPPI: 2 Code 1942 Ann., §1733. MONTANA: Sec. 93-1101-8, Repl. Vol. 7, Revised Codes of Montana 1947. NEVADA: NRS 52.070. NEW YORK: C.P.L.R. 4522. NORTH CAROLINA: Gen. Stat. §§8-14, 8-15 and 8-19. OREGON: ORS 41.670. TEXAS: Vernon's Tex. Civ. Stat., Art. 3726. WASHINGTON: RCWA 5.44.070.

[54] FLORIDA: F.S.A. §§92.25–92.28. MINNESOTA: M.S.A. §600.19. NEW MEXICO: §20-2-13, N.M.S.A. 1953. NEW YORK: C.P.L.R. 4523. WYOMING: Stat. 1957, §§1-162 to 1-163.

[55] ARKANSAS: Stat. Ann., §28-932. CALIFORNIA: Evidence Code §1532 (Deering's). IDAHO: Code, §9-302. ILLINOIS: Smith-Hurd Ill. St. Ch. 51, §56. INDIANA: Burns' Stat. §2-1607. IOWA: 43 Code Ann., §622.44. KANSAS: K.S.A. 60-465. KENTUCKY: KRS 422.020. MARYLAND: Code, art. 35, §38. MICHIGAN: Stat. Ann., §27A.2107. MINNESOTA: M.S.A. §600.22. NEVADA: NRCP, Rule 44(a). NEW HAMPSHIRE: RSA 516:32. NEW JERSEY: N.J.S.A. 2A:84A, Rules of Evidence, Rule 63(19). NEW YORK: C.P.L.R. 4525. OREGON: ORS 43.340–43.360. SOUTH CAROLINA: Code 1962, §26-101. TEXAS: Vernon's Tex. Civ. Stat., Art. 3726b. UTAH: 9 Code Ann. 1953, §78-25-4. WASHINGTON: RCWA 5.44.060–5.44.070.

nal entry thereof made pursuant to law in the office of the clerk of a city or a town is *prima facie* evidence of the marriage.[56] Some statutes, while not specifically so providing, do so by clear inference.[57]

In some states, the marriage certificate, as such, is not acceptable as proof of the marriage, but an entry in a marriage record book is sufficient.[58]

Although some statutes do not provide that the certificate or record is *prima facie* evidence of the marriage,[59] this omission is not significant. Since the record is admissible, one who contests its effectiveness as *prima facie* proof of marriage has the burden of going forward with the contesting proof. In a few jurisdictions, the certificate, itself, does not constitute *prima facie* proof of marriage unless it is recorded.[60]

Sec. 11:14 Proof of death or other status of missing person.

One of the most troublesome problems of proof is the establishment of the status of a missing person. This creates a particular hardship when it concerns persons in the armed forces or members of the merchant marine (where, for example, a ship has been lost at sea). Many states have enacted statutes to ameliorate this hardship.[61]

---

[56] ALABAMA: Code, Title 7, §386. ARIZONA: A.R.S. §12-2265. CONNECTICUT: C.G.S.A. §§46-5 and 46-8. COLORADO: CRS, §90-1-20. HAWAII: Rev. L. Hawaii 1955, §323-13. IDAHO: Code, §32-309. MARYLAND: Code, art. 62, §13. MASSACHUSETTS: Ann. L. Mass., c. 46, §19 and c. 207, §§45–46. MICHIGAN: Stat. Ann., §§27A.2132–27A.2133. MINNESOTA: M.S.A. §600.20. MONTANA: Sec. 48-126, Repl. Vol. 3 (Part 2), Revised Codes of Montana 1947. NEBRASKA: R.R.S. 1943, §42-116. NEVADA: NRS 122.030. NEW HAMPSHIRE: RSA 457:38. NEW JERSEY: N.J.S.A. 2A:84A, Rules of Evidence, Rule 63(18). NEW YORK: C.P.L.R. 4526. WISCONSIN: W.S.A. 327.18 and 328.09.

[57] FEDERAL: 28 U.S.C. §1739. FLORIDA: F.S.A. §741.10. IOWA: 9 Code Ann., §144.48. KENTUCKY: KRS 422.020, 422.050 and 422.080. SOUTH CAROLINA: Code 1962, §26-101. TEXAS: Vernon's Tex. Civ. Stat., Art. 4606. UTAH: 9 Code Ann. 1953, §78-25-3. WEST VIRGINIA: Michies W.Va. Code 1961, §1342.

[58] DELAWARE: 8 Code Ann.; Title 13, §119. MISSOURI: V.A.M.S. §490.58. OREGON: ORS 43.380.

[59] CALIFORNIA: Evidence Code §1316 (Deering's). ILLINOIS: Smith-Hurd Ill. St. Ch. 89, §§9–12. KANSAS: K.S.A. 60-460 to 60-461. MAINE: 19 M.R.S.A. §121. MISSISSIPPI: 2 Code 1942 Ann., §1734. RHODE ISLAND: Gen. L. 1956, §23-3-31. VERMONT: 12 V.S.A. §1695.

[60] VIRGINIA: §20-20, Code 1950, 1960 Repl. Vol. WASHINGTON: RCWA 26.04.100 and 26.04.120. WYOMING: Stat. 1957, §20-14. In Pennsylvania, a certified copy of a marriage license record is required. 48 P.S. §1-20.

[61] FEDERAL: 50 U.S.C. §1009. ALABAMA: Code, Title 7, §386(1–3). CALIFORNIA: Code Civ. Proc., §§1928.1–1928.4 (Deering's); Evidence Code §§1282–1283 (Deering's). CONNECTICUT: C.G.S.A. §52-181. COLORADO: CRS,

A typical statute is section 4527 of the New York Civil Practice Law and Rules, which reads as follows:

"§4527.   Death or other status of missing person.

(a) Presumed death.   A written finding of presumed death, made by any person authorized to make such findings by the federal missing persons act is prima facie evidence of the death, and the date, circumstances and place of disappearance. In the case of a merchant seaman, a written finding of presumed death, made by the maritime war emergency board or by the war shipping administration or the successors or assigns of such board or administration in connection with war risk insurance is prima facie evidence of the death, and the date, circumstances and place of disappearance.

(b) Death, internment, capture and other status.   An official written report or record that a person is missing, missing in action, interned in a neutral country, or beleaguered, besieged or captured by an enemy, or is dead, or is alive, made by an officer or employee of the United States authorized by law of the United States to make it is prima facie evidence of such fact."

The special statutes here under discussion are, in the truest sense, statutory aids to proof. The establishment of *prima facie* evidence of the status of missing persons in circumstances other than those covered by these statutes is dependent on the decisional law of individual jurisdictions.

---

§§52-1-22 to 52-1-23. DELAWARE: 5 Code Ann.; Title 10, §4316. FLORIDA: F.S.A. §§92.30–92.32. GEORGIA: Code Ann., §§38-632 to 38-635. HAWAII: Rev. L. Hawaii 1955, §§224-19 to 224-21. INDIANA: Burns' Stat. §§2-4901 to 2-4903. IOWA: 47 Code Ann., §633.517. LOUISIANA: LSA-R.S. 9:1441–1443. MICHIGAN: Stat. Ann., §27.966(1–3). MINNESOTA: M.S.A. §600.24. MISSISSIPPI: 2 Code 1942 Ann., §1698-01. MONTANA: Sec. 93-1001-39 and 93-1001-40, Repl. Vol. 7, Revised Codes of Montana 1947. NEVADA: NRS 55.010–.030. NEW HAMPSHIRE: RSA 523:1–3. NEW JERSEY: N.J.S.A. 2A:83-4 to 83-6. NORTH CAROLINA: Gen. Stat. §§8-37.1–.3. NORTH DAKOTA: NDCC 31-11-04.1 to 04.3. OREGON: ORS 43.450–43.460. PENNSYLVANIA: 51 P.S. §§630–632. RHODE ISLAND: Gen. L. 1956, §§9-19-19 to 9-19-22. SOUTH CAROLINA: Code 1962, §§26-131 to 26-133. TENNESSEE: T.C.A. §§24-512 to 24-514. VERMONT: 12 V.S.A. §§1702–1704. WASHINGTON: RCWA 5.40.020–5.40.040. WYOMING: Stat. 1957, §§1-186 to 1-188.

Sec. 11:15   Proof of weather conditions.

Where the condition of the weather on a given date, or at a given time within that date, is important in a litigation, it is obvious that an individual, who personally remembers the condition of the weather at the critical time, can testify with respect thereto. However, the average finder of the facts (court or jury) is apt to take a jaundiced view of the ability of a witness to pinpoint whether, at a given moment, it was clear, sunny, cloudy, rainy or snowy.

The United States Weather Bureau takes regular observations of the weather and is able to furnish, upon mere request, a precise record. In practice, the record is subpoenaed and a weather bureau employee brings to court a certified copy thereof (very often printed).

In all probability, such a record would be admissible under the business records or official reports exceptions to the hearsay rule.[62] However, to make assurance doubly sure, some states specifically provide by statute that any record of the observations of the weather, taken under the direction of the United States Weather Bureau, is *prima facie* evidence of the facts therein stated.[63]

Sec. 11:16   Proof of population.

The Secretary of Commerce of the United States is authorized by statute to furnish "transcripts or copies of tables and other census records." [64]

In a great many states, these general census figures are indirectly admissible in evidence because the courts take judicial notice thereof basing such notice on the official census reports.[65]

It should be noted that we are here referring to *general* census reports, whose admissibility is limited to the population figures. It is very doubtful whether census reports can be used for the purpose

---

[62] *Cf., Beaty Shopping Center, Inc. v. Monarch Ins. Co. of Ohio,* 315 F. 2d 467, 470.

[63] MICHIGAN: Stat. Ann., §27A.2124. NEW JERSEY: N.J.S.A. 2A:84A, Rules of Evidence, Rule 63(15). NEW YORK: C.P.L.R. 4528. VERMONT: 12 V.S.A. §1693.

[64] 13 U.S.C. §8(b).

[65] *Wigmore on Evidence* (3rd Ed., 1940) §2577, footnote 4, and 1964 pocket supplement, p. 293.

of establishing facts as to the status, occupation and the like of individual citizens.[66] However, if by special authority a local census is taken for the purpose of registering individuals, much of the material therein contained is admissible because "[s]uch an official enumeration becomes virtually a register."[67]

Unless general census reports were admissible in evidence (either directly or through the medium of judicial notice), it would be virtually impossible to prove the population of a given state, county, city, town or other political subdivision. New York, by special statute, provides that a certificate of the officer in charge of the census of the United States, attested by the United States Secretary of Commerce, giving the result of the census is *prima facie* evidence of such result.[68] In many other states, general statutes permitting the introduction of records regularly maintained by the state, inferentially allow the use in evidence of census records.[69]

Sec. 11:17 Market reports.

The value of commodities, other goods and investment securities at a given time and place is an important issue in many cases. Unless some means were afforded to make simple proof on this subject, the burden of establishing the facts would obviously be cumbersome and costly.

Although a person familiar with a given market (sometimes inaccurately termed "an expert") will be heard to give direct testimony of his own knowledge, the courts have, by decisions without the

---

[66] *Wigmore on Evidence* (3rd Ed., 1940) §1671.

[67] *Doto v. United States*, 223 F. 2d 309, 311, referring to a census taken pursuant to a special provision of the New York State constitution and admitted in evidence for the purpose of showing the name, residence and status as an alien of a defendant in a criminal case.

[68] C.P.L.R. 4530(a). Subdivision (b) of the same section provides that where the population of the state or a subdivision thereof is required to be determined according to the Federal or State census, the result reached and officially certified "is conclusive evidence of such population."

[69] FEDERAL: 28 U.S.C. §§1732(a) and 1733(a). ALABAMA: Code, Title 7, §§428 and 432. ARKANSAS: Stat. Ann., §28-930. CALIFORNIA: Evidence Code §1280 (Deering's). COLORADO: R.C.P., Rule 44(a). DELAWARE: 5 Code Ann.; Title 10, §4308. FLORIDA: F.S.A. §92.20. GEORGIA: Code Ann., §38-630. IDAHO: Code, §9-315. INDIANA: Burns' Stat. §55-111. KENTUCKY: KRS 422.050. LOUISIANA: LSA-C.C.P. art. 1393. MINNESOTA: M.S.A. §§600.13 and 600.18. MISSOURI: V.A.M.S. §490.700. NEW JERSEY: N.J.S.A. 2A:84A, Rules of Evidence, Rule 63(15). OREGON: ORS 43.360–43.370. WISCONSIN: W.S.A. 327.18.

use of statutory aids to proof, permitted the use of standard compilations to establish value and prevailing prices.[70]

The Uniform Commercial Code [71] contains the following provision:

> "Whenever the prevailing price or value of any goods regularly bought and sold in any established commodity market is in issue, reports in official publications or trade journals or in newspapers or periodicals of general circulation published as the reports of such market shall be admissible in evidence. The circumstances of the preparation of such a report may be shown to affect its weight but not its admissibility."

This provision has been substantially adopted in many American jurisdictions.[72] As its text states, the applicability of the uniform statute is confined to establishing the prevailing price or value "of any goods regularly bought and sold in any established commodity market." The definition of the word "goods" in the Uniform Commercial Code specifically excludes "investment securities" and choses in action.[73]

As we have noted at the beginning of this section, stock exchange quotations and similar reports are admissible under decisional law

---

[70] *G. E. Employees Securities Corporation v. Manning*, 137 Fed. 2d 637, 641 [stock exchange market quotations]; *McKenzie v. Perdue*, 67 Ga. App. 202, 215 ["Cotton Year Book" of New York Cotton Exchange]; *Associated Metals & Mineral Corp. v. Dixon Chemical & Res.*, 82 N.J. Super. 281, 313, cert. den. 42 N.J. 501 ["Iron Age," steel industry weekly publication reflecting prices].

[71] Section 2-724.

[72] ARKANSAS: Stat. Ann., §85-2-724. CALIFORNIA: Cal. U.C.C. §2724. CONNECTICUT: C.G.S.A. §42a-2-724. GEORGIA: Code Ann., §109A-2-724. ILLINOIS: Smith-Hurd Ill. St. Ch. 26, §2-724. INDIANA: Burns' Stat. §19-2-724. KENTUCKY: KRS 355.2-724. MAINE: 11 M.R.S.A. §2-724. MARYLAND: Code, art. 95B, §2-724. MASSACHUSETTS: Ann. L. Mass., c. 106, §2-724. MICHIGAN: Stat. Ann., §19.2724. MISSOURI: V.A.M.S. §400.2-724. MONTANA: Sec. 87A-2-724, Revised Codes of Montana. NEBRASKA: R.R.S. UCC §2-724. NEW HAMPSHIRE: RSA 382-A:2-724. NEW JERSEY: N.J.S.A. 12A:2-724. NEW MEXICO: §50A-2-724, N.M.S.A. NEW YORK: Uniform Commercial Code, §2-724 (McKinney's). NORTH DAKOTA: Uniform Commercial Code §2-724. OHIO: Page's Rev. Code Ann., §1302.97. OKLAHOMA: 12A Okl. St. Ann. §2-724. OREGON: ORS 71.2724. PENNSYLVANIA: 12A P.S. §2-724. RHODE ISLAND: Gen. L. §6A-2-724. TENNESSEE: T.C.A. §47-2-724. UTAH: Uniform Commercial Code, §2-724. VIRGINIA: §8.2-724, Code 1950, 1965 added vol. WEST VIRGINIA: Michies W.Va. Code Supp. 1963, §46-2-724. WISCONSIN: W.S.A. 402.724. WYOMING: Stat. 1962, §40A:2-724.

[73] Uniform Commercial Code, §2-105.

without statutory sanction. New York, which has adopted the Uniform Commercial Code, has an additional special statute, which makes admissible reports of stock exchanges as well as reports of commodity markets. This statute reads as follows: [74]

> "A report of a regularly organized stock or commodity market published in a newspaper or periodical of general circulation or in an official publication or trade journal is admissible in evidence to prove the market price or value of any article regularly sold or dealt in on such market. The circumstances of the preparation of such a report may be shown to affect its weight, but they shall not affect its admissibility."

Section 20.2031–2 of the regulations of the United States Internal Revenue Service covering estate taxes provides that in determining the valuation of stocks and bonds both on a stock exchange and in an over-the-counter market "the mean between the highest and lowest quoted selling prices on the valuation date is the fair market value per share or bond."

Sec. 11:18 Lack of record.

Instances often arise in the trial of a case where the fact that there is no official record of a given transaction or happening becomes important. It is possible to prove this fact by the testimony of a competent witness to the effect that he has personally searched the records and found none applicable to the situation of the case at bar. However, particularly where the records of a number of jurisdictions and political subdivisions are involved, the cost of making such direct proof might be prohibitive and a vast number of witnesses competent to make a search would have to be called.

To obviate this hardship, many jurisdictions have, by statute, provided a method for having a lack of record proved by the certificate of a responsible officer.[75]

---

[74] C.P.L.R. 4533.

[75] ALABAMA: Code, Title 7, §394(i). ARIZONA: R.C.P. Rule 44(h). COLORADO: R.C.P., Rule 44(b). DELAWARE: 13 Code Ann.; Super. Civ. Rule 44(b), Chan. Rule 44(b). INDIANA: Burns' Stat. §2-1617a. KANSAS: K.S.A. 60-466. KENTUCKY: R.C.P., Rule 44.02. LOUISIANA: LSA-C.C.P. art. 1396. MAINE: 16 M.R.S.A. §461; R.C.P., Rule 44. MICHIGAN: Stat. Ann., §27A.2108. MINNESOTA: R.C.P., Rule 44.02. MONTANA: Rule 44(b), M.R.C.P., Repl. Vol. 7, Revised Codes of Montana 1947. NEBRASKA: R.R.S. 1943, §25-1282.

The texts of these statutes vary in detail, but they may be regarded (except as to formal details) as practically identical. Typical of the variations are the Federal and New York State statutes. They read, as follows:

"A written statement that after diligent search no record or entry of a specified tenor is found to exist in the records designated by the statement, authenticated as provided in subdivision (a)(1) of this rule in the case of a domestic record, or complying with the requirements of subdivision (a)(2) of this rule for a summary in the case of a foreign record, is admissible as evidence that the records contain no such record or entry." [76]

"A statement signed by an officer or a deputy of an officer having legal custody of specified official records of the United States or of any state, territory or jurisdiction of the United States, or of any court thereof, or kept in any public office thereof, that he has made diligent search of the records and has found no record or entry of a specified nature, is prima facie evidence that the records contain no such record or entry, provided that the statement is accompanied by a certificate that legal custody of the specified official records belongs to such person, which certificates shall be made by a person described in rule 4540." [77]

Nevada: NRCP, Rule 44(b). New Jersey: N.J.S.A. 2A:84A, Rules of Evidence, Rule 69. New Mexico: §21-1-1(44)(b), N.M.S.A. 1953. North Dakota: R.C.P., Rule 44(b). Pennsylvania: 28 P.S. §125. Tennessee: T.C.A. §24-624. Texas: Vernon's Tex. Civ. Stat., Art. 3731a, Sec. 5. Utah: 9 Code Ann. 1953, R.C.P., Rule 44(b). Virginia: §8-272(b), Code 1950, 1957 Repl. Vol. West Virginia: R.C.P., Rule 44(b) Wisconsin: W.S.A. 327.09. Wyoming: R.C.P., Rule 44(b).

[76] F.R.C.P., rule 44(b).

[77] New York C.P.L.R. 4521. Rule 4540, referred to in this section, describes the methods by which official records of courts or government offices in the United States may be authenticated

Chapter XII

REDIRECT EXAMINATION AND
REBUTTAL PROOF

Sec. 12:1 Permissible scope of redirect examination and re-buttal proof.

Redirect examination of a witness is that which is undertaken by the attorney originally calling him after the witness has been cross-examined.

Rebuttal testimony is that which is introduced by a party after his opponent has completed his main proof. Of course, after a plaintiff's main case has been presented, the defendant puts in his main case. This is not rebuttal proof, which occurs only after the second party has completed his main proof.

The scope of permissible redirect examination and of rebuttal proof rests in the sound discretion of the court.[1] However, this dis-

---

[1] *Wigmore on Evidence* (3rd edition, 1940), §1873 and Pocket Part.

269

cretion must rest upon the necessities of the case and cannot be arbitrarily exercised. The general rule prevailing in the United States was set forth in an old case, which has been practically uniformly followed throughout the years, as follows: [2]

> "The rule upon this subject is a familiar one. When, by the pleadings, the burden of proof of any matter in issue is thrown upon the plaintiff, he must in the first instance introduce all the evidence upon which he relies to establish his case. He cannot, as said by Lord Ellenborough, go into half his case and reserve the remainder. The same rule applies to the defence. After the plaintiff has closed his testimony, the defendant must then bring forward all the evidence upon which he relies to meet the claim on the part of the plaintiff. He cannot introduce a part and reserve the residue for some future occasion. After he has rested, neither party can as a matter of right introduce any further testimony which may properly be considered testimony in chief. . . . But this rule is not in all cases an inflexible one. There is and of necessity must be a discretionary power, vested in the Court before which a trial is had, to relax the operation of the rule, when great injustice will be done by a strict adherence to it. If a party, by a mere mistake or inadvertence, omit to introduce a piece of testimony constituting an essential link in his chain of evidence, and does not discover the mistake until after he has closed his testimony, the Court in its discretion will, rather than that his cause should be sacrificed, permit him to supply the omission; taking care, however, to see that the adverse party is not prejudiced by the relaxation of the rule. This discretionary power, however, is to be exercised with great caution. While the rule may be departed from for the sake of preventing great and manifest injustice, it ought not to be so frequently disregarded as to render it a rule in name and not in reality."

The possible variations of this rule are discussed in another old case, thus: [3]

---

[2] *Hathaway v. Hemingway,* 20 Conn. 191, 195.
[3] *Mueller v. Rebhan,* 94 Ill. 142, 150.

"As a matter of practice, the rulings of Courts are not uniform upon this question. In some Courts it is held that neither party is called upon to produce all his testimony in support of any allegation in issue until it has been developed on the trial that an issue in the evidence is made upon that question. . . . That rule has not prevailed in the Courts of this State; but the more usual rule is, that the party upon whom the burden of proof rests must, in the first instance, produce all the proof he proposes to offer in support of his allegation; and after his adversary has closed his proof, he may only be heard in adducing proof directly rebutting the proofs given by his adversary. This question of practice must, to a greater or less degree, be left to the discretion of the Court trying the case. This discretion should be exercised in such a manner that neither party shall be taken by surprise and deprived, without notice, of an opportunity of producing any material proof."

The loosest rule has been enunciated as follows: [4]

"It is understood to be now the universal practice of the Courts of this State, in both civil and criminal proceedings, to permit a witness, after having been examined in chief, consigned and cross-examined, to be again examined by the party introducing him, upon points touching which he had not before testified, and subsequently to be recalled and interrogated in regard to facts material to the issue, which had not been previously elicited or referred to, either from inadvertence or ignorance that they were within the knowledge of the witness. In civil cases it has been held that it is discretionary with the Court to permit witnesses to be introduced, even after both parties had announced that the evidence had been closed; the exercise of such a discretion may frequently be as important to the safety of the accused as to the interest of the State."

In the event a court sustains objections to questions on redirect, the record will be clear and, upon proper exception, the sustaining of the objection may be reviewed on appeal. If the necessity for recalling a witness for redirect examination arises and the court

---

[4] *State v. Duncan*, 8 Rob. La. 562, 563.

refuses to permit such recall, the record of such refusal is sufficiently clear to permit appellate review. However, to make assurance doubly sure, counsel should spread on the record a statement of what he intends to establish by the recalled witness.

If the court refuses to accept rebuttal testimony (or refuses, upon proper request of counsel, to permit a rebuttal witness to be called), counsel should make an offer of proof on the record so that the matter will appear in proper perspective for appellate review.

In the balance of the present chapter, we shall treat redirect examination and rebuttable testimony interchangeably, since the principles, practice, strategy and tactics involved in each situation are practically identical.

Sec. 12:2 Additional preparation for redirect examination and rebuttal proof.

By their nature, redirect examination and rebuttal proof depend upon testimony elicited by one's opponent either on cross-examination or during the course of his main case. It follows that, except for one's general knowledge of his case and the data at hand to prove it, the only special preparation for either redirect or cross-examination or the introduction of proof in rebuttal is a careful notation of the testimony in the case up to the time that counsel is called upon to act.

In some important cases counsel order "overnight copy" from the court reporter and, from a perusal of this material, counsel is able to frame his future conduct. But this is an extremely expensive performance and, in a vast majority of cases, is not employed.

The method of making notes of testimony as the trial progresses is often peculiar to the attorney trying the case. There are few investments more worthwhile than to have a trial assistant, whose major duties are to make a note of the testimony as the trial progresses and to keep track of all exhibits.[5] If a trial assistant is not available, counsel must take it upon himself to make notes of the testimony.

Some counsel prepare (or have their assistant prepare) a running account of all of the testimony. This has the triple advantage of permitting ready reference for redirect examination and rebuttal testimony, of allowing review, during recesses of the trial, in order to

---

[5] See sections 6:5 and 6:6, *supra.*

prepare further steps, and of being tremendously helpful in preparing summation or a post-trial memorandum. Other counsel, particularly in a short trial, merely note the highlights of testimony. Still others do not attempt to note the testimony, as such, but merely take notes in the nature of memoranda as to what they intend to ask on redirect examination or use for rebuttal testimony.

If the method of making notes followed by counsel is to outline the testimony, it is important that the name of the witness be prominently displayed in these notes and that it be clearly indicated whether the testimony outlined at a given point came on direct or cross-examination.

The most important factor in outlining the evidence is to make sure that, to the extent that counsel deems it wise,[6] no testimony of the opponent is left uncontradicted; because, as a general matter, uncontradicted proof must be accepted by the fact-finder as true.[7]

In cases tried to the court without a jury, it is the unfortunate practice of some judges to "take everything" that is offered in evidence, subject to a deferred ruling on whether, upon final analysis, all of this evidence should be received.[8] In such a situation, counsel is confronted by a difficult decision in connection with the production of rebuttal testimony. If the evidence taken subject to final ruling is voluminous, counsel should make every effort prior to his rebuttal to force a ruling. If he cannot do so, he may be compelled to ask for an adjournment in order to meet this "take everything" evidence. He certainly should be given time to consider what portion of this evidence he desires to meet and to find out what proof he can produce for this purpose. If a reasonable adjournment is refused, counsel should state on the record his reasons for asking it and take an exception to the refusal to grant it.

Sec. 12:3   Choice of subjects for redirect examination and rebuttal proof.

Although counsel should always be careful to avoid leaving in the record uncontradicted proof harmful to his cause,[9] the choice of subjects to be adverted to either on redirect examination or to be

---

[6] See section 12:3, *post.*
[7] See footnotes 7, 8 and 9 in section 1:2, *supra.*
[8] See section 3:4, *supra.*
[9] See text accompanying footnotes 7, 8 and 9 in section 1:2, *supra.*

used in rebuttal proof is a highly selective process. This is particularly true where the pleaded issues have been enlarged by happenings during the trial.[10]

It is not necessary that *every* fact testified to on cross-examination or during a defendant's case should be rebutted. However, on the major issues of the case and on all questions affecting credibility, it is wise to meet even minor proof.

Redirect examination should be as short as possible. There should be a concentration on the major issues and on those minor issues which affect the credibility of the witness being examined. This can usually be accomplished in a minimum of time and, if so accomplished, has a maximum effect because the fact-finder will be relieved instantly of doubts he may have had.

As to major issues concerning which a witness can do no more than deny them, the simplest kind of question suffices. Counsel may ask the witness whether, as testified to by another witness, a certain thing happened. All the witness need do is answer in the negative.

It is particularly important that counsel constantly draw attention by the nature of his questions as to what is a main issue and what is a side (and probably unimportant) matter. Two examples are enlightening.

In one case, a witness on cross-examination was asked how many talks he had had with the defendant before a certain date. It turned out that, although the witness had remembered three such conversations, there were actually three more. On redirect examination, the witness was asked this simple question: "Whether you had three or six talks with the defendant before November 15, was it after all such conversations that you received the letter which has been marked in evidence as exhibit 15?" When the witness replied in the affirmative, the number of talks became unimportant and, what is more vital, the jury realized that this number was unimportant.

In section 5:7, *supra*, we have referred at some length to a case where, on cross examination, it was established that letters offered in evidence seemed to belie a contention of the plaintiff and that he had written these letters more than a year after he had claimed that he presented an idea, which was later pirated, to a defendant who used that idea. On redirect examination, counsel merely asked him

---

[10] See section 3:3, *supra*.

whether he now realized that he was mistaken about the dates of the letters. He answered affirmatively. Counsel then asked him whether he had kept copies of the letters and he testified that he had not done so. With this simple redirect examination, counsel not only was able to belittle the importance of the date of the letters but was able to turn the event to his own benefit by his method of summation.

If it is decided to meet an issue on rebuttal, the criterion for use of this rebuttal should be how strong the evidence is at the command of counsel. It is better to leave a matter untouched than to attempt to meet it by weak proof. Particularly is this true, since the rebuttal evidence is ordinarily the last thing that the fact-finder hears before the taking of testimony is concluded.

If strong rebuttal evidence is available, however, it should be employed to the utmost, particularly where it has the strength of adding to a party's attack.[11]

Sec. 12:4 Redirect examination as a technique for "saving" a witness.

When a witness has been subjected to severe cross-examination (whether lengthy or short), the main purpose of redirect examination should be to restore both the previous testimony and his credibility. If in the course of establishing that the witness is the type of person who should be believed, counsel can also add strength to his own case in general, he should, of course, follow this path. But the important thing is for counsel to show that, despite what occurred on cross-examination, his witness is telling the truth. If there has been a strong attack on the witness' credibility at the close of his cross-examination, counsel should *immediately* take up the subject of this attack and meet it.

Where there has been an implication of recent fabrication, counsel may, under certain conditions, introduce evidence that the witness had, prior to taking the stand, made a friendly statement corroborative of his original testimony.[12]

Where the witness seems to have been confused by the questions propounded to him on cross-examination, counsel may be in a position to clear up the confusion and to prove that, if the witness had

---

[11] See section 12:5, *post.*
[12] See text accompanying footnotes 13 and 14 of section 2:3, *supra.*

understood the questions addressed to him, his answers would have been consistent with his original testimony.

The re-examination of a witness is more difficult, by far, than cross-examination. The following excerpt from an interesting book is apposite to our present subject: [13]

"Herein the object of the advocate is to overcome the effect of a destructive cross-examination. This object is attained by a miracle; if you can't perform them, you had much better allow your witness to go out of the box without further question. I once heard Sir Edward Carson perform that miracle in this country, shortly after the war. His client had been grievously defamed; the defendants had justified, and in furtherance of their defence endeavoured to shew that he was something of an adventurer, living entirely upon his wife's fortune. Carson's case was that there is every difference in the world between the man who exploits his rich wife and the man who, having married a rich wife, allows her to help him. The plaintiff had been handled very severely; his wife was asked on the threshold of the cross-examination: 'When did your husband last do a day's work?' and she had to answer that she didn't know. Then began a terrific bombardment. 'Your husband is wearing a very handsome astrachan coat; where did he get it?' 'I gave it to him.' 'Who paid for the Rolls-Royce you arrived in this morning?' 'I did.' 'How much money did he put towards the purchase of your mansion in the country?' 'Nothing.' And so on, through a minute examination of all the daily expenses of the married couple. Cross-examining counsel sat down with a very satisfied expression. Carson slowly lifted up his long, lean body, smoothed his silk gown, turned his melancholy face towards the lady, and said: 'Mrs. X.' He paused a moment to let the musical voice obtain its effect. Then in a sad, weary tone, as though the whole matter were very painful to him, 'Mrs. X,' he asked, 'were you in love with your husband?' In the circumstances, no answer but one was possible, and therein lay the skill of the advocate. 'I was,' she replied, faintly. Carson looked at the jury for a moment; then lifting his eyes towards her he asked gently: 'Is there any one of these things about which my friend has asked

---

[13] Healy, *The Old Munster Circuit*, p. 72, as quoted in *Wigmore on Evidence* (3rd edition, 1940), §1896.

you which you regret?' Once again, only one answer was possible. 'No,' she replied. Carson paused for a moment, he appeared to be thinking. 'Mrs. X,' he said, 'if the opportunity arose again today, would you be proud and happy to do it all again?' 'I would,' she cried, lifted by her advocate to enthusiasm. 'Thank-ye, Mrs. X,' said Carson, and sat down. The jury gave his client £5000, and it was those three questions that won the verdict."

Sec. 12:5 Redirect examination and rebuttal testimony as an attack technique.

In many cases, the nature of cross-examination or of proof adduced by an opponent opens the field to the ability of counsel to attack his opponent's case in a manner which would not have been permissible during the presentation of his own main case.[14] The opportunity thus afforded should be avidly seized.

Where redirect examination or rebuttal proof or both are used as an instrument of attack the points raised should be vigorously presented. It may be possible for the witness who has been cross-examined to establish the falsity of inferences which that cross-examination may have brought forth. By all means, including the submission of documentary proof, the witness' prior testimony should be enlarged. There can be no legitimate objection to this type of questioning if it can be seen that it is necessary or desirable to rebut inferences as well as adverse factual proof.

If, in order to rebut inferences it is deemed wise by counsel to call additional witnesses, whom he had not originally intended to produce, he should not hesitate to apply for a reasonable adjournment in order to bring these witnesses into court.

Where a witness who has been cross-examined can, himself, destroy any part of the effect of that cross-examination, his redirect examination should be as long as is necessary to produce this result. When the witness, himself, is the means of rebuttal and if his testimony is convincing the effect thereof is often much stronger than if he had so testified during his original examination.

A dramatic example of the ability of a witness to destroy what appeared to be an effective cross-examination occurred in a New

---

[14] As to the widening of triable issues by proceedings during the trial, see section 3:3, *supra.*

York action, wherein the wife sued her husband for a separation. In her complaint, the wife had alleged, as one of the acts of cruelty with which she charged her husband, that he had refused to pay for an appropriate wedding ceremony and reception for her daughter, although he could well afford to do so. On cross-examination, the defendant was asked whether he had, in fact, so refused and whether he had told his wife that her daughter should elope. To the surprise of both examining counsel and of the court, the defendant admitted these facts. Then, on redirect examination, the following occurred:

Q. Mr. R, you have admitted during cross-examination that you refused to provide an elaborate wedding reception for your stepdaughter. Is this the fact? **A.** Yes.

Q. When did this refusal take place? **A.** About a month before the marriage.

Q. Will you please relate to us, in substance, what conversation you had with the plaintiff, your wife, on that occasion? **A.** My wife and I were going over the list of proposed guests to be invited to the wedding reception. In going over this list I noticed that my wife had not included her own sister and her brother-in-law. I called her attention to this omission. She told me that it was deliberate. She said that the reason she was not inviting them to the reception was because, a year ago when our son was confirmed, her sister and her brother-in-law had come to the reception so poorly dressed that she was ashamed of the effect they made on the other guests and that she would not subject herself to this type of humiliation again.

Q. What did you say to her? **A.** I told her that if she was going to treat her own flesh and blood in this manner, her daughter could elope and that I would have nothing to do with providing a wedding reception.

Q. What happened after that? **A.** My wife gave in and agreed to include her sister and brother-in-law in the list of guests.

Q. Was the reception held? **A.** Yes.

Where there has been a counterclaim in a case, the witnesses establishing the counterclaim are produced after plaintiff's main case. Rebuttal testimony, in such an instance, is equivalent to a defendant's main case in an action brought against him. Obviously, whatever testimony is available should be produced in defense of the counterclaim.

INDEX